Stopping the Noise in Your Head

To Bentha

The new way to overcome
anxiety and worry

Stopping
the Noise in
Your Head

DR REID WILSON

Vermilion
LONDON

1 3 5 7 9 10 8 6 4 2

Vermilion, an imprint of Ebury Publishing,
20 Vauxhall Bridge Road,
London SW1V 2SA

Vermilion is part of the Penguin Random House group of companies whose
addresses can be found at global.penguinrandomhouse.com

First published in the United Kingdom by Vermilion in 2016

www.penguin.co.uk

A CIP catalogue record for this book is available from the British Library

ISBN 9781785041044

Printed and bound in Great Britain by Clays Ltd, St Ives PLC

Penguin Random House is committed to a sustainable future for our business,
our readers and our planet. This book is made from Forest Stewardship
Council® certified paper.

CONTENTS

CHAPTER 1: Worry Works for Me   ~ 1

CHAPTER 2: It's a Competition   ~ 7

PART ONE: The Dominant Strategy of Anxiety

CHAPTER 3: Ahhh . . . the Comfort of Certainty   ~ 15

CHAPTER 4: An Amygdala, a Priest, and a Rabbi . . .   ~ 33

PART TWO: Your Winning Strategy

Step Back

CHAPTER 5: Noise Pollution   ~ 47

CHAPTER 6: Make It NOT About Your Content   ~ 57

CHAPTER 7: Content and Competition   ~ 75

CHAPTER 8: Move the Massive   ~ 83

CHAPTER 9: Be Mindful of the Moment   ~ 95

WANT IT

CHAPTER 10: Taking the Paradoxical Point of View   ⌒ 113

CHAPTER 11: A Profound Experience with the Toilet   ⌒ 135

CHAPTER 12: Message to Self: I *Want* This   ⌒ 151

STEP FORWARD

CHAPTER 13: Dangling by Fingertips   ⌒ 177

CHAPTER 14: An Olympic Attitude   ⌒ 185

CHAPTER 15: How to Talk like a First Responder   ⌒ 199

CHAPTER 16: "I Made It as Unpleasant as I Could
            and Then I Waited"   ⌒ 217

BE CUNNING

CHAPTER 17: The Art of Cunning: Rope-a-Dope
            and the Brer Rabbit Offense   ⌒ 233

CHAPTER 18: Act as Though This Is Such a Clever Tactic   ⌒ 241

CHAPTER 19: Talking to Anxiety   ⌒ 253

CHAPTER 20: "Give Me Your Threats—Let Them Come"   ⌒ 263

PART THREE: Make Your Play

CHAPTER 21: You're Going Where?   ⌒ 279

CHAPTER 22: Plan Your Strategy   ⌒ 287

CHAPTER 23: Change Your Voice   ⌒ 307

CHAPTER 24: Shift Your Attitude   ⌒ 325

CHAPTER 25: Make Your Play   ⌒ 339

Appendix A: Need Coaching? Get Treatment ⌒ 357

Appendix B: Resources ⌒ 365

About the Author ⌒ 367

Index ⌒ 369

CHAPTER 1

Worry Works for Me

Where would we be without our worries? How would the dishes get done, children get fed, bills get paid? With all that we have going on in our lives, how would the floors get swept, homework get done, birthday cards get mailed on time? How would we get enough sleep each night unless we worried about *not* getting enough sleep?

Perhaps there's some truth in all that (save the bit about sleeping —I'm fairly certain worry won't help with that). Our worries serve a purpose in our daily lives. They aren't just instruments of torture.

I imagine when you purchased this book you assumed that I'm here to help you defeat and cast out your worries, to provide the tools you need to kick that worry addiction once and for all. But the truth is that worry and I have a love-hate relationship. Not unlike my relationship with chocolate-covered almonds (dark). I've had to set some serious boundaries and limitations with these pleasures. The desire for almonds pops into my mind from time to time, and I have to respond. "Look here," I say in a stern voice, "there is a time and a place for chocolate-covered almonds (dark), and right now, in the middle of a conference in Austria, is neither the time nor the place."

When worry plays a role in helping us to solve our problems, it does a fantastic job. (Just like when the almond-to-dark-chocolate ratio is more like 3:1 than 1:1.) So I want you to *love* worry when it serves you. But when it becomes a bothersome noise in your head, it has no redeeming value and you need to kick it to the curb.

TWO-HEADED WORRY

I have spent most of my thirty-five-year career working with anxious clients. When people ask what drew me to this field, one of my playful answers is, "It takes one to treat one." And I guess that's right. Although I have never had an anxiety disorder, I sure know how to worry. In fact, I am skilled at generating lots of bad feelings alongside many wonderful feelings. I can distinctly remember a moment in college when I concluded that I was likely to be a lifelong expert at generating worrisome thoughts. I figured that the best way to keep track of my own mental health was to make psychology my profession.

Various resources helped produce the book you're holding in your hands—investments such as time, research, years of study and practice, drafts, proposals, and perhaps 4,000 cups of various forms of caffeine—and among all of those was *worry*. My worry shows up in one of two forms: either incredibly helpful . . . or dreadfully bothersome.

When I continually remind myself that I should be working on this project, and yet I don't set aside time to focus on it, I use up part of my consciousness fretting because I'm not getting around to the task. I experience a combination of guilt (that I'm not being productive enough) and worry (that I am making a mistake by not addressing the project at this very moment), both wrapped up in a tidy little package padded with a thick layer of self-criticism.

When the task is my writing, it sounds a bit like this: "Geez, I gotta get focused on writing the book. I gotta be more efficient with my time. I gotta stop doing these *little* productive things and focus on the *big* productive stuff. And I gotta find a synonym for gotta." And then, "If I don't devote time and energy to this, it'll never get done. I waste so much time during the day. I need to start focusing. I should do all of these things today . . . simultaneously." This is not a loud noise in my head, mind you. It's more like a kind of muttering. It gnaws away at me in the background and brings a taste of unhappiness into my mental palette each day.

Here's the other way my worry works, and this I highly recommend. The thought pops up again: "I gotta get back to working on the book if I'm ever going to get it done." But this time it's wired into my disposition about this project. It's important to me, I want to accomplish it, and I absolutely want to devote time in the immediate future to work on it. I can use that thought as a signal to move into action. Relatively quickly I shift into problem-solving mode: I decide when I'm going to set aside a chunk of time, and I literally mark off that half day or so in my calendar.

Did you notice how I just said, "Relatively quickly I shift into problem-solving mode"? That happens on a really, really good day. Usually it's somewhere between "You'd better get back to work!" and "I'll mark off some time soon."

Granted, worry isn't the only way I get myself to work. Lucky for me, most of the time I feel inspired about my day. I have interesting projects that motivate me, and I can keep my attention focused on the positive outcomes I want from my creative efforts. (The caffeine helps too.)

But juggling and prioritizing tasks is not smooth sailing for any of us. Worry helps us through the rough waters by motivating us to stay on task and solve problems both big and small in our lives. Very simply, I would not want to lose the benefits of worry. But I also don't want to kick around in the wading pool of worry. I want to dive into the deep end and tackle the real challenges in life.

How about you?

WORRY WORKS

Worry, of course, has long been critical to our survival. Our cavemen ancestors who took leisurely strolls down by the stream, enjoying the pleasures of a beautiful fall morning, were eaten by the saber-toothed tigers (dinosaurs were mainly vegetarians). Their genes were lost. Our paranoid, there-could-be-danger-around-any-corner, defender-of-the-family-tribe ancestors lived to procreate, passing on to us that ever-present protective mode of worry.

Some degree of worry is actually good for us, for it can help jump-start us out of our denial, and it can drive us to prioritize our tasks. Most important, worry is designed to be an *initial* response, as Step One in the problem-solving process. It should initiate our efforts to find solutions by triggering our analytic process: evaluating the current situation, generating response options, choosing among them, selecting one, and then implementing it. When this progression works well, we get to conclude our analysis with a message like, "I'm worried about finishing this project, and now I'm going to take action. This is how I'm going to get it done—here's my plan." See, that's the usefulness of worry.

We bastardize the process when we operate as though worry *is* the problem-solving process. We keep naming the problem over and over again without productively addressing solutions. We say, "I've got to get this done. If I don't get it done, I'll be in trouble. I'm not sure I'm going to make it." During stressful times—if our steady income seems threatened, if an unfamiliar physical symptom is persisting, if a son begins driving or a daughter begins dating—most of us fret a little too much. It's as though worry becomes our talisman to ward off the trouble, the mistakes, the dangers. We believe that if we can just worry *enough*, we will come up with ways to prevent the bad things from happening. We feel threatened, so we operate as though all this thinking will protect us from committing any errors of judgment, and that it will ensure we make the right choice. Then once we decide on a plan of action, we worry as a way to verify that it's the *right* action, which really becomes a process of second-guessing our decisions.

But we have it wrong. Worry isn't supposed to solve problems. Its job is to *generate* problems in the front of our minds so we know what to fix. And it causes us to think more about how things might go *wrong* than about how to correct difficulties. After all, one way to *avoid* trouble is to imagine ourselves *in* that trouble! Imagine you are late for an appointment and driving in a rush. As you approach the traffic light, it turns yellow. You momentarily consider taking the risk of running through the light, because that will save you precious minutes. Then up pops an image of things going *really* badly for you and others in the middle of that intersection. You immediately act on your instantaneous decision to stop. That's worry at its best.

What happens if we don't place our worries within the problem-solving process? When we start paying a high emotional cost for unnecessary worry, and when our worries pop up in our minds too frequently, then those thoughts hurt us. Worry leads to anxiety. The more we worry, the more anxious we will become, whether it's about family, financial issues, work or school, or illness. If we don't address this type of worry and find ways to control it, we will continue to be anxious.

And worry will absolutely inhibit our performance. During any project, we should focus our attention on the *task*. But when our attention keeps getting redirected toward unhelpful worry, we become self-absorbed. "How will I do? What if I fail? That will be too painful for me. Must avoid failure!" These are compelling thoughts, and anyone would have trouble disengaging from them. But if you want your inner resources available for the activities you value, you need to find a way.

That's what this book is for. Yes, worry serves an essential function by helping us solve legitimate problems, and in Chapters 5, 6, and 7 we will discuss that. But through the rest of the book, we will look at times when anxious worrying disturbs us instead of helps us. We are going to study problematic worry and how we limit our successes in service of this dominant challenger. Then I will show you how to win that challenge.

CHAPTER 2

It's a Competition

I am going to compare our struggles with worry and anxiety to a boxing match. Yes, I am. And to a chess game. To Monopoly, bridge, the ancient adversarial competition of Go, and any of the martial arts. To tennis and poker. How can I dare compare your significant psychological struggles with a board game? Because I believe it is the most pragmatic, efficient way to gain your life back.

All competitions apply strategies: the flexible and fluid broad designs for gaining control over the challenger in order to reach your goal. And all competitions include tactics: the powerful short-term actions used to gain that control or force the challenger to make an undesirable move. You implement your broad strategies by applying tactics moment-by-moment.

In the game of chess, one strong opening strategy is to occupy and control the center of the board, because your pieces tend to be more mobile the closer they are to the center. Tactically speaking, how might you begin implementing that strategy? Start by advancing one or two of your pawns. First, move the pawn in front of either your king or queen. Then develop your knights before their respective bishops, because it's easier to find a good square on the chessboard for your knights. Don't move any of your pieces twice. Develop both sides of your board equally. Strategies in chess are not the *exact* move you make; instead, they are general principles to follow.

In that same way, to win over our needless worries and unhelpful anxiety, it's best to consider that we are engaged in a mental competition with broad strategies and more precise tactics. You will have *lots* of options for specific moves within this challenge.

Competitions are structured, with rules and rituals. They are organized to test our skills, our courage, and our cunning. And they can be won. But if you are losing now, how do you start winning? Make-believe is at the heart of all games, and we will absolutely engage our imaginations to accomplish our goals here. You and I must influence your neurology, and we will accomplish this through metaphors for how your neurology operates and how it changes. We begin our make-believe by externalizing and personifying the part of you that generates unhelpful worries and distress, and I'm going to refer to that competitor as Anxiety with a capital A.

A LOSING STRATEGY

You win a competition by applying the best tactics that implement the cleverest set of strategies. I can promise you that if you are troubled by worries and anxieties—whether it's general worries, panic, phobias, social anxieties, or OCD—Anxiety has been winning this game because it has an ingenious set of strategies. Brilliant, really. (I will explain them to you in detail as we move along.) Anxiety's best strategy is to convince you to spend most of your energy worrying about how to protect yourself or someone else against harm. It scores points by getting you to worry and then step back instead of step forward into the action.

If you organize your actions around only a defensive strategy, you will continue to lose to this skilled tactician. I assume you are *great* at playing defense: you can back up, avoid, tense up, worry about the future, and stick with the tried-and-true. But you cannot win a competition by only playing defense. If you are *reacting to* your symptoms, trying to *quiet* your worries and attempting *to get rid of* any threats that show up, you are at a great disadvantage.

You must have an offensive plan that pushes you *into* the territory of your challenger. (I will explain the method behind this madness soon enough.) And then you must act within that plan, over and over again. That's a scary thought. And crazy, really. Who in their right mind would want to step *into* the fire? Here's that kind of crazy for you: Chris Sharma. In Chapter 13 I'll tell you how he is one of our many models as a competitor.

To become a winning player, you need a good coach. That's me. Obviously, I have to prove myself to you, and that's my intention. I'll explain the nature of this competition, show you exactly how Anxiety is using worry and distress to beat you now, offer you a clear understanding of the mistakes you are making (and, yes, you are making mistakes, because we *all* do), unfold the strategies that will give you your life back, and help you engage in the proper tactics within those strategies.

You probably have guessed this already but winning this competition requires that you change. And what should surprise you is that the most important change you must make is at the level of your *attitude*, not your behavior. Yes, you will change your actions. But the actions you take will be in service of your new attitude. Your job will be to purposely and voluntarily *choose* to *seek out* uncertainty and distress. This sounds crazy, because it's paradoxical. And it will be hard for you, because to move purposefully into unknown territory under Anxiety's control, you must *willingly choose* to feel clumsy, awkward, unsure, and afraid. You will know you are aggressing into new, unfamiliar territory when you *voluntarily* and *purposely* decide to scare yourself.

To win this competition is hard. But the good news is that it's not complex. I will coach you on how to face your fears with a simple frame of mind that no longer feeds your anxious worrying and your avoidance.

Do you know you are already competing with Anxiety? Your challenger is winning, and you haven't even been given the rules. That's not fair. That's going to change now. We'll begin by studying the moves of Anxiety to know your play. But first, a story.

Only two competitors remain at the final table in the eleventh hour of gameplay: twenty-two-year-old Welsh poker sensation John Tabatabai, the current chip leader, and this new Norwegian girl whom no one was betting on earlier in the day.

The main floor of the casino is teeming with tourists, but it's standing room only here in the disco room at the Casino at the Empire in central London. The TV lights are blinding, the roving cameras are an added distraction, and media members mill about. They must sense an imminent victory. By now the blinds are a steep £15,000/£30,000. At stake are one million pounds and, almost more gratifying, a coveted World Series of Poker bracelet.

Two months prior, "Annette_15" was playing online almost exclusively. She's played thousands of Internet poker tournaments, winning more than twenty-three major online tournaments and earning just shy of $850,000. But today, on the eighth day of the World Series of Poker Europe inaugural event, Annette Obrestad is live and in the flesh, the calm and collected mystery girl at the final table.

Obrestad is holding pocket sevens (7♥ 7♠), and John Tabatabai has a five of spades and a six of diamonds (5♠ 6♦). Annette raises to £100,000. Tabatabai calls. The place reeks of men's cologne; the air buzzes with electricity. After the flop (7♣ 6♣ 5♥), Obrestad has three of a kind, and Tabatabai has two pair. Obrestad bets £250,000, Tabatabai raises to £750,000, and Obrestad responds, "I'm all in."

The seated onlookers, unable to contain themselves, stand in unison. Tabatabai removes his glasses. "I call," he says, smiling but visibly uneasy. Both final table competitors are all in. The winner will be decided in the next two cards. The World Series of Poker will all be over in a matter of seconds.

The "15" in Obrestad's username signifies when she started playing Internet poker. Annette_15 was a high school teenager with an online gaming presence, winning free tournaments while learning patience and stamina. In the summer of 2007, Obrestad won a 180-person sit-and-go online tournament and asserts that she looked at her cards only once during the event. She'll often play this way, with her cards hidden, which forces her to put 100 percent of her attention on the other players at the table.

An integral part of the game of poker is studying each of your challengers, and Annette Obrestad is a scholar of observation. Whether or not she's involved in a particular hand, she scans the table, reads intentions, and picks up what to the layperson is completely indiscernible. Not unlike a skilled chess player, when Obrestad is on top of her game, she considers every possible play in every unique scenario. She knows which hands are typically played and which are not. She weighs small bets versus big bets and deliberates on the meaning behind every action, every raise, every fold. Predicting your competitors' moves is near impossible, but if you can identify their trademarks and tendencies—aggressive or timid, raising or calling, playing too many hands or not enough—you can use this information against them. This is where the game is played for those who truly know how to play it.

Obrestad learned the game at the keyboard, battling a sea of faceless virtual opponents. She assesses her opponents before the first card is even dealt. "People give away 'tells' way too often," she says. "If you're good at picking up that stuff, you can win so many more pots." It's this attitude that gives Obrestad a reputation as an aggressive player.

Watching her compete one-on-one against veterans like Phil Hellmuth, wearing her thick black sunglasses that mask her eyes, Obrestad's confidence and stillness is almost unsettling. She's not mugging for the camera. She's not visiting players at other tables, shaking hands, making friends. She's too busy reading her competitors' cues and anticipating their next moves. That's not aggression; that's careful attention.

Right now it's roughly a quarter past midnight. Obrestad clasps her hands together and bows her head, the same thick black glasses concealing her emotions. The turn is the two of spades (2♣). Obrestad still has the lead. This corner of the casino is silent. The entire room is on its feet. The river is the queen of hearts (Q♥). Obrestad cracks a smile—the first "tell" she's let slip in the last eleven hours. As stacks are counted and the winner is determined, Obrestad sits back in her chair, her eyes welling with the realization that she is now the youngest competitor *and* the first female player to win a World Series of Poker bracelet. The poker world has crowned a new champion. Her name is Annette Obrestad, and tomorrow is her nineteenth birthday.

Anxiety is the cleverest of challengers. Why? Because it studies our weaknesses, our vulnerabilities, our needs. It captures our natural responses to threat, exaggerates them, and turns them against us. It hijacks any softness in our personality traits. It feeds us false information, conveying that certain activities are more threatening than they actually are. And it creates a set of beliefs that causes us to back away to safety instead of step forward into the face of threat. Your challenger is looking to exploit *any* vulnerability you might have within these domains.

Using Annette as our model, we are going to study these moves of Anxiety so we can create a winning set of strategies. Are you game?

PART ONE

The Dominant Strategy of Anxiety

CHAPTER 3

Ahhh . . . the Comfort of Certainty

I admit that I carry around a set of high standards for myself and my world. You and I have not met, but my guess is that you hold a set of standards that aren't so different. How do these sound to you?

✧ To feel physically and psychologically comfortable
✧ To perceive my world as safe enough
✧ To spend my time and energy on tasks and relationships I enjoy
✧ To feel confident in my decisions and that I am heading in the right direction
✧ To avoid mistakes
✧ To experience a sense of success
✧ To feel satisfied and content in my moment-by-moment experiences

These idealized goals are sitting there inside me, a core part of my psychological makeup. Here's the problem: if I am not paying close attention, I adopt these as my *expected* standards. Of course, I can never accomplish these goals on a consistent basis, especially since the universe fails to line up according to my wishes. So when I invest in these standards, I will end up disappointing myself more often than I feel pleased. As though that weren't enough, when I guide my daily activities by the hopes that I will *immediately* gain access to these outcomes, I usually suffer more than I celebrate.

A PERFECT PAIR

Of all these standards, two seem primary to us all. We want certainty, and we want comfort. Anytime we are engaged in that mind-set, we believe that maintaining a sense of confidence and comfort will make our lives more satisfying. We want to *know* what's coming next, because that makes us comfortable.

By establishing these priorities, we inevitably create an enemy of any doubt or distress that arises. When we want to feel secure and confident, and we start feeling insecure, we then respond accordingly: we feel an urge to get rid of it. When we are doubtful, we rapidly act to remove it, because doubt breeds the distress of not knowing. The message "I don't want this" appears in a variety of contexts. We develop a low tolerance for losing, being in conflict, being misunderstood, or feeling confused. We don't want to have to cook dinner when we're tired, or pull a muscle during exercise, or lie in bed sick.

I definitely fit into this tribe. I don't want to sit with financial insecurity, or the worry of an undiagnosed condition, or traffic that's stopped moving. I don't want the pain of crying, when with each passing second I sob harder.

We want security. We want to feel confident and certain, because then we can relax. We feel at ease when we know what's coming next. Who wouldn't want that? So we are consciously motivated and unconsciously driven to seek the comfort of certainty.

These desires will always be sitting inside of us, tugging at us, calling for our attention, beckoning to us like the siren songs called to Odysseus in Homer's *Odyssey*. And they can quickly transform into demands. "Seek control *now*. Find comfort *now*. Doubt and distress are unwanted. Banish them as soon as possible. Seek the relief of certainty." I have developed deep respect for their permanent presence and their powerful influence over my decisions.

I surrender to the fact that I will *never* get rid of these desires (and I suggest you do the same). I'm like you and everybody else in that we are forever going to *want* to feel safe and sure and comfortably in control. These are unconscious drives, built into our psyches. The unconscious will seek to eliminate negative thoughts and feelings. Moment-by-moment it monitors for doubt and discomfort and periodically will send us a message to remove those inner disturbances. When our doubt registers consciously, we will automatically feel that urge to remove it, because our unconscious wants it gone. That's one of the reasons we start feeling distressed. And it makes sense through deductive reasoning: "I am experiencing something unpleasant. Unpleasant experiences should be removed. I am justified in trying to remove this unpleasantness." That goal is built right into our psyches.

CAN THIS DECISION COME WITH A GUARANTEE?

If we aren't sure and we *need* to be, our emotions are going to give us trouble, and they will often be expressed through questions. Am I 100 percent positive that I didn't make a bad mistake back there? Am I sure my children are safe at school right now? Am I certain yet that buying this house is better than renting? When our desire for the comfort of security and confidence turns into a requirement, it will drive a great deal of our worries, fears, self-criticisms, and disappointments.

Why? Because the world does not comply with our wishes. Complex adult life will not allow us to actively engage in making decisions while simultaneously maintaining a sense of comfort and certainty as well as requiring some kind of assurance of the outcome.

Who wouldn't want to feel confident in each decision? But it doesn't work that way. When we must have that kind of control, we are going to feel out of control more often than not. It will disrupt our ability to solve problems, and it will definitely stifle our intellectual and emotional growth. Since there are no guarantees yet we seek them, we will back away from decisions, we will back away from action, and we will move increasingly farther away from a satisfying life. And we will suffer. It's ironic and even seems counterintuitive, but by seeking control we lose control. It's true.

THE FAILURE OF BACKING AWAY

At any given time, I am avoiding several projects of differing levels of importance. Right now my list of ought-to-do-but-don't-get-around-to activities looks like this: call Bill back, fit in a workout, master my new Dragon Natural Speaking software, pull my receipts together from last week's trip. Then I have a set of tasks that have been sitting around for quite a while: reading from my stacks of journals and professional books (continual project), watching Steve's video demonstration (two years overdue), fixing the woofer on the home theater (two years), finishing the soundproofing and replacing the broken track lighting in the new office (eighteen months and seven months, respectively), cleaning the water cooler (six months), and meditating (who's got the time!).

While procrastinating, if I think about one of these tasks, I evaluate it as just too unpleasant, confusing, awkward, boring, time-consuming, and/or stressful. I appraise whatever I *am* doing at the moment as easier, more enjoyable, and more comfortable. This is outright self-deception. Why? I am convincing myself that choosing the "easier" and "more comfortable" option will make me happier. With that standard, of course I'll avoid tasks like meditating or repairing the track lighting; they require effort and awkwardness. But I think we can find lots of data that says "easy and comfortable" do not equal "happy."

My second self-deception? I am predicting that the (more difficult) task I avoid will not be as satisfying as what I am doing now. And yet I have shown myself again and again that mastering a new skill, or accomplishing a task that requires my concentration and effort, brings me a sense of fulfillment. Checking a long-standing chore off my list gives me satisfaction. So I have *data* to prove I'm wrong! Geez, fulfillment and satisfaction sound pretty close to happiness. And yet, when I'm in that mind-set of "choose safe and comfortable," that information isn't available to me.

The third way I fool myself is to think that such avoidance helps me stay comfortable. But when I avoid tasks that belong on my list, I *don't* feel more comfortable. I'm not capable of blocking the list from my mind. Items flow right up to burden my consciousness through worry and self-criticism.

Can you relate to these three self-deceptions? You look at your tasks as just too unpleasant, confusing, awkward, boring, time-consuming, and/or stressful. You believe that you shouldn't do the more difficult task in front of you because it won't be satisfying, it will just be hard. And you fool yourself into thinking that such avoidance helps you stay comfortable.

By momentarily thinking about the more difficult task and then avoiding it instead of approaching it, we fail to identify any creative solutions. Choices are lost to us. For instance, we might be able to delegate a chore, or invite someone to join us in a task, or reward ourselves after completing an item. But not when we turn a blind eye to difficulties.

Why do we miss the mark here? Because when this frame of mind dominates our actions (or lack thereof), we are run by our automatic mind-set of "stay comfortable, remain confident, and keep in control."

GIVING ANXIETY A HELPING HAND

I have learned over the years that I must actively, consciously challenge that mind-set with a competing stance of equal or greater force. As I face a challenge, into my mind must come a message such as, "When I finish, I will be glad I started," or "I'm taking this off my list by the end of the day." If I act on these messages as though they are commands ("Where are you going? Sit back down!"), I am typically rewarded. And yet I all too often operate in the world as though I haven't learned that lesson. That's how deeply embedded these messages are.

Just to set the record straight, I'm no slacker, and no one would ever list "lazy" as one of my personality traits. I am a driven high achiever. Yet when my actions are dominated by unconsciously mediated, hardly audible self-instructions to maintain the familiar and easy status quo and avoid any risk, I am trapped and not free.

Remember, we are studying the moves of Anxiety right now. And its biggest move is that Anxiety takes advantage of your underlying beliefs and tendencies, especially those sending you a message that you must stay safe, comfortable, and certain. It is parasitic, thriving when you avoid anything difficult, feeding off of your natural predisposition to seek safety and comfort. It can survive only when attached to someone who has little tolerance for risk, uncertainty, and distress, whether this is a global stance or a worry about a specific fear or phobia. (Here is a little foreshadowing: if Anxiety thrives within someone who has little tolerance for uncertainty and distress, then to win this competition, what must one learn to tolerate?)

ATTRACTING WORRY

Alongside this desire for comfort and certainty sits our tendency to avoid any actions that cause us to struggle.

Any of us can unknowingly structure most of our days around the intent to increase what we can control and to enhance our comfort. Imagine you are facing a difficulty. Perhaps you have a big decision, or you have a project that requires a significant amount of your time and effort. Now imagine that, at the same time, your tendency is to avoid any struggles and to remove all doubt and distress *before* you step forward. This circumstance *attracts* anxious worrying, and it can operate with stealth, on autopilot. You will more likely stand still or back away rather than step forward.

After suffering a trauma, all of us will struggle. We will respond in one of two broad ways. In the first way, we eventually make some sense of the trauma and then respect our emotional and behavioral responses. When we get to that point, we then work through our emotions so that we have a chance to spring back toward our normal self.

Or we get stuck in our reactions to the trauma and quickly develop a general framework on how to operate in the world. Safety becomes of paramount importance, and we believe that losing control of our feelings or circumstances can come quickly and easily. Given that frame of mind, avoidance is an easily adopted strategy, and vigilance serves as our early warning system. When we sense a potentially troubling situation, our first task is to end it immediately. We start by what we mistakenly consider a problem-solving process—worry. If our worry doesn't solve the threat, then we avoid the risk by escaping. Now we become the pawns of Anxiety.

GENERATING WORRY
Common Stances That Can Turn Against You

- I need to know what the right decision is. There *is* a right decision, and I've got to figure that out before I can act.
- How do I know what to do now? What's the absolute right decision here?
- Did I make the right decision? Will that decision cause harm? Am I going to be hurt in the future because of that decision?
- I've got to stay on guard. I can't let anything bad happen. There's a chance that something bad is going to happen.
- I can't handle that.
- Will I fail?
- I need to be careful. I need to watch out.
- Above all, I need to avoid the symptoms.
- I *must* relax, *right now*.
- I have to do it perfectly.
- I must be sure that there is no risk here.
- This is too much for me. I can't do it. I don't have what it takes.
- There's something wrong with me.
- I can't let anybody know.

Even more troublesome for all of us are the threatening events in which no easy solutions are evident. When we don't know how to fix these problems—to get our heart to stop beating so fast when we think of taking a commercial flight, to make certain our children are safe at school, or to guarantee that buying this house is better than renting it—we're going to worry. We can't know how these activities will turn out, we don't want them to go wrong, and we're afraid they might. But what if we add to the mix this specific frame of mind: I need to see clearly the outcome of a difficult event before I step forward. When we generate such an internal demand, we add distress in an already distressing situation.

This is what you and I are going to work on. Let's figure out a way to reduce your suffering when you are already facing hard times.

If we're worried about our children's safety, we get them to text us when they're on the bus, then again when they get off the bus, and when they've made it through that tough gym class, and then when they're finally safely back at home. In this same way, if we believe a right answer is out there regarding whether to rent or buy, and we must be *certain* about what that right decision is, then we keep researching about home values instead of making that purchase. What's the most common (but not helpful) strategy to reduce worry? It is to stay away from the stimulus that produces our distress. When we are run by our need to avoid difficulty, then if things begin to get a little dicey—if things heat up—we will seek the quickest, easiest escape route. So if we're afraid to fly, we take a flight only when we "have to," and we avoid all the others, even if it means driving to the destination wedding and turning down that new, better paying job that requires frequent travel.

THE "GET RID OF" PROBLEM

For a moment, imagine that you struggle with social anxiety. That means you will avoid specific difficulties, often related to people's opinions of you. You don't want people to judge you because you fear their judgment will be harsh and lead to negative consequences you won't be able to cope with. So you may decide not to speak up in a meeting unless you are positive you will come across "looking good" in the eyes of everyone in the room. You worry that if you come across poorly, you will end up feeling ashamed. Plus, you can never undo that terrible mistake. Or, as you are buying your groceries, you might avoid paying with your credit card in case your signature looks shaky to the cashier, who may then think there's something wrong with you. You might then feel like you could never return to that grocery store and face the humiliation of that event again. You get rid of that potential problem by backing away.

What if you are prone to panic attacks and you never, ever want to have another one (that's certainly understandable)? Now, as you're walking into a new classroom, your heart starts racing and your head gets woozy. If your goal is to get rid of that discomfort as fast as you can, you will probably turn around and walk right back out of the class before it even begins.

If you are unwilling to feel awkward, clumsy, insecure, and sometimes even terribly uncomfortable, you will back away instead of engage in activities that otherwise might give value to your life. Here is a little foreshadowing of what's to come in this book: If it is true that being unwilling to feel awkward, clumsy, insecure, and uncomfortable is a significant contribution to your problem, then allowing those feelings must be a part of the solution.

If we simply worry about an upcoming problem instead of solving it, or if we back away to get rid of our distress, we are inviting Anxiety to take advantage of us, and we are on a path of suffering. Anxiety *thrives* on worry and avoidance. It is parasitic, and it lives off what we do with our natural predisposition to seek safety and comfort. Our urge to remove uncomfortable sensations actually strengthens those symptoms. How?

Once we are stuck in a repetitive relationship with Anxiety, a fascinating pattern emerges: Anxiety doesn't have to do much work. It has only to scare us enough to trigger our fears. Then we'll do anything not to be scared like that again. We will expend all the energy while it sits back and wins the day.

Check out Figure 1 and think about our relationship with Anxiety as similar to a pendulum. What happens when we push a child on a playground swing? She gets to continue to enjoy swinging. What happens

Figure 1. The "Getting Rid" of the problem.

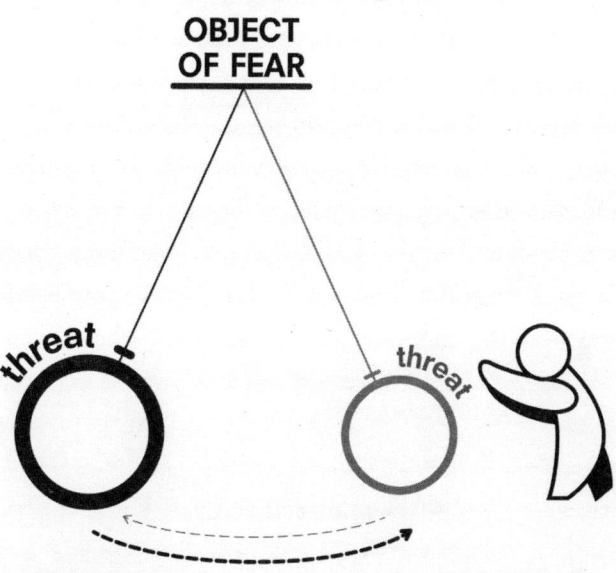

OBJECT
OF FEAR

threat

threat

- more symptoms
- more fear
- stronger urge to avoid

when we try to push away a difficulty that stands in front of us? Just like a pendulum, it will gather more energy and come back at us with more vigor. Whenever we face a threat, if we decide "I don't want this" and try to get rid of it or push it away, we give Anxiety energy to hurt us.

It's true that when we feel threatened, our instinct is to protect ourselves. Feeling that urge is not the problem. However, we get into trouble when we decide that we *never* want to feel threatened like that again, and when we elect to get safe and comfortable by getting rid of any scary doubt that pops up about that theme. Once we make that decision, then any time the threat gets close, we push it away. If the threat returns, we push it away again. When we act on our intention to avoid the difficulties we need to face, we manufacture more fear, more symptoms, *stronger* symptoms, and a greater urge to avoid. Eventually we end up in a never-ending cycle of feeling threatened and then trying to get rid of that feeling. And now we have our pendulum.

So if you are nervous about your presentation skills, you might think, "I can't allow the audience to see my hands shake," or, "I can't permit myself to stumble over my words." PUSH! And now you are more anxious and worried. If you suffer from obsessive-compulsive disorder (OCD), you may declare your unwillingness to endure the sensation that your hands are dirty. So when you sense your hands are dirty—PUSH! You get more anxious and have the urge to wash your hands. Or you step away from the front door and then question whether you remembered to lock it—PUSH! You get anxious and have the urge to check again.

Illustrations of Anxious Worrying

Work or school

- I have to be sure that I succeed. What if I fail? What if I'm demoted?
- I can never make a mistake. But I think I made a mistake. It may be a big mistake.
- I have to figure it out. But I'm not smart enough. I don't think I can figure it out.
- I have to get an A on this test. But I didn't study enough.
- I can't do poorly in that presentation. If I do, I'm sure I'll be fired.
- I'm not going to have enough money.

Relationships

- Are they going to accept me? I'll never perform to their expectations. I'll disappoint them. I can't let them discover how little I know.
- What are they thinking about me?
- I'm not sure whether he's the right one for me. I don't know what to do if he leaves me.

- I can't stumble over my words or make a mistake. They'll think I'm stupid.
- If my face turns red, I'll be humiliated.
- If my signature is shaky, I'll be so embarrassed.
- If I walk in now, everybody will stare at me.
- What if I can't think of anything to say?
- I might stumble over my words while I'm leaving the message, and I won't be able to erase it.

Panic and phobias

- What if there's a spider out there, and I don't see it?
- How can I be sure that dog won't bite?
- I have to know whether a tornado is coming.
- I can't let myself have a panic attack.
- If I don't know how crowded it's going to be, I'm not going to go.
- What if I start panicking while I'm on the bridge?
- If my heart starts beating too fast, I'll panic.
- How do I know whether he's going to get mad? If he gets angry, I won't be able to tolerate it.
- I have no idea when I'm going to start feeling trapped again.

Obsessive-compulsive disorder (OCD)

- Am I certain my hands are clean?
- I think that spot might've been blood.
- I felt a bump. I need to turn around and make sure I didn't run over someone.
- If I don't undo that, something bad may happen.
- There's a chance I just offended God. Can I gain his forgiveness?
- What if I did something terrible without knowing it?
- This doesn't feel right, and I can't move on until this feels right.

You generate a pushing-away force when your stance becomes a demanding one: "I *must* worry and avoid because I don't know how to solve this problem, and it *must* be solved or something terrible will happen." If you're fighting against your difficulties, if you're begging for them to go away, if you are disengaging from activities to keep yourself safe, then you are stepping into a trap. Anxiety feeds off of this attitude.

Let me repeat. Pushing away difficulties makes Anxiety stronger, just like pushing that playground swing away from you will guarantee that it comes back to you with equal or greater force. That's why pendulums are so highly stable. Did you know that pendulums, just like the one you see in a grandfather clock, provided the world's most accurate timekeeping technology from the mid-1600s until the 1930s? Push Anxiety away? It comes back with equal or greater force. You cannot win this competition by continuing to invest in worry and avoidance and a "getting rid of" mind-set that pushes away difficulty. We are going to have to make some clever maneuvers to break up this relationship.

"THIS SHOULDN'T BE HAPPENING"

As we experiment with some new project, we are stepping away from our usual and customary activities, and that puts us at risk of making a mistake. We all entertain the possibility that something could go wrong as we engage in life. Accidents happen. We stumble, we screw up, and we might even embarrass ourselves when we act in certain ways.

But when we get *preoccupied* with this concern, we become vulnerable. If everything must go according to our preconceived standard of perfection, then our point of view is going against basic nature. Life offers no guarantees. The more precise we are about how things must unfold, the more vulnerable we become. Unrealistic expectations and absolute standards create the fertile ground in which anxious worrying grows.

As you face one of your difficulties, imagine holding this view: "Something may go wrong, and if it does, I won't be able to handle it." You now have two choices: you can step away from the task, or you can step toward it. If you move toward that difficulty, you will now most likely decide, "I need to stay alert for danger! Something could go wrong, it could happen at any moment, it could be pretty bad, and I won't be able to handle it. So I had better be vigilant against any kind of threat." When we are looking out for negative events, and we think it's likely they will occur, and we think we won't be able to cope with them, then we brace for impact. That's basic human nature.

So if you step forward with those worries, do you know what happens next? You start noticing what the average person is oblivious to: sensations inside your body, or expressions on other people's faces, or some small thing that just doesn't seem right. If you then react from an "I don't want that" stance, then—PUSH!—you become even more anxious.

If you choose to avoid instead of approach, the threat diminishes, and you feel more at ease. Avoidance begins to seem like a more attractive option. When you allow safety to become paramount . . . and you can't be certain everything's going to go according to your plan . . . and if things go wrong, you predict they will go *terribly* wrong . . . and you believe you can't handle that . . . then *of course* you will likely back away.

And that's how Anxiety flourishes: when you worry about trouble and begin to pay inordinate attention to any signs of threat. Whether you keep stepping forward with dread or you back away, your challenger still wins that round.

SAFETY CRUTCHES

The most common way we solve the issue of threat, whether real or false, is by relying on what the anxiety-treatment literature calls safety behaviors. Let's call these safety crutches, since we lean on them in times of need. We have just been talking about the number-one safety crutch we all use: avoidance. But we can lean on lots of other crutches, like staying close to people who can take care of us; never changing up our routines; or continuing to think, research, and ask questions instead of acting. If we have been depending on these crutches for a long time, we may hardly notice them. But if we study them more closely, we will see that all of them are a form of avoidance.

We are especially likely to feel that urge to grab on to some sense of safety and security when we think about expanding our territory, since when we explore new arenas, we could end up stumbling or falling. If we are nervous fliers, we might get a prescription for a benzodiazepine to help us survive the twenty-four-hour flight to Asia. While giving a toast in a foreign language, we relieve the pressure by prefacing it with an apology for any butchered expressions.

We rely on safety crutches to get us through those fearful situations. Someone who is claustrophobic will arrive at the theater early to grab an aisle seat, one close to an exit, a seat where he can easily duck out of the theater should he become anxious. And the comfort of that seat, adjacent to the exit, will (over time) mute the symptoms of fear. The rumbling in the stomach, the cold sweat, the shaky knees, the trembling hands—those physical indicators are prevented, or at the very least subdued, thanks to the proximity of the exit door.

Here's an interesting finding in the research literature: it doesn't matter if the moviegoer *uses* that exit at any point during the picture. The availability of the safety crutch can be just as problematic. "Ah, thank goodness that the exit is just a few steps behind me and that I can use it at any time. If I was sitting at the opposite side of the theater, or if—God forbid—I was stuck in the middle of the row with people on both sides of me, I would literally be trapped. That would be terrible. But thank goodness I've got my exit. I'll be fine here." Do you see what happens? To use a crutch requires us to predict that something could go wrong if we *didn't* use it. That means we mentally rehearse things going wrong, and mental rehearsal will reinforce fear. Leaning on safety strategies may reduce fear in the moment, but it helps maintain the fear over time. If our predicted catastrophe doesn't occur, we will assume it was because we used that safety crutch, so we're more likely to use it again next time.

You can assume that you have at least made an unconscious decision to avoid doubt and distress, because that's human nature. Therefore, if you challenge your commitment to feeling comfortable and certain, you must purposely and voluntarily *choose* to put yourself into territory that provokes distress and doubt. You will need support for that endeavor, so you and I are going to work explicitly on this pattern of seeking the comfort of certainty. I'll help you learn to recognize your tendencies in the moment and to challenge them with a new set of beliefs that support the many choices you have in your valued future. I'm going to teach you the skills and perspectives necessary to push your activity into areas that feel difficult, uncomfortable, or threatening. You'll learn ways to view these tasks as you would a competition you have the ability to win. And I will teach you how to set up experiments that match the skills you have now to the challenges that lie ahead.

Our strategy will sound crazy because it's paradoxical. As I mentioned in Chapter 2, my job will be to convince you to purposely and voluntarily choose to *seek out* uncertainty and distress. Uncertainty and distress is the game board on which we are playing. When you resist them and when you fight against them, you give up territory to Anxiety. If you worry about your heart, you stop strenuous exercise. If you fear needles, you refuse to get your annual flu shot. If you are afraid of getting rejected, you do not ask anyone for a date. When you back away in the face of any of these threats, you give up ground.

Keep this in mind: Anxiety scores points against you whenever it can get you to move *away* from doubt and distress and *toward* comfort and certainty. We are going to *push into* doubt and discomfort so we can take back your territory.

CHAPTER 4

An Amygdala, a Priest, and a Rabbi . . .

T he mind has a brilliant capacity to respond to threat instantly and subconsciously. If you think of your brain as a high-functioning control board, receiving and distributing information at an almost inconceivable rate of speed, then the amygdala is the ESC key. Escape. Control-Alt-Delete. In an *Interstellar*-esque summer blockbuster, the amygdala is that bright red panic button at the far corner of the will, the control panel, shielded by a clear plastic casing that Matthew McConaughey must smash open with the butt of a fire extinguisher before the Earth is demolished by the [insert object of impending doom here].

In reality, these two almond-shaped emergency responders, each of them about an inch long, have no plastic casing, no protective cover, no barrier whatsoever. The pair of them just hang out in the midbrain, exposed in the temporal lobe with all of the other controls of the limbic system: the hippocampus button, which forms long-term memories; the cingulate gyrus switch, which regulates aggressive behavior; the dentate gyrus knob, which regulates happiness; and the Staples "Easy" button, which provides stress relief in the form of a catch phrase. The amygdala is working in the background, constantly monitoring for answers to "Am I safe?"

As you go about your daily life, you constantly receive data from the outside world through all the senses: vision, hearing, smell, touch, and taste. This data enters the brain via the thalamus, a structure sitting on top of your brain stem that both processes and transmits sensory input. If the data received is potentially threatening, the thalamus tosses it over to the amygdala. The amygdala analyzes the perceived threat, deciding just how threatening it might be and how much epinephrine (think: adrenaline) is needed to deal with it. The amygdala pages the hypothalamus; the hypothalamus texts the adrenal gland; the adrenal gland sends an e-mail confirmation; and after that series of split-second exchanges, epinephrine is tweeted (actually, it's secreted).

That's why you experience the fear response within milliseconds of any perceived threat. Now you are protected. You have averted disaster yet again.

The amygdala commandeers the entire brain and every major system of the body to respond to the threat. Adrenaline courses through your body. Your heart is pumping, your blood pressure rises, and you might even be able to lift a compact vehicle. If you begin to slip on the ice while walking, or see something slither in front of you on the path, or suddenly become lightheaded, you will be controlled by this magnificent and spontaneous first responder. Thanks to the amygdala, you can now manage this potentially threatening situation, whether it's a visit to the DMV or a minor fender bender or even [insert object of impending doom here].

As you peel back the layers and begin to understand the origin of and chemistry behind worry, it's likely that you'll develop a love-hate relationship with your amygdala. Much like a beckoning carton of ice cream in the freezer, the amygdala simultaneously comforts and aggra-vates. But like all components of our minds and bodies that play some part in our anxiety, the amygdala is doing precisely what it's supposed to do. It's behaving impeccably, as a matter of fact. And for that alone we should be thankful.

Thank you, amygdala.
Thank you for playing such a crucial role in making me a huge, worry-making machine. I really appreciate you. As much as I resent you. Love, Me

If there's one thing we all have in common, it's that every one of us has survived a (seemingly) life-threatening car backfire. That POW sounds quickly and unexpectedly. In instances like these, the amygdala receives incoming data (the auditory *POW*) and (knowing that sound indicates a *possible* danger, like a firearm discharge) immediately instructs the body to assume a guarded state. "Escape mode!" We turn without thinking, seeking the source of the explosion. We cover our heads. We overreact. If our guard is down, we might even stumble forward, crouch close to the ground, or cover our heads, shielding ourselves from stray firework shells and imaginary bullets. And then we feel like total idiots when we realize that the perpetrator behind this near-death experience was an old Ford with a clogged fuel filter. We stand up, shake off the threat, and pray no one saw that rather dramatic reaction. But still, the amygdala is doing precisely what it's intended to do. And it deserves our appreciation.

This characteristic is more than human nature. It's universal to the ani-mal kingdom, in the world of predator and prey. Somewhere on the open savannahs of Africa, an impala explodes into a spectacle of zigzag leaps to confuse and outrun the claws of a cheetah. Once the cheetah gives up the chase, the impala will shake and tremble to release the leftover bodily tension after narrowly escaping death. Then it will gracefully dash off to rejoin the herd. And don't we act just as quickly when a car backfires, when the plane we're riding experiences sudden turbulence, and when we trip on that crack in the sidewalk? That response is ingrained in us.

We can call this arousal of the amygdala the fast-track method. When the car momentarily loses traction as it hits ice, we are thrust into emergency response mode before we even have time to think, "Holy crap, here comes the ditch!" That's the shortcut to the amygdala via the thalamus. It's the amygdala functioning at its finest, in both worriers and non-worriers alike, in both the healthiest of us and those with mental health disorders. Whether you consciously observe it or not, you probably employ the fast-track method daily.

New Yorkers know this reaction in a special way. Any New Yorker can easily recall at least one experience of stepping on an uneven subway grate. Walking through Times Square, the metal grill beneath you will suddenly sway and shift and sink perhaps an inch into the sidewalk, but it still gives you the impression for one fleeting second that you're going to fall straight through the ground and onto the gritty train tracks below. And for the next month or so, you step over or around every grill, grate, plate, or manhole cover you encounter. You're reminded of that terrifying feeling of (as you imagined it) falling through that hole in the ground and becoming a permanent fixture of Times Square's subterranean transit system. For a few weeks your amygdala has a built-in message: "This may be unstable, and I could fall through. DANGER!"

FROM SUBWAY GRATES TO SNAKES

One of my offices is out of my home, back on a few acres in the woods. It is a beautiful setting, but occasionally, maybe once every two years, if you were walking down the sidewalk to the entrance, you will be greeted by a snake draped across the stone walk in front of you. Let's play this out. You're strolling down the sidewalk, totally relaxed. You're not on guard, for there's no reason to be. Suddenly and unexpectedly you spot a snake directly in front of you on the sidewalk. If you're like me, you jump back and squeal like a child. You can imagine what happens next. You momentarily freeze while your heart races, then you back away slowly and hope you can find another path to the door.

Let's slow that instant reaction and look at it from your mental processing. As your brain receives the stimulus of the snake, its monitoring function searches your memory banks to make sense of the scene, as it does every moment of your waking life. In this case, it concludes "Dangerous mismatch! You and this object at this close proximity in this environment equal threat." In literally the blink of an eye, your brain considers and rules out the response options of jumping over the snake, stomping on it, grabbing something with which to hit it, or standing there screaming at the top of your lungs. It picks "Freeze, then back away slowly." (The little squeal you let out is not a required part of the package, but it does seem like the right thing to do.) The bodily sensations that go along with being scared can be uncomfortable. But they are a required component of a vital system of learning. When you become surprised by a threat and you let your brain's automatic response take over, it will serve you well. Its most important task will be to generate and then sort through ideas about how to solve the problem.

Once you've had that mini-trauma (just like the subway grate misstep), for the next three or four days, every stick on the ground is a snake. Every garden hose is a snake. Every rustle in the leaves is a snake. Why? Because with both the subway grate and the sidewalk snake, the unconscious was caught off guard. It's as though your defensive system is in the "everything seems pretty safe here" mode, and all of a sudden it is as surprised as you are by this little threat. When you are traumatized by that sort of thing, the unconscious says, "I am so sorry, boss. I let you down. I was operating as though everything was fine when a true threat was present. I promise I'm on guard now! I'll protect you! I'm on the lookout full time for snakes now!" Your amygdala decides it's smarter to suspect that more objects are snakes than to let down its guard and allow you to step on a snake and get bitten. So it modifies your sense of threat. "Okay, when I sense anything resembling a snake or a location where a snake might be present, I'm gonna be on guard for snakes."

Since the amygdala's motto is "better safe than sorry," we all will be on the receiving end of plenty of false positives, reacting as though threat is present when no threat exists. We'll gasp and freeze when suddenly spotting the dog leash on the ground because it looks similar enough to the snake we saw three days ago—just so the amygdala doesn't allow us to unknowingly step on a copperhead that might be within reach of us.

As we have an increasing number of false positive experiences, the amygdala will learn that encounters with snakes are actually pretty rare, and eventually it will back down to its pre-snake encounter state. In fact, that's exactly how our amygdala will quiet down. We place it into a safe, reasonable facsimile of the scene in which we were frightened, and we let it hang out and learn that *this* scene (the dog leash, the rustling leaves, the garden hose) is actually not a threat, so it is different from *that* scene (the snake on the sidewalk). This system works pretty darn well, unless we continue to tell ourselves that a threat is imminent. Let me explain.

We can arouse the amygdala through a second set of circuitry, from the brain's prefrontal cortex, which interprets events and generates opinions about the possibility of pending danger. Since this circuitry involves a higher level processing from outside the limbic system, it triggers an alarm response more slowly, in about a couple of seconds. (That may not sound very slow, but you have to compare it with a few-hundredths of a second when cortical response is uninvolved.) The slow track arousal of the amygdala is the result of talking yourself into worrying.

"Talk myself into worrying?" you might say. "Trust me, I worry enough without prompting. I don't need to talk myself into more worry, thank you very much."

Well, you may not always do it consciously, but I bet you've talked yourself into worrying about a meeting or an encounter or an occasion before the moment has even arrived.

"Baloney. Give me an example."

Okay, I will. Let's say you've been invited to a dinner party. En route to said party, you think to yourself, "Oh, no. I just realized that the host invited Ashley, and I can't *stand* Ashley." It's less that you can't *stand* Ashley and more that you and Ashley aren't on the best of terms these days. The last time you and she were in the same room together, you got into a heated argument about politics or religion or *Dancing with the Stars* . . . some hot-button issue. "I can't deal with this tonight," you tell yourself. "She's going to bring up that fight we had, and she'll want to talk about it and 'fix things.' It's going to be so awkward." Within seconds, another frightening realization hits you. "OMG, what if she doesn't want to resolve things? What if she got there early so she could tell everyone what a nasty person I am? I'll walk into the front door, and she'll have turned all the dinner guests against me over one stupid argument that happened three months ago. Ugh. I just *can't tolerate* facing that embarrassment. I should call and tell them that I got stuck at work or something. I should avoid the situation altogether." You haven't even parked the car and already you're catastrophizing about a situation that might be threatening but just as easily could be harmless. You've predetermined that this dinner will be a dismal failure, and this prediction hinges on a person who may or may not be invited, who may or may not arrive early with the intention of soiling your good name, and who may or may not even recall the aforementioned argument.

Sound familiar? "Uh, oh. This could be trouble. Should I avoid the situation? I should at least get on guard for threat." It may not be a dinner party, and it may not be about Ashley, but we talk up these types of scenarios all the time. Meanwhile, our amygdala hears only one message, "Danger," and secretes that energizing adrenaline.

Of course, this train of thought is perfectly logical, in fact vital, if your job is to seek out worst-case scenarios. A firefighter walking into a burning building, for instance, cannot assume that things will go smoothly. Firefighters have been trained to adopt this kind of thinking and to plan for the worst. A SWAT team leader knows that he cannot turn any corners lightly, that he needs backup, and that he must have all necessary resources at his disposable in the event that this forcible entry gets ugly.

As for the rest of us—those who aren't police officers or specialists in risk analysis—this direct link between catastrophizing and the amygdala gets us nowhere. This incessant "talking" can only put us into an unwarranted state of distress. We pull into the parking lot of a local bar. We tell ourselves, "Oh, no. This parking lot is crowded. That means it's going to be just as crowded inside. What if it's so crowded that I become trapped? When I get anxious, I have trouble concentrating. Then I have trouble putting sentences together. What if I get flustered and then embarrass myself? What if I feel trapped in a conversation with someone as it starts going south? I can't handle that. I shouldn't even bother. I should just go home."

Talk, talk, talk, talk, talk, talk.

And where does all of this talking get us? Well, it doesn't make us calmer or more comfortable. All we do when we're into nonstop worrying is get our amygdala riled up for all the wrong reasons. This catastrophic self-talk gets our worry juices flowing and causes the amygdala to release epinephrine before we arrive at the dinner party, before we enter the potentially crowded local bar, before we step onto the plane. You see, this is the scenic route. This is the long road worry travels down.

An amygdala walks into a bar, and the bartender says, "Hey, don't come in here looking for trouble!" (That one kills at psychology conferences.)

The worst part of talking ourselves into a freaked-out state? The neo-cortex—the talking, thinking, interpreting brain—has no hard wiring to the amygdala that says, "Whoops, my bad. No cause for alarm. You don't have to prepare for panic anymore." That "Just kidding!" message comes back undeliverable. Remember, this is the brain's limbic system, which developed early in the evolution of mammals, the neocortex is trying to communicate with. Hence, the simple structure of the amyg-dala is built with an economy of action. Like a mother watching her toddler swim for the first time, the amygdala (once triggered) is con-stantly on alert, ready to offset any threatening situation with a healthy dose of epinephrine. That is its primary, simple function, love it or hate it. No just kidding button is available.

Even if a situation is safe but you *tell* yourself it's dangerous, your amygdala will come to the rescue like Dudley Do-Right of the Royal Canadian Mounted Police. (You don't remember that cartoon? He was all about liberating the damsel in distress. "I'll save you, Nell!") The amyg-dala is your Dudley Do-Right. Let's use a flying example again. Imagine you're on a commercial flight that passes through moderate turbulence. Such turbulence is completely safe for the plane. But if you *interpret* the experience as dangerous, then your amygdala will set off its alarm to protect you. If you want to be less anxious on a plane, we don't have to change anything about the flight. We have to change your interpretation.

So how, then, are we going to get your amygdala to chill out when you are in your catastrophizer mode? How do we get those almond-shaped epinephrine pushers to realize that everything is as it should be, that you don't need all this worrying, that you don't *want* all this worrying?

We're going to get to all that before we're done.

PART TWO

Your Winning Strategy

STEP BACK

CHAPTER 5

Noise Pollution

You're nineteen years old, wrapping up your sophomore year of college. That term paper you're writing, the one that has to be hand-delivered to your professor's mailbox by end of day, is a dozen pages short. As of this moment, while you stare mindlessly at the screen, you've got today's date at the top and a title you're unhappy with. And the reason you're stalling and surfing through Facebook status updates is that you didn't read two of the three texts required to form a proper response.

And you skimmed the third.

If you're not worried at this moment, the content of this book is of no use to you. I envy your cold detachment. You'll achieve great things.

Of course you're worried! You've got seven hours to push out twelve pages of material on a subject you know very little about. No, it's not an impossible feat, but it's certainly stirring up some nerves. We can all agree that this is a legitimate worry, and for the purposes of this book (and your study of and battle with Anxiety), we're going to call this type of worry a signal.

SIGNAL

"I have a final paper due before dinner
on two texts I haven't read!
And I haven't started!"

Why a signal? Well, because at that moment, the knocking knees, knot in your throat, cold sweats, and affected breathing—all physical manifestations of your worry—are prompting you to put out effort. Your body is signaling you to **TAKE ACTION**. "Move it! DO something!" You must own up to the difficult situation you've put yourself in, acknowledge the worry and the physical symptoms associated with it, and develop an abbreviated plan of attack. Take action! Accept the mediocre title and move on! Get off Facebook and start writing! You call a classmate who's read the assigned texts and invite him or her over for breakfast. You call your professor (commence sobbing) and beg for an extension on account of the three final exams you've endured this week. Or, alternatively, you call your professor (still sobbing) and invent a semi-plausible story about a computer virus . . . or an unpleasant breakup . . . or a dormitory fire that destroyed all of your possessions, including the hard drive on which your paper was saved, and thank God you weren't in the building at the time!

Whatever moral standard you choose to live by, no matter how much sobbing you choose to employ, the signal is still **TAKE ACTION**: move, work, write, create, call, plead, invent, lie (anything *except* stay still, sulk, stare, stall, succumb).

Anything worth worrying about is worth problem solving. (Of course, the key to living by my motto is to know what is worth worrying about and what is not.) Either the worry pops up and it's a signal that we have some problem solving to do . . . or it's plain old noise.

Noise is what its name suggests. Buzzing. Nuisance. Interference. It's irrelevant. It's repetitive. It's downright irritating at times. It's not productive or useful or worth listening to. Noise is static.

SIGNAL

Your teenage daughter is out on a date.
She was due home at midnight.
It's now 2 AM.

NOISE

You have OCD, and unnecessary "checking" is your thing.
As you hear the hotel door close behind you, you think,
"Did I lock the front door when I left home this morning?"

Let's give a more in-depth example of noise.

You, an overachieving nineteen-year-old sophomore, completed your term paper days in advance of the due date. To say you were comfortable with the assigned texts would be an understatement; you could probably recite them from memory. Rather than handing in the paper early, you used that spare time to review your essay response, making minor changes and correcting some overlooked grammatical errors. You deliver the final draft eight hours before the deadline and e-mail your professor a copy as well.

You awaken at 3 AM, panicking. *Wait—what if I totally missed the point of the assignment? What if I misread the prompt? What if I summarized too much and analyzed too little? What if I forgot to include the bibliography? What if I get a D on this paper?! That would really bring down my final grade and my GPA. My parents would be really disappointed.*

Talk, talk, talk. Worry, worry, worry.

What tells us that this is noise as opposed to a signal? First, it's three o'clock in the morning. You (like most of us) have declared three o'clock in the morning as sleep time. Pursuing the worry at 3 AM brings you no benefits, even if it is a valid concern. You've got to treat it as irrelevant noise.

Second, must I remind you that you are *not* the procrastinating, underprepared college freshman? You are the diligent, bright student who is mindful of the deadline and goes above and beyond as opposed to doing just enough. Having reexamined the paper multiple times, you most likely would have noticed if your response was off target. Don't you agree? See where I'm headed here? You have found nothing tangible to substantiate your worry, nothing to legitimize the fear that you've "blown it" and put a big, ugly dent in your GPA. Earning a D is not impossible, sure, but it's unlikely.

Mark this one as noise and go back to bed.

SIGNAL
You and your partner had an argument at breakfast.
You both said some mean things and then
stormed off to work. Neither of you has apologized.

NOISE
You called your partner at 10 AM, apologized,
and scheduled to talk when you both get home.
But you are still dwelling on the argument
instead of focusing on your work.

Or let's imagine that your son (or your daughter, niece, whoever) has been accepted to their top choice school in New York City. And while you know that this is an accomplishment worth celebrating, you're overcome by worry. *What if another terrorist group attacks New York? It happened once. It can happen again. If my daughter [son, niece, relative] goes to New York, she won't be able to protect herself from something like that. I don't want her to go. It's too dangerous. There are plenty of other schools* . . . and so on.

You're right. She won't be able to protect herself. And you can't protect her either. We have no control over the fate of New York City or its residents. We can't predict the future. And unless you are employed by the CIA and are privy to information that states otherwise, no one has detected a current threat on the City of New York. Yes, 9/11 was a horrific, devastating, tragic event. But it was also a *singular* event. Its impact on our minds and memories, and our spirits and families does not substantiate the worry that it will happen again, in New York City or in Toledo or Kansas or anywhere in between. No signal exists here; no call to action. Here is that irrelevant, repetitious noise, *posing* as a signal, *posing* as something worth worrying about.

STEP BACK

Worry is supposed to be only a trigger for problem solving. It is not supposed to last a long time. But Anxiety's goal is to get you confused as to what is a valid concern and what is noise and then to get you to dwell on the worry instead of solving the problem.

As long as you're actively engaged in that worry, you'll never be able to decipher whether it's a signal or noise. So when a worried thought pops up, take a step back, disengage from your upset about the specifics. Examine the worry and then decide if it's a signal or if it's noise. If you conclude that it's a signal, that's wonderful! You can do something about a signal. Signals come with solutions. Signals we can handle.

On the other hand, if that worry pops up and sounds like noise, you can't solve it. No solution exists. The paper's been handed in (twice!).

No changes can be made at this point. Getting out of bed at 3 AM and rereading the response is caving in to the noise. Your easy-listening station is picking up static, and you're turning up the volume, trying to decipher the lyrics to the song you can barely make out beneath all the *noise*. It's time to change the station.

"What if I'm wrong?" you might ask. "What if I decide something is noise, but it's actually a signal? What then?"

What then? Well, in most cases, your head would roll right off of your body.

Of course you might be wrong! Parked on an inclined road, you worry that you've left your car in neutral. You choose to dismiss this pesky worry, treat it as noise, and keep walking. Hours later, you return to that same spot and find that your car is missing—or, rather, that it's rolled down the hill and into a tree . . . or another vehicle . . . or several other vehicles. It turns out the car was in neutral. *Whoops!* You screwed up.

I won't sugarcoat it. There's always the risk that you're wrong when you decide a worry is noise. More important, you have to be willing to take that risk. "Nuts! I left my car in neutral. I'll have to get that bumper replaced. Well, that was stupid. I won't make that mistake again."

SIGNAL
"I'm supposed to move the car by 7 AM.
It's 7:15 AM. I hope it didn't get towed!
I had better go move it!"

NOISE
"I'm supposed to move the car by 7 AM. It's 5:45 AM.
I hope it doesn't get towed! What if the alarm fails?
I had better wake up in an hour!"

Warning: What I'm about to say might just blow your mind. This right here might disrupt the whole worry system you've sculpted and perfected over the years. Ready? Brace yourself. Here it comes:

What you often worry about isn't worth your attention.

Astonishing, I know, but ultimately true. The things your mind cooks up (the flawed term paper) aren't always valid concerns. The burdens you take on (the pending terrorist attack) don't necessarily need your shoulders to rest upon. And here's the best part: If you happen to treat noise as a signal, you'll hit a dead end as soon as you begin to problem solve. How reassuring is that! It's foolproof! As soon as you give your noisy worry some undue attention by actively exploring solutions, you hit a wall. *SMACK!*

Signals require actions. Noise requires nothing. It's that simple.

Try to resolve a noisy worry. I dare you. Try to wake up at 3 AM, rewrite that twelve-page paper, sneak past security and into the administration building, break in to your professor's office, retrieve the old paper from the desk, replace it with the revised copy, hack your professor's e-mail, delete the digital copy you had e-mailed previously, sneak out, return home, go back in time, and resend the document. It makes for a *great* intellectual thriller, but in reality, it's static. Change that station.

Either a worry represents a valid concern and therefore becomes the first step in your problem-solving process, or that worry is irrelevant, distress-provoking noise you should not address. Anxiety needs you to respond to a noisy worry as though it is an alarming signal. It would *love* for you to think, "This might be serious. It could cause me harm. I've got to pay attention. Even if it turns out to be noise, I need to feel certain that it *is* noise. Besides, I trust my feelings, and I'm uncomfortable right now, so something must be wrong. Why would these worried thoughts pop up in my mind unless there *was* a threat?"

Exhausting, eh?

For all of us, needless worries will blast away at us with content that, on the surface, sounds so serious. If you struggle with OCD, you might become compelled to wash your hands, based on this belief: "If I don't wash my hands, I might make someone else dangerously ill." If you become focused on the fear that you might bring salmonella home from the grocery store to your children, causing them grave illness or death, you're going to feel highly threatened. Who wouldn't become distressed if they believed in the imminent possibility of such catastrophic outcomes? If I thought it was highly probable that I would catch the flu by not washing my hands, I guarantee you that I would wash my hands thoroughly. I'd support my actions with this stance: "I've got a hectic life right now. I can't cancel a week's worth of writing or treatment sessions or conferences to fight off the flu. Not right now. I can't handle that!"

But in this OCD example, contamination is the *topic* of your obsession, but contamination isn't the issue. The issue is that Anxiety has you treating noise as though it's a signal. Suppose I were to say to myself, "I've just imagined something inappropriate. That means I'm a bad person." If I fall for that thought, I'd be highly distressed. I can't handle the belief that I am inherently a bad person! If you suffer from OCD, then the topic of your obsessions is irrelevant; it's noise. But OCD doesn't let you understand that. It keeps you focused on the noise and makes you interpret it as a signal.

Well, if OCD isn't about germs or being a bad person (or any of the other topics it generates in your mind), what's it about? OCD is about you not being able to tolerate doubt and distress related to your theme. If you understood that, then the more accurate thought would be "If I don't wash my hands, I'll feel uncertain and anxious." When an obsession pops up, it is a signal—a signal that you are having an obsession! And that obsession is designed to produce doubt and discomfort. It's not a signal that something terrible is about to happen. I'm going to help you learn to handle uncertainty and distress. I can't help you if you believe your obsession is truly about contamination or about being a bad person, because those messages are unhelpful noise that should not be addressed.

Maybe OCD has never messed with you, but you are generally a worrier. Then you likely dwell on a broad set of issues, particularly health concerns, your finances, relationships, and work or school performance. Anxiety has the ability to take a legitimate concern, such as being able to pay this month's mortgage, and cause you to worry about it all day, every day, instead of focusing your attention on productive problem solving.

If I am a single father of three and I just lost my job, I am going to worry about how to put food on the table and pay the monthly rent. It wouldn't be surprising for me to think, "If I can't pay the mortgage at the end of the month, I could lose the house. The kids and I could end up out in the street. I can't let that happen!" This is certainly a relevant concern. And my worry should trigger my creative intelligence to help me solve this problem. But if instead I fall into a subroutine of worry-without-an-action-plan, that will have no redeeming value. I'm not coming up with options to solve the problem. I'm not figuring out where my money is going to come from. I'm simply distressing myself by repeatedly reciting the nature of my problem. When we create a subroutine in which we worry throughout the day about such a topic, disconnected from taking problem-solving actions regarding a legitimate concern, then we are making a serious error in strategy.

If I can help you accomplish three essential tasks, you can win this competition. The first is to distinguish worries that are important signals from those that are irrelevant noise. Second is to make sure you act on the signals instead of simply worrying. We've been talking about these two tasks here, and we will continue in these next two chapters.

Your third task is to stop paying attention to the noise. We will spend the rest of the book learning some very interesting ways to handle those useless, irrelevant, unhelpful, and even hurtful worries.

We have already talked about the surefire way to get rid of worries, which is to avoid any actions that will provoke your distress. That's why people stop flying, or never take the elevator, or refuse to touch anything that might be "contaminated." When you avoid because of your irrational fears, Anxiety scores big-time points. So I'm going to show you how to step forward again, which means that those worries you silenced by your passivity will now return. When you start worrying unnecessarily—when you fret over some difficulty without the intention or ability to problem solve—Anxiety is manipulating you.

The quickest, easiest, and most helpful way to handle a noisy worry is simply to drop it and focus on anything else. If that intervention fails you and those thoughts become like a boom box blaring in your head, you will need a more nuanced response. Then it's time to engage in our strategy. And our first task is to decide that attending to the topic of your noisy worry is the worst move you can make, one that *guarantees* you will lose.

CHAPTER 6

Make It NOT About Your Content

A struggling small business owner is facing some difficult decisions. With a seemingly insurmountable debt and no promising prospects, he's thinking he might need to lay off some if not all of his employees. Even more troubling, he doesn't know how long he can maintain this business when he has little income, no new leads, and a swarm of creditors breathing down his neck. His worries—about the livelihoods of the people who work for him, about his own livelihood, about impending bankruptcy, about finding a job in this economy—all of these bothersome, muttering worries, have forged together to form a big, ugly ball of anxiety that hounds him day in and day out.

Of course, our small business owner doesn't expect his worries to solve his problems. They are a *signal* of his problems but offer no solution. None of us believe that worrying brings instant gratification or pays off our credit card bills. "This is unpleasant," we tell ourselves, "but at least I'm worrying. That's a step in the right direction." Worrying about all of these potential negative outcomes seems a heck of a lot better than losing everything/going to pieces/going crazy/having a heart attack/disappointing everyone/humiliating myself. We have no need to adjust our intentions (which are good) or the logic behind them (which is sound). Instead, we must figure out new ways to respond to our distress signal. We need an alternative approach.

Presently, our fictional (but all too real) small business owner is stuck in what we can call the Problem Identification phase, in which we acknowledge the hurdle(s) we're facing. It's not uncommon that we'll get trapped here, sitting down and staring at our problems like we're staring at a blank page, asking ourselves, "Well, now what?" Worrying helps us to identify those challenges. But when we don't do anything about them, worry starts to remind and nag us, stressing just how important each of these problems is, painting a bleak picture of our present situation.

SOLVING PROBLEMS

So how do we get out of that Problem Identification phase? Well, our worries are designed to motivate us. They are there to drive us toward creating a problem-solving plan and then acting on it. Instead of standing in those problems and wading into worry, we need to set in motion a strategy to solve those challenges by taking one step at a time. Our small business owner needs to call his financial advisor and look into loan options, or call his father-in-law in Toledo to ask him for loan options, or seek new job procurement services at a free business seminar. Or perhaps all of these things. When we are staring at a problem, even something as simple as setting aside a specific time on a specific date to address the issue is a better option than allowing worry to gnaw, gnaw, gnaw away at us.

That doesn't mean worries will now disappear. Yes, we can still feel troubled even while taking action to solve our problems. We may start to question the plan while we are midway through implementing it. Our small business owner can set a date and time to meet with his CPA, but that won't stop worry from creeping in. "What am I going to do between then and now? What if the CPA has no options for me? What if setting this appointment is not *enough*?"

That's our goal: for signals, we are to create a plan and act on that plan. Worry is absolutely beneficial when it is integrated into the overall strategy. But that means, of course, that we've got to *create* a strategy. If you believe you're dealing with a signal, then let worry provoke you into taking action to address the problem. That means you've got to have a plan you are *willing* to act on. And that means you need worry to trigger you into *doing* something.

"GET PREPARED!"

Hurricane preparedness is a common discussion thread in the East Coast of the United States, particularly when July and August roll around. Frank, a South Florida resident, has been bombarded with reminders on local news programs about purchasing supplies in advance. At the end of each evening broadcast, meteorologists urge homeowners to "Get prepared!" Frank's go-to supermarket has stocked up on water, canned food, flashlights, and batteries, even going so far as to display these emergency items in an obvious and convenient location near the front of the store.

If there's one thing Frank's stocked up on, it's worries. You might say he's "mentally prepared" for any tropical storms or hurricanes that might sweep through. He hasn't actually purchased window shutters or the recommended disaster supplies—nonperishables, first aid kit, battery-operated radio—but he's got enough worry stored up to last him three months. And he has worried a heck of a lot about that old tree out back, the one that in 125 mph winds could easily be uprooted and come crashing down on his screened-in patio . . . but, no, he hasn't actually done anything about it. His legitimate worrying never triggered action, never impelled him to make a supply run, never prompted him to pull that old chainsaw out of the shed and cut down that looming liability.

Through all of this worrying, Frank has anticipated most of the negative events that might occur. He does this because he believes that when he worries, he is readying himself for any calamity that might befall him. His pattern reflects this false belief: "If I worry about it, then when something bad happens, I'll be better prepared for it." Or, on a similar note, "If I worry about this, I'm more likely to figure out how to avoid or prevent something bad from happening." What Frank hasn't done, despite all of his fretting and stressing and ideological defense of worrying, is take any action to prevent these negatives outcomes.

Listen up: When you worry about a legitimate concern and then *do not act* on that worry, you transfer it from a signal to noise. We all do this. We identify a problem that's worth worrying about, and then all we do is worry. That's noise. If it doesn't kick you into problem solving, it's noise. If you want to get stronger, you must stop doing that.

Remember that worry has a legitimate role in motivating us to take action on our plans, to stay on task, and to solve problems both big and small in our lives. It has the *potential* to trigger planning, preparation, and action, but worrying in itself is not acting. Acting is checking inventory, purchasing supplies, and putting up shutters. Acting means we've got ourselves moving. Worrying is sitting still.

When faced with a challenge (be it a hurricane or a struggling business or a reluctance to start writing), we must *decide* to act and then we must act. We should perceive our worries as an indication that we should meet our challenges head on, cut right to the heart of them, and *take action*. Otherwise, we'll be in the aftermath of the storm, sitting and staring at that old tree that's collapsed onto our patio, and asking, "Well, what now?"

✧ ✧ ✧

Shall we try another example? Yes, we shall.

You have an interview scheduled for tomorrow morning, and you're understandably anxious about it. You've been unemployed for a year now, and this position could prove to be very lucrative. You don't want to blow it.

Let's take a minute and jot down all of the worries that are spinning around in your mind.

WORRIES	There'll be a lot of people in the room.
My hands will be sweaty/clammy.	I won't know the answer to a question.
Someone else will be more qualified.	I'll be overdressed.
I'll be late.	I'll be underdressed.
My mouth will dry out.	I'll make a bad first impression.
I'll misrepresent myself.	I'll have to pee mid-interview.
I'll sweat through my shirt.	They'll think I'm boring.
I'll forget my resume.	I suck at interviewing.

I'd say those are pretty typical worries that most people relate to. Now let's take another minute and distinguish the noise from the signals.

WORRIES	~~There'll be a lot of people in the room.~~
~~Hands will be sweaty/clammy.~~	I won't know the answer to a question.
~~Someone else will be more qualified.~~	I'll be overdressed.
I'll be late.	I'll be underdressed.
My mouth will dry out.	~~I'll make a bad first impression.~~
~~I'll misrepresent myself.~~	I'll have to pee mid-interview.
~~I'll sweat through my shirt.~~	~~They'll think I'm boring.~~
I'll forget my resume.	I suck at interviewing.

That's right. Only seven of the fifteen worries cycling through your mind are actually in your control (i.e., signals). And—good news—all seven can be addressed rather easily.

I'll be late: Map the distance beforehand, estimate travel time, and leave an additional thirty minutes for unexpected traffic, locating the building, parking, etc.

My mouth will dry out: Bring a small cup of water in with you to the interview. You can even buy a special chewing gum at the pharmacy that promotes saliva production (but take it out before you enter the room!).

I'll forget my resume: Keep an extra copy of your resume in your car. Additionally, pack your suitcase/portfolio the night before so it's not a last-minute concern.

I won't know the answer to a question: Consider the questions that might be asked at a job interview. If you're interviewing for a corporate position, you may want to know the history of the corporation, their mission statement, their clients and services, etc. Do whatever research you need to prepare for whatever they might toss your way.

I'll be overdressed/underdressed: Ask friends for their opinions about attire for an interview. Search monster.com for "The 6 Worst Things to Wear to a Job Interview."

I'll have to pee mid-interview: Seek out a bathroom just before you enter the office.

I suck at interviewing: Practice! Conduct several mock interviews with a friend or family member, and try thinking on your feet.

As for the other seven concerns—well, there's not much you can do about those. How can you ensure that no other candidate will be more qualified than you? *You can't!* So unless you're willing to camp out in the hallway and discourage all incoming interviewees to give up this swell opportunity on your behalf, you can do nothing except mark it as noise.

ELEVATE YOUR GAME!

What does this chapter title mean, "Make It NOT About Your Content"? When you find yourself repeatedly worrying about a specific topic, I'm going to refer to that topic as your content. Anything at all that you're stuck on and worried about is your content, whether it's a medical procedure, walking into open spaces, making mistakes, having conflicts or being rejected, asking someone for a date, being the center of attention, or forgetting to lock the door.

Now we've settled what the term *content* means. But I'm telling you to make it NOT about your content. This means you must put effort into correcting any misinformation you have about the topic of your worry. It means you need to gather any knowledge you might be missing before you can step forward into the arena that threatens you. When we worry, all of us make some errors in assessment of what is truly at risk. Noisy worries pop up that exaggerate the problem, defining it as horrific, intolerable, humiliating, or life threatening. When facing a difficulty while those worries are in control, negative thoughts will intrude into our days and nights, and we will tend to back away as the only way we know to quiet our worries. Your task is to answer those worries. You've got to figure which ones are signals and which are noise, because you must determine your true risk and then decide whether you want to take that risk.

But this work will not only be about correcting misinformation. Whether you worry about only a specific topic or you dwell on lots of themes, if you want to feel stronger and more resilient, then we need to get underneath your specific content so we can address your tendencies. On page 22 in Chapter 3, you saw the chart called "Generating Worry: Common Stances That Can Turn Against You." That gives you a good sense of the tendencies Anxiety takes advantage of. One of the most important stances to address is "I can't handle this." Your task will be to adopt a new attitude: "This is hard. I'm not sure I can handle it, but I'm going to move toward it anyway." To do that, you must be willing to tolerate uncertainty and cope with distress. Why? Because Anxiety will not *allow* you to feel sure that you can handle these situations. You must step forward *at the same time* you're feeling uncomfortably doubtful.

There are two big reasons you need to begin this process by addressing your questions about the specific topic of your worry. First, if you firmly believe "I shouldn't step forward and engage because it's not safe," then you're stuck. Why would you pursue this task and simultaneously resist it?

The second reason, and the one I want you to pay closest attention to in this book, is that Anxiety *needs* you to stay distracted by your content, by the topic of your worry, in order for it to dominate you. Anxiety does not want you to discover that the core theme in this competition is a *generic* sense of doubt and distress, not a specific one. As long as Anxiety can keep your attention on your content, it wins and you will continue to lose out. Elevate the game! Get above your content, up to the real challenge you must face.

Let me be clear. It's *fine* for a part of you to think that the threat is too much. But your executive, the one you put in charge of making decisions and acting on them, needs to think otherwise.

Let's say you want to work on your continuing panic attacks, but every time you begin to panic, you think you're having a heart attack. You have to resolve that misinformation. Otherwise, the thought of having another panic attack will terrify you. Why would anyone step forward if a heart attack is the risk? If I thought at any moment I could provoke my own heart attack, I'd be very cautious, too. When you decide a panic attack is dangerous, you're likely to avoid strenuous physical activity, make sure you have anti-anxiety medications available, only go to the grocery store with a companion, frequently check your pulse, and so forth. Why would you change any of those behaviors if you believed they were saving you from harm? So either you stay stuck, or you change what you believe about panic attacks.

If you want to work on your fear of flying, and your fear is the possibility of your plane crashing, you need to change your perspective on this issue. Decide that you are *not* actually putting your life at significant risk when you fly. Your job is to move fearful thoughts about air travel out of the category of signal and into the category of noise. It is the only possible way you can start winning. And don't give anyone else the responsibility of making you feel safe. You can talk to a pilot or work with a therapist who specializes in the fear of flying. But don't turn the task over to them of convincing you that flying is safe. It's not their job; it's your job. You have to commit yourself to finding ways to trust the industry. (And, by the way, it absolutely deserves your trust.)

Even when you come to a rational conclusion, your worried self is still going to generate spontaneous fearful thoughts about dying on the plane. You simply cannot extinguish them; the mind does not work that way. Those thoughts will show up as you consider approaching a flight. Once you make your informed decision that flying is safe enough for you, then when any further worries pop up, your task is to label them as irrelevant noise (that still has the ability to make you scared). You won't *feel* like it's irrelevant noise. But you have to *act* as though it's noise. (We'll be talking about this "act as though" theme in Chapter 18.) Your job is to allow those noisy worries to pop up and then not believe them. When the worried thoughts arise, view them from the perspective of "*Of course* I'm going to have these thoughts. I'm doing something that has frightened me in the past. My mind hasn't quite caught up to my understanding that everything is safe. It's okay that these thoughts show up, and I don't need to act on them." (You don't need to literally say such a long message to yourself in the moment. But whatever you do say will be some simplified version of that point of view. We'll address all this talking-to-yourself stuff in Chapters 15 and 16.)

Once you catch yourself worrying and then decide to let those thoughts go, turn your attention to something else of interest. It's likely that the worry will pop up again, maybe within just a few seconds, and that needs to be acceptable, too. What do you do then? Again turn your attention to something else of interest . . . until you get disturbed again.

Let me give you another example. If you believe it's time to ask for a raise but you're too afraid your supervisor will fire you if you speak up, you will need to handle that fear. You can convey to yourself something like, "It'd be crazy for her to react that way. But I guess it's conceivable. And I'm willing to take that risk, because this issue is important to me." Or you can make a different decision: "It's too risky for me right now. Even though I deserve a raise, she laid off three people this quarter. I can't afford the chance that I could be next." Our job here is not to figure out which decision is best; it is to encourage you to make a timely decision so that you can quiet all that noise in your head.

Maybe you are afraid of humiliating yourself in front of coworkers, of blacking out while driving, or of contaminating the house and thus causing your children to be sick. Few people can cope with those kinds of fears. However, if you want to step into one of these activities, you have to figure out how to step away from those interpretations. Whether you worry about lots of little things or a specific phobia, panic disorder, social anxiety, or OCD, if you don't change your perspective about the threat, those activities will quickly and easily end up in the "I can't handle that" bin.

MARY

The ten-hour flight back from London was uneventful, but sitting in the very back row meant that Mary had a non-reclining chair and two bathroom doors directly behind her. And she was a *long* way from the escape exit doors. As the plane landed at the Phoenix airport and taxied to the gate, the air inside the plane seemed to stop circulating. As everyone got up to retrieve their luggage from the overhead bins, Mary could no longer see the front of the plane, and it seemed like *eons* before anyone started moving down the aisle. Suddenly, her heart started racing and her knees started shaking. Everything was escalating rapidly.

Within two breaths, Mary was in full-blown panic mode. Up popped this danger message inside her mind: *There's not enough air! I'm going to suffocate in here!* Despite her whole body feeling weak, as though she was moments away from collapsing, she thought about climbing over the seats to get out of there as quickly as possible, and she came close to screaming. She felt caught between a likely death experience and social humiliation. "Well, if I push ahead of everybody . . . I can't really do that. They're going to think I'm rude. But do they really know I'm in danger? I'm in danger! They have to move and let me out."*

She survived the next ten intense minutes, but by the time she got off the airplane, she collapsed in a chair and wept. She didn't know how she'd get on the next flight to make it home.

She began to have more and more trouble flying. Worried anticipation. Panic attacks on the plane. Her trouble spread to other arenas that offered no immediate escape. "I was revisiting Boston—I hadn't been there in years—and my daughter was using the map to navigate for me. Two big highways had portions that were now underground, and it was really, really bad for me. I'm ashamed to say that at one point I started screaming at my daughter to keep us away from the tunnels. Only twelve at the time, my daughter was trying to read the map and accidentally put me into a three-and-a-half-mile long tunnel. I kept yelling at her. When we finally got out, she started crying. She said, 'I didn't know you were so mean.' In my mind I said, 'Well, I'm never, ever driving in Boston again.'"

Now Mary sits in front of me, frustrated that this problem has extended for ten years. We will have only two appointments, one today and one tomorrow, to address her classic symptoms of claustrophobia: the fear of restriction and suffocation. Mary has a flight tomorrow night, and she is not at all comfortable stepping onto that plane. "I love to

---

*Reid Wilson, *Exposure Therapy for Phobias*, video, psychotherapy.net, *http://www.psychotherapy .net/video/Exposure-Therapy-Phobias*, 2012. See Appendix B.

travel. But it takes so much out of me because when I get on an airplane and the hatch door closes, I suddenly realize that there is no outside air source. There's no way for me to leave. And my heart starts racing, and sometimes it's been so bad, I felt like I was going to have a heart attack. Because it feels like it's jumping out of my chest and almost like it's going to rip out. It's pounding so hard, and I'm stuck in one little place. Because people do have heart attacks from shock and really strong duress, right?"

Parking structures are tough. "With their low ceilings I feel like I'm going to be crushed in there. The concrete above me looks really heavy, and I think if it fell . . . well, I think the worst possible death would be to be buried alive. If they're big and they're like a labyrinth, or if the ramps get crowded and the traffic's not moving, that really panics me. And basically I just don't park inside parking structures anymore."

Elevators are a struggle, too. "If they're really modern, go fast, and no one else is in them, I'm not too bad. But I don't like elevators if they're slow and kind of clunky, or if too many people crowd on. I'm afraid it's going to get stuck, and then I won't be able to breathe. And I won't be able to get out. I don't like to be in those kinds of situations. Anytime I feel trapped, I get really panicky."

Mary focuses her attention on some substantial threats.

- ❖ She absolutely does *not* want to get stuck in a place where she might have a panic attack. She doesn't trust that the human heart can tolerate the stress of a highly anxious situation, so when she gets panicky and her heart starts pounding, she believes that's a *signal* of danger. She believes a panic attack has the potential to damage her heart.
- ❖ She believes there's a finite amount of air on an airplane or in an elevator or parking garage, and that air can be used up easily. So when she starts feeling trapped on the plane, she treats that as a *signal* of danger, just like when she has those feelings in an

elevator or parking garage. Every time she flies, she is reminded of the possibility that she might get stuck on an airplane, sitting on the tarmac, causing her and all the rest of the passengers to suffocate. She does *not* want that suffocation fear to come true, whether on an airplane, in a tunnel, or in an elevator.

✧ She can remember past times when she has had a full-blown panic attack as soon as she felt trapped on an airplane and in a tunnel. She doesn't want to provoke those terrifying feelings again! So any circumstance where she might start feeling trapped becomes a *signal* of danger.

✧ On many occasions while driving through a parking garage, she has felt confined, and her imagination creates a scenario where either she suffocates inside there or the heavy concrete ceiling falls on top of her car. She *certainly* doesn't want that to happen. She has concluded that parking decks are a *signal* of danger, and she simply won't go into parking garages anymore.

And now her world is smaller.

That's Mary's content in a nutshell. And she has strong, valid reasons to be afraid! But wait a minute. Mary is diagnosed with claustrophobia. How can her reasoning be valid? It's not because these situations are inherently dangerous. It's because she has experienced such threatening moments of impending doom that she has constructed a belief system that perceives those situations as dangerous. Plus, those traumas alone convinced her limbic system's amygdala that it should automatically move into alarm when it senses these types of stimuli. Mary struggles with commercial flight, tunnels, and parking decks. Her fear of suffocation and restriction illustrates how Anxiety can take advantage of us after traumatic events in which we have felt threatened.

Our job—hers and mine together—is to *push that content away*. She has generated some strong signals that automatically provoke her sense of threat. She, of course, doesn't want to keep generating that fear response. More important, if Mary wants to reach her goals, she needs to turn these signals into noise so she will be able to dismiss them more easily. When her anxious worries pop up, she needs to develop her ability to mentally step back and label them as irrelevant clatter. When she starts to feel panicky, again she needs to mentally step back and then say (and believe), "I can handle these feelings."

Can we push that content away—the suffocation, the threat to her heart, the collapsing garage—into the category of extraneous noise? If Mary and I can accomplish that task, our work will not be done. She will then need to attend to the core work: letting herself feel her doubt and her physical discomfort. That will be hard for her, but at least she will be focusing on her primary task. We will return to Mary again, starting in Chapter 10. She has a lot to teach us.

Coping with feelings of uncertainty and distress is hard enough. Coping with some of the content of fears—Suffocating! Being humiliated! Falling from the balcony! Running someone over!—can seem impossible. So your job is the same as Mary's. Your *first task* is to do whatever it takes to shift the topic of your fear from signal to noise. You might not be able to accomplish that by yourself, and you probably can't do it instantly, but you do have to get it done.

Here are two topics we won't be addressing in this book: worries that are signals and the specific content within your worries. When you hear worries that you believe are signals, you should take actions that move you toward resolving the problem. And you'll have to study some other book if you are looking to figure out what to do with the specific worries of your specific content (your job loss, a medical condition, a bad decision, the best glasses for the shape of your face). In this book, you and I will design tactics to respond to distressing, noisy worry in all its forms.

By the way, let me remind you that your challenger doesn't care about the topic of your worries. The goal of Anxiety is to take advantage of your feared content *in order to bother you.* That's the game it has constructed, and it has coerced you into becoming the weaker player. One way it does that is to confuse you about whether a specific concern is a signal or noise. You need to sort that out. So let's review what I was explaining just before I talked about Mary. Your mission should be to sweep content out of the way by correcting any misinformation so you can focus only on being willing to feel intimidated and insecure. Handle your legitimate concerns. What specific fears are threatening you? Get your questions answered. Find out whether you are misinformed about a subject. How stable are ladders, and how do you safely climb a stable ladder? Can anyone teach you the signs that help distinguish a friendly dog from an aggressive one? How frequently does one need to check The Weather Channel to be ready for a storm? How dangerous is it to stand near a railing of the balcony? Does a person need to worry about a panic attack turning into a heart attack? How long does the HIV virus live outside the body? Could asking for a raise be grounds for dismissal?

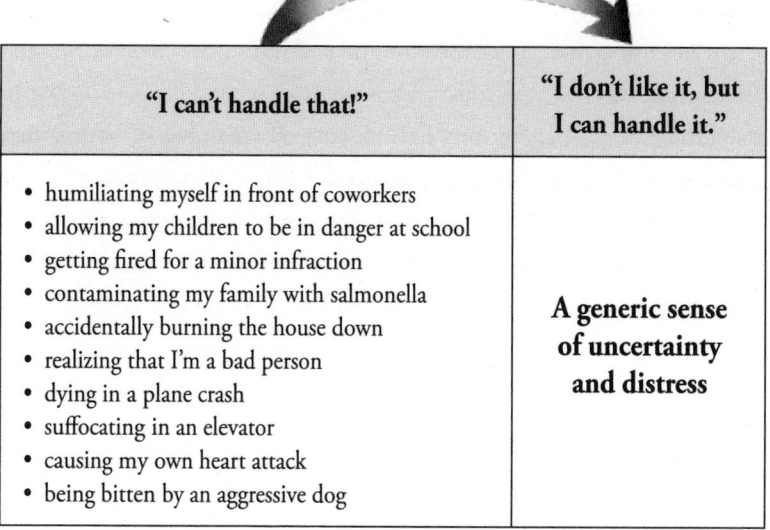

"I can't handle that!"	"I don't like it, but I can handle it."
• humiliating myself in front of coworkers • allowing my children to be in danger at school • getting fired for a minor infraction • contaminating my family with salmonella • accidentally burning the house down • realizing that I'm a bad person • dying in a plane crash • suffocating in an elevator • causing my own heart attack • being bitten by an aggressive dog	**A generic sense of uncertainty and distress**

When skills are necessary, develop your skills. If you worry about drowning, taking swimming lessons might be in order. If you are awkward about public speaking but you need that skill at work, you might consider attending a skill-development group like Toastmasters.*

Once you have made an informed decision, corrected the misinformation, and settled on a plan of action, then when your worries pop up, you can move them into the category of useless noise instead of signals. It doesn't mean they won't pop up again. It just means you don't need to pay attention to them. If you have a fear of heights that keeps you from climbing a ladder but you *want* to be able to climb a ladder, then get your safety concerns handled. Even after you settle your concerns, once you're stepping up onto rung three, with shaking hands and shaking legs, your worries are still going to pop up, and they may sound something like: "This ladder isn't safe! I'm going to fall and crack my head open!" That is the moment when you need to act as though these thoughts are noise, reflecting your anxious insecurity, and not a signal of your impending doom. You really can handle feeling anxious and uncertain. Cracking your head open? Not so much.

Keep in mind that if Anxiety is *dominating* you, no amount of preparation or information or reassurance will feel sufficient. OCD represents the embodiment of this problem. If you are a checker, you probably know that it ought to be sufficient to turn off the stove and then confirm once that it's off. If contamination is your issue, you can gather all kinds of data that reinforces washing your hands for twenty seconds in warm soapy water should be sufficient to prevent germs from spreading. You may know, as an orderer, that you can tolerate the housecleaner moving the magazines on your coffee table three inches to the left. If you are caught up in thinking rituals, then you probably know that having a bad thought shouldn't require you to counterbalance it with

---

*Visit *https://www.toastmasters.org/* for more information.

a good thought. But if OCD is dominating you, all of that clarity of mind is utterly useless once your obsessions kick in. At that point, you will feel compelled to remove your doubt, and you won't stop until you do. That's why you and I must focus on how to manage the distress of uncertainty. But hold on, because we have to build that system from the ground up, and we're just getting started.

The struggles of those with OCD show us unquestionably that if you want to take back control of your life from Anxiety, you cannot wait until you are certain that everything is safe or that you know what the perfect decision is. You cannot continue to gather more and more reassurance until you finally feel settled. You must learn how to step toward the threat while a part of you is still feeling insecure. Trying to close all the loopholes, attempting to erect a secure safety net, waiting for a clear indication that everything is going to work out, waiting until you feel confident . . . these options are not available to you while you are still being challenged by Anxiety. You have to step forward, into the proverbial fire, while some part of you is predicting that this is a really bad idea.

CHAPTER 7

Content and Competition

I s the game Monopoly about real estate? Of course not. It's about chance and strategy. It's about shoring up enough fake money to build little toy houses and hotels on a game board (and hopefully being the first player to do so), forcing the other players into "bankruptcy" and shame. It's about cleverness and careful investment of this fake money and choosing between an old shoe and an iron. It has little to nothing to do with the real-life principles, risks, or rewards of property ownership, mortgage, and development.

Is chess about clashing regimes? No, it's about the strategic placement of game pieces. In the words of chess master Bobby Fischer, "All that matters on the chessboard is good moves." It's as much about kings and queens as Chutes and Ladders is about chutes. Or ladders, for that matter.

These elements of our most cherished board games—real estate, clashing regimes, even the complex characters in Clue—are further examples of what we defined as *content* in the last chapter. Content is the story built around a well-designed game board and a pair of dice, a story that gives names to the game pieces (rook, knight, Professor Plum) and makes the game more attractive, particularly to children. In most cases, it's the content (two fleets of warring battleships) that sells the product.

To focus on the content of one of these competitions as opposed to the rules and goals of the game itself would be a serious error in strategy. Imagine while playing Monopoly that you slip into some altered state of reality and begin to think, *Oh, no! I've landed on Park Place and it has three houses! That's $1100! Where am I going to get that kind of money? My boyfriend is going to be furious. We can't afford this!* This kind of fixation on the story of the game seems absurd. But it's not uncommon for us to give this much time and attention to the content of our noisy worries. How? By believing that they are signals.

Our work is to keep you from getting tricked into focusing on the *wrong* topic. So let's put aside for right now the concern that Park Avenue is nowhere near true market value. Instead, let's concentrate on engaging in, and eventually winning, the real challenge in front of you.

Anxiety has four ways to take advantage of your natural, normal (and important!) tendency to worry. First (and this is its greatest manipulation), it tricks you into thinking that every time a worry about some particular theme pops up, you should take it seriously. Of course, it cleverly picks a topic that has significance to you. Anxiety knows this is a highly effective means to hook you with worried content by making it always relevant to your life, to your need for comfort, to your financial security or self-esteem, the importance of your image with others, or your sense of safety. So don't be surprised if the topic of your worry appears to be especially suited for you.

Second, as I explained in the last chapter, Anxiety *doesn't care* about the topic it selects. It picks this content only to make you scared and worried. And then it wins if it can get you to work hard to get rid of those feelings. In fact, it picks that topic because it *knows* it will get you upset and it *knows* you will want to get rid of your upset feelings.

Third, it convinces you that you don't have what it takes to handle this problem, and therefore it's best that you back away, that you avoid attempting to solve the difficulty by facing it head-on.

The Rules of Anxiety's Game

1) If *any* fearful thought pops up, take it seriously.
2) Once you are scared and worried, try to get rid of those feelings.
3) Assume you don't have what it takes to solve this problem, so back away.
4) Anytime you start feeling anxious, take that as a signal of danger.

Fourth, Anxiety trains you to use your distress as a gauge to measure impending danger. If you feel uncomfortable, it gets you to assume that your discomfort is a signal that you are not safe, that some threat is probably lurking about. It reminds you that your highest priority is the comfort of safety.

You are losing this mental competition by believing that a true threat exists whenever a worry or an anxious feeling pops up, by believing that you should get rid of distress and worry when they show up, and by believing that you don't have what it takes to face your problems directly. You can't get stronger if you keep thinking and acting this way.

STEP BACK THEN CLIMB UP

Therefore, I propose that you adopt what you will probably consider an illogical strategy. Whatever you are afraid of, if you have decided to treat it as the noise of an irrational fear, then I encourage you to step back from the details of that specific topic when they pop up. In fact, I want you to get completely away from focusing on that as your primary topic.

For example, imagine that you struggle with the possibility you might have caused an accident while driving, so you are prone to repeatedly checking anytime such a worry pops into your mind. You've decided that such obsessions (your worries) and compulsions (your actions) are generated by OCD. Now you are driving into a parking garage and suddenly the thought pops in your mind, *Did I just hit a pedestrian?* How might you apply our strategy? Your first move could be to say to yourself, "It's fine I just had that thought." And then focus your attention back on driving to your desired parking spot. Don't let yourself look in your rearview mirror, and don't loop back around "just to check once, for safety's sake." Tolerate the doubt and distress you are now feeling.

Crazy, right? You have some powerful sense that you might've hurt someone, and I'm suggesting that you don't act on the worry?

Now you'll be stuck feeling anxious, and a part of you continues to think, *What am I doing? I've got to go back! I can't stand this feeling! It will take me only two minutes to loop back around. That's no time at all. What kind of fool would I be not to take those few minutes to double back, just to be sure? That's better than being arrested for a hit-and-run. I've got to go back!* You hear that voice inside you, and you feel all that tension and anxiety, but you nod your head and keep driving forward. What an insane way to respond to your fear that you've hit a person with a 1.5-ton vehicle! But if you have OCD, that's what you need to do: take actions as though the content of your worry is irrelevant (which means to keep driving). Expect that your worry will continue to show up, trying to get your attention. Expect that you will continue to be anxious. Allow your worry and permit yourself to feel anxious, just don't let them run the show. That's how you will win this competition.

I'm going to go through this kind of response a zillion times with you. You will clearly know how to undertake this tactic when we are done. Whether you engage in it or not will be up to you. I'm fine with that. After all, you are in charge of your life, not me. I'm just a consultant. But I take our job seriously, and it is to help you elevate your game to a level where you have a fighting chance to succeed. You need to climb up one level of abstraction, up where the winners play, and completely detach yourself from *any* specific content. You must engage in this competition at the level of a broad (not specific) sense of uncertainty and distress. You need to move toward what scares you for the sole purpose of generating a basic feeling of doubt and discomfort. Pull yourself away from the specific topic of your doubt so you can embrace the general feeling of doubt itself. *Now* you can win.

How does it sound when you go up one level? Let's use another OCD example regarding germs. To remain down on the content level,

Figure 2. Step UP to a new perspective.

"I wash my hands to get rid of contamination."

"I do a repetitive behavior to get rid of my doubt about something that seems risky or dangerous."

where Anxiety dominates, you would say, "I wash my hands to get rid of contamination." Your job is to move *up* one level of abstraction so you truly comprehend why you feel the urge to compulsively clean. That statement would sound something like this: "I do a repetitive behavior to get rid of my doubt about something that seems risky or dangerous." You stepped up onto a new platform, one that has *nothing* to do with germs or safety. And, therefore, we can now do business. Your next move is to realize that you keep trying to *get rid* of your doubt. That's just what Anxiety wants, for you to do whatever you must to stop feeling unsure. So to score points in this competition, you pull your attention away from contamination and you turn your attention toward allowing your feelings of doubt. In fact, as soon as you permit those feelings, even invite them, you will score big points.

Your challenger will not like this one bit. It wants you to slide back down into the content. Anxiety has hijacked your values and is using them against you. In whatever shape, size, or storyline it comes, Anxiety always provides content to distract you from the real competition. It uses content to continually tug at your attention, trying to pull your focus away from our task of learning to tolerate intimidation and insecurity. It expects you to say, "But, wait, I can't let my kids get sick from my negligence."

Here's the caveat: *of course* you must address the topic of your worry. Remember the title of Chapter 6? "Make It NOT About Your Content." You have to resolve the content questions, because they are stopping you from learning how to handle the intimidation of feeling uncertain. If you are afraid the plane may run out of air while you sit on the tarmac and you will then die of suffocation, you need to learn that that's not even possible. If every time you get panicky and you start fearing your heart can't handle beating 120 beats a minute, then you need to learn that, yes, of course, it's designed to *create* an accelerated heartbeat during emergencies. What happens if you continue to believe that every dog has the potential suddenly to turn vicious and lunge at you, or that you can't cope with seeing someone vomit? What if you keep holding the frame of mind that getting fired would be the worst thing that could ever happen to you, and it could happen any day for any number of minor infractions? How about if you believe that when you have a momentary abhorrent thought, it means you are someone who will act in an abhorrent way? If you keep a tight hold on those beliefs, there is no way we can get you stronger. Playing at the content level is a loser's game.

OCD has an interesting twist. There is very little you need to figure out about the content of the various OCD themes. Yes, you can learn the medically recommended hand-washing routine, and you can confirm how long the AIDS virus lives outside of the body. But you are going to find that this information will never be sufficient. For the vast majority of obsessions, the content is simply irrelevant, and if your early attempts at education and reassurance fail to satisfy you, then you should not try to figure *anything* out about the theme of your obsessions. If you start drilling down into the details of your obsession, trying to prove to yourself that you're not a pedophile, or confirm that your office building doesn't contain asbestos, or ensure that God has forgiven you for some blasphemous thought, then you will become tangled in the vines of the disorder. Content is *really* not relevant in OCD.

Once you degrade your content (that's what we want to do) and you lower your sense of actual risk (even though you will still *feel* at risk), you will be able to elevate your sense of competence by engaging in new experiences. Your skill set must include the ability to remind yourself that you are not going to dwell on your content. Stepping up one level of abstraction means that you work on your frame of reference, your point of view, your orientation to this topic. At this level, to win over anxious worrying, you must go toward what scares you and then embrace the feeling of doubt and distress. Yes, you will not have to wash as thoroughly as OCD demands, or you'll have to climb that ladder a few more scary rungs, or elevate your heart rate faster than is comfortable. But you should engage in these behaviors so you can face the generic sensations of uncertainty and discomfort. Get away from thinking that you must resolve some legitimate uncertainty. If you have a phobia of heights and we arrange for ten people to hold that ladder for you, and we cover the floor with three feet of foam to protect you if you fall, you would still feel intimidated and insecure as you climb up a few rungs of the ladder. That's what I'm talking about. After we resolve the legitimate concerns, you will now face capital-A Anxiety, and it will generate that uncomfortable uncertainty. Decide to *seek out* that discomfort and doubt! *Now* you can win.

You've already heard me express this a few times, yet I repeat it here because Anxiety makes it quite difficult for you to comprehend what I'm saying. (And I promise that you will hear it a few more times before we're done.) I sincerely believe that if you can give yourself messages that manifest from that higher frame of reference—"I need to go toward what I'm afraid of"—and you are willing to believe those messages, then you can direct your actions moment-by-moment in such a way that you get your life back.

If I can help you grasp the true nature of this mental competition, and if you can lift your sights up to the real work of purposely choosing to feel insecure, uncertain, and anxious, then we will be focusing our attention on the proper tasks. If you will decide to push forward, knowing that intimidating doubt and distress will follow you, then I will help you learn that you actually *can* cope with those feelings. That will be your ticket out of suffering. Let's give you that opportunity, shall we?

CHAPTER 8

Move the Massive

I n his lifetime, Sir Isaac Newton made innumerable achievements in various fields of science, though psychology was not among them; in fact, Newton famously suffered from mental illness.

It was not, as myth suggests, a fortuitous collision with an apple that inspired Newton's revolutionary theory of gravity. The year was 1666, and the twenty-three-year-old physicist had temporarily left Cambridge University for his childhood home in Lincolnshire, England. Unlike most scholarly boys in their early twenties, young Isaac didn't come home to do laundry; rather, Newton had abandoned his studies because the Great Plague was sweeping across London.

While no one knows for sure which anecdote bears the greatest resemblance to the truth, we can assume that Newton was indoors. He preferred to work in isolation, and prior attempts at farming and manual labor were utter disasters. He was seated perhaps at a grand desk that overlooked the lush garden at Woolsthorpe Manor. Like any young lad home on college break, he was probably avoiding his mother like the plague (pun intended), overeating, musing on typical twenty-three-year-old topics such as physics, astronomy, alchemy, and infinitesimal calculus when suddenly the thud of an apple just outside the window caught his attention. It was from this, from the simple act of an apple descending from its branch to the earth below, that Newton conceived gravity as a force acting upon the apple, pulling it downward, causing it to fall. He extended this insight into his formula for universal gravitation, which he believed could even be holding the planets of our solar system in line.

One of the several purposes of this Step Back section is to help you call into question some of your beliefs about how to respond to your difficulties. If you can step away from those viewpoints long enough, you will have a chance to imagine the possibility of stepping forward with a new perspective. So let's step away from psychology for a moment to look at the Big Picture. Newton's discoveries in the areas of motion, force, and resistance are the *really* Big Picture. His theory, developed 350 years ago and coined the Three Laws of Motion, forms the foundation of the huge scientific field of classical mechanics. Together these laws represent one of the principal concepts in today's engineering and technology.

This is heady stuff, but don't abandon the project quite yet. Believe it or not, the Three Laws of Motion offer us a clear path out of your suffering. Following is what is most valuable to us.

Every object in the world (including you and me) will keep doing what it's currently doing until something forces it to change. Newton's First Law of Motion introduces the concept of *inertia*: an object will continue moving at its current speed and direction, or it will continue to stand still, until some force causes it to alter its course. Imagine rolling a ball across a field. Your ball will roll on and on at the same speed for eternity unless something gets in its way. And, of course, something will always get in its way: the friction caused by contact with the ground and air, any bumps it encounters, the pull of gravity with any uphill climbs, etc. *All* objects on Earth have inertia.

This explains why your beliefs, the ones that have kept you from tackling this problem, will remain in place until you force them to change.

Everyone's beliefs and convictions have inertia. How might this inertia be playing a part in your feeling stuck? Perhaps you have decided that your worries are valid. Maybe you think that change is too difficult for you. Or you've concluded that there is no point in changing, so why bother expending any energy to try. You could believe that you don't have the skill, motivation, strength, confidence, or courage to put any effort toward changing. You will continue to take actions (or do nothing) according to these beliefs. Once these beliefs are solidly in place, they justify your decisions even as they keep you from moving toward new desired goals, such as having children, or taking a job that requires public speaking or air travel, or simply relaxing. Why step forward if you believe you're going to be hurt and you can't tolerate that hurt? Why put out effort to change if you believe you can't really produce a long-lasting change? And so you don't change . . . unless we mess with your point of view in some way. And that's exactly what we're going to do in this book.

The more massive the body, the more it will resist change. So a greater force will be required to move it in a different direction. Inertia states that an object will keep doing what it's doing until it's forced to change. But there's more to it than that. Newton showed us that the mass of a body—how substantial it is—makes it more capable of resisting change. It is simply more difficult to move. If a baseball is made from iron, for instance, it will require much greater force to change its motion than a standard baseball made from cork and rubber. An eight-year-old child will not be capable of knocking over a sumo wrestler, even if he uses all of his strength and 100 percent of his effort.

Therefore, if the beliefs in your way are *strong*, if they have *big* mass, then they're going to put up a strong fight against your efforts to change them. If you are *certain* that you are right to avoid some difficulty, if you are *convinced* that you might put yourself in great harm if you stepped forward, if you are *positive* that you don't have what it takes to change, then you will resist the idea of stepping toward what intimidates you, even if it's the very best way to get stronger.

And why would you *want* to entertain such a possibility? It's dangerous. You could get hurt. You have traumatic memories of *getting* hurt. You're not strong enough to handle such consequences again. It's not worth it to put yourself through more suffering since nothing is really going to change. Doing what you're doing now—avoiding the challenge, using crutches to get by, stepping back from unknown territory—makes the best sense to you. You do not want to move in a different direction. It takes too much effort, and it is too threatening. That's basic nature! That's basic science!

So if you are holding on tightly to your beliefs, then you and I have our work cut out for us. In this Step Back section I'm tell you that you need to start this work by deciding what is a signal and what is noise. If you keep believing that it's too dangerous to step forward, or that you don't have what it takes to do this work, or "why bother" doing the work because change is not possible, then you are treating these messages as signals that tell you that you should not make any change. When that is your stance, then I can talk until I'm blue in the face but it still won't have any influence on you. Your mass is too big.

If you want the benefits this book offers, then you need to actively work on shrinking your mass, which means calling a number of your assumptions into question. Simply moving yourself to a position of uncertainty can be sufficient for what we need to accomplish. How would that sound? Like this:

- ✧ Maybe I'm telling myself a story, and it actually *isn't* so dangerous. Maybe.
- ✧ I wonder if this approach *can* work for me. I wonder.
- ✧ Perhaps I actually *do* have what it takes, and I just don't know it because I don't push myself. It's possible.

✧ Could it be that I've been deceiving myself and I really *can* handle getting hurt, even though I won't like it? I'm not sure.

✧ Is it possible that *somewhere* within me I have the ability to change? I haven't considered that lately.

✧ Maybe these ideas are worth exploring, even though I have my doubts.

If you can introduce this kind of curiosity into the equation, you will shrink your mass. Once you do that, you will have an easier time applying our tactics.

How You Can Change According to the Laws of Motion

1) Every object in the world (including you and me) will keep doing what it's currently doing until something forces it to change.

2) **This explains why** your beliefs, the ones that have kept you from tackling this problem, will remain in place until you force them to change.

3) The more massive the body, the more it will resist change, so greater force will be required to move it in a different direction.

4) **Therefore**, if the beliefs that are in your way are *strong*, if they have *big* mass, then they will put up a strong fight against your efforts to change them.

5) To alter the direction a body is moving, you have to use force as strong as or stronger than the force that's causing it. The body will then change in the direction of your force.

6) **This means** you have to act in a powerful way that is opposite of what Anxiety expects, so you can force it to change direction. This same action is probably going to scare you, and a part of you does *not* want to get scared. Your courage and your determination must become equal to or larger than your scared feelings. And then you have to take action.

7) The most disruptive force is a sudden, hard push in a new direction.

8) **Therefore**, if you want Anxiety to change, you must practice changing your point of view at a moment's notice, for at least a few moments, so you can welcome what you fear. That is not the direction Anxiety was taking you. Now you're suddenly pushing Anxiety in a different direction.

9) Once force is applied, how fast an object changes is inversely proportional to the mass of the object.

10) **So if** you have trouble applying the skills you learn in this book, or if you apply them but you don't make much progress, then explore the possibility that some of your beliefs are still keeping you from stepping forward.

11) For every action there is an equal and opposite reaction.

12) **That's why** you should expect that Anxiety will resist your efforts. It's going to fight back. And a part of *you* that's vulnerable to Anxiety's messages will resist your efforts. A part of *you* will fight against change because change is disruptive.

To alter the direction a body is moving, you have to use force as strong as or stronger than the force that's acting on it. The body will then change in the direction of your force. For example, let's say you have a soccer ball sitting on the ground in front of you. Gravity is holding the ball down, and the earth is holding it up; it's in a stationary position of inertia. You now decide to kick it. The harder you kick that soccer ball, the faster and farther the ball will travel across the field. This part of Newton's Second Law of Motion states that an object changes its velocity in the *direction* of the applied force.

How about a moving target instead of a stationary one? Picture yourself playing a friendly game of tennis. Your challenger just served the ball into your court. When your tennis racket strikes the approaching ball, it applies a new force to the ball, disrupting the speed and direction your challenger's racket initiated. The ball will now move where your racket instructs it to move. Of course, if you don't match the power of your challenger's swing, then the ball won't get back over the net. But if you smack it with an equal force and the proper direction, it will head back over the net and into the challenger's court. That's matching power with power.

This means you have to act in a powerful way that is opposite of what Anxiety expects, so you can force it to change direction. This same action will probably scare you, and a part of you does not want to get scared. Your courage and your determination must become equal to or larger than your scared feelings. And then you have to take action. When Anxiety threatens you, it expects you to back away. I'm going to teach you how to step forward instead. And if you step forward, Anxiety expects you to go toe-to-toe with it, to openly fight it, and it knows it can beat you like that. Beginning in the next chapter, I will explain how to do the opposite of what Anxiety expects, by dropping your guard, feeling scared, and courageously welcoming the threat. This work is not for the meek or the weak of heart. But it is for those who are clever and open to applying cunning, manipulation, and trickery.

Ah, but there is more to this Second Law.

The most disruptive force is a sudden, hard push in a new direction. Imagine Misty May-Treanor, three-time Olympic beach volleyball gold medalist, with her hands clasped together, ready to meet the ball with enough opposing force to send it back over the net and ground it on the opponent's court. Her goal is to *pop* the ball over the net. She wants her hands to become a hard surface that will quickly punch the ball up with just enough energy. Now visualize a weight lifter who is about to complete an overhead press of a heavy barbell. She bends her knees, drops down a little, and then uses her whole body to thrust upward, driving the barbell from her shoulders up over her head. A sudden, hard push in a new direction.

Picture a regulation bowling pin, fifteen inches tall, three and a half pounds, constructed from hard rock maple wood and molded in white plastic. The pin stands upright and remains grounded, fixed to the solid maple floorboard by gravity pushing down on it and the floor simultaneously holding it up. We call that a balanced force. (Hold on: I'm about to introduce an *un*balanced force or a disruptive force.) Now visualize a mechanical arm introducing ten of these pins, all of them the same cut and size. It positions them to form a perfect triangle sitting at the far end of the bowling lane. You make your approach, drawing near the foul line, likely with no understanding of the intricate physics involved or the makings of a perfect strike, focused instead on throwing that bowling ball *nice and hard*. After all, if you're trying to knock over one pin, you can concentrate on aim and entry. But if you're trying to knock over ten pins at once, you've got to smack 'em. This is one big mass, and you've got to *smack it* with a force that will disrupt its balance. After all, you're trying to knock them all down!

Hit them fast and hard. Knock them off balance.

Therefore, if you want Anxiety to change, you must practice changing your point of view at a moment's notice, for at least a few moments, so you can welcome what you fear. That is not the direction Anxiety was taking you. Now you're suddenly pushing Anxiety in a different direction. You don't need to understand yet what I mean by this approach. But here are the key phrases to begin absorbing: "change your point of view," "change direction," and "welcome what you fear."

You and I are not going to focus on fixing everything. We are going to pay attention to only a few moments in time. But in those few moments, Newton would likely agree that it's best to move swiftly and efficiently over to a new point of view and then act on that point of view. There's nothing gradual or gentle about this. Your goal will be to hit Anxiety fast and hard, to knock it off balance. All you will need to pay attention to is to engage in a new pattern that disrupts the pattern Anxiety has instilled in you, and then learn what happens next.

Once force is applied, how fast that object changes is inversely proportional to the mass of the object. Imagine that two soccer balls sit in front of you. You now kick each of the two balls with the same amount of force. But soccer ball A has twice the mass of soccer ball B, so ball A will travel at *half* the speed of ball B. (This, in simplified terms, is why we don't play soccer with bowling balls.)

So if you have trouble applying the skills you learn in this book, or if you apply them but you don't make much progress, then explore the possibility that some of your beliefs are still keeping you from stepping forward. Remember, big mass = big resistance, so the change process slows down. Strong negative beliefs = big resistance. And that will slow your progress unless, of course, you smack that belief hard by doing something aggressively opposite.

By the way, your job is not to *get rid* of any unhelpful current beliefs. They are going to be hanging around and influencing your actions until your experience teaches you that those beliefs are wrong. So what *will* your job be? You will learn about an entirely new point of view, and then I'm going to ask you to focus your attention on that point of view as you take actions. Believe it or not (and you certainly don't have to believe it yet), your old belief system will fade away through lack of attention, and your actions will teach you the benefits of your new mind-set. (You will learn all about belief systems, points of view, mind-sets, and the like in Chapter 10.)

For every action there is an equal and opposite reaction. Newton's popular Third Law of Motion explains why your rear bumper and trunk might need replacing if somebody backs into you in the parking lot. That car may have struck yours, but in that split second, your car pushed back with an equal and opposite force. So his bumper and trunk should have taken just as much punishment as yours. (Unless, of course, it had big mass: like a half-ton pickup with an armor-plated steel bar in place of a rear bumper. Then they'll drive away without a scratch.) We see this same principle applied when a cannon fires a ball, causing the cannon itself to roll backward across the deck of the pirate ship. The backward recoil of the cannon is equal to the force of the projectile ejected from the cannon. Why? Because every action provokes an opposite reaction. Remember how you used to fool around with balloons when you were a kid? (No, I don't mean when you inhaled the helium so you could talk like Donald Duck.) You blew up the balloon as big as you could tolerate. And then, instead of tying it off (which was too difficult anyway), you let the end go. And the balloon flew all over the room in every which way. The air rushes out of the opening, and the balloon moves rapidly in the opposite direction. Action . . . reaction.

That's why you should expect that Anxiety will resist your efforts. It's going to fight back. And a part of you will resist your efforts. A part of *you* will fight against change because change is disruptive. If you shove Anxiety, it may very well shove you back. For instance, let's say you decide to practice my suggestion of tolerating uncertainty, so you choose to drive to work after checking twice, instead of your usual fourteen times, that the front door is locked. That action makes you uncomfortably doubtful, but you seem to tolerate it well enough. Then you arrive at work forty minutes later, and suddenly your anxious worrying intensifies. The image of someone walking right into your front door pops into your head. This person is stealing all of your valuables! *What have I done? How stupid can I be, taking that guy's advice? What does he know?! Ack! I've got to go back home!* There's Anxiety trying to kick your butt. And unless you step back and recognize it as such, you will be Anxiety's pawn, telling the office manager that you're feeling ill and driving all the way back home to check one more time "just to be safe."

Physics tells us that the only way to get any work done is to apply effort to overcome resistance. (Not surprisingly, resistance is measured in newtons.) Hey, wait a minute. Isn't that what we have to do, too? Except we have to apply effort to overcome our *own* resistance so we can get our work done. We want to sleep longer instead of getting out of bed and preparing for work. We'd like to finish watching the movie on Netflix instead of grabbing the gym bag and heading out for a workout. We'd rather check e-mails a little while longer before we start writing that report. To overcome this resistance, we have to activate our determination and willpower.

The bigger the change you attempt, the greater resistance you will experience. If Congress ever tries to overhaul our tax system (don't hold your breath), they will be overwhelmed with intense lobbying by 1.2 zillion influential stakeholders who feel threatened by such a change. The United States suffers mass casualties from gun massacres with the frequency seen nowhere else in the developing world. Yet, if Congress attempted to pass a law imposing greater gun control . . . well, you know how that would turn out.

✧   ✧   ✧

Don't worry, I won't give you a pop quiz about these concepts at the end of this book. But we will develop our strategy based on these ideas. That means we are taking on a project that goes against our basic nature, so it won't feel easy to you. The good news is that we have science on our side, and we are going to use a scientific method to help you work, love, and play more freely.

Before we leave this section, we have one more chapter with one more step: a big step back taken at a moment's notice.

CHAPTER 9

Be Mindful of the Moment

All I knew was that Phill thought it would be "cool." It was the fall of 1970, my sophomore year at the University of North Carolina, and my big brother, Phill, a senior at Duke University, suggested, "Let's fool around with the biofeedback machine." Biofeedback is a treatment technique that uses electronic monitoring to help you quiet your mind and body. Today these machines are roughly the size of your palm, but in 1970, biofeedback was just developing. This machine, constructed and housed in Duke's School of Engineering, took up all four walls, floor to ceiling, in a 13 × 20-foot room. That didn't surprise me. The UNC sociology department's sole computer was a crude stack of machinery that occupied every inch of a 500-square-foot room (otherwise known as a Manhattan studio apartment). Now, of course, the little computer we can hold in our hands is 100 times more powerful.

The following Saturday, Phill and I spent several hours exploring this electromyography (EMG) phenomenon, attaching electrodes to our foreheads and listening to the feedback, to the rise and fall of sound that alerts us to the tension in our frontalis muscle. Our goal was to deepen the tone, because a deeper tone reflects a muscle with less tension. And as that tone deepens and the frontalis muscle quiets, the rest of the body and mind tend to follow suit.

My most fascinating discovery on that day was that I could "do" things to deepen the tone. By making minute adjustments, like how I was sitting, how I was breathing, what I was focusing on, I could alter the feedback. But to get my mind and body *really* quiet, I needed to listen to the tone, notice when it deepened, and then invite my mind and body to "keep doing whatever you are doing." I didn't know *how* it was happening; I just tried to catch that wave and ride it. I was quite captivated by the whole experience.

After a few Saturdays in the Engineering lab, electrodes taped to our foreheads, our ability to control that tone became exquisite. And then . . . I got it! My body and mind developed a memory of this state of physical and mental tranquility. I could call it up on cue, simply by taking a calming breath and quieting my thoughts (in addition to some subtle, visceral shifts in my consciousness that I still can't describe). Today, more than forty years later, I can still return to that peaceful place with about half a minute of attention.

That profound experience was the beginning of my appreciation of the stepping back process, the ability to mentally separate ourselves from the ongoing thoughts and feelings of daily life. By the time I finished college, I was a daily meditator, and I continued that practice for several more years. In the late 1970s I worked as a staff psychologist at the Boston Pain Unit, one of the first in-patient therapeutic communities for chronic pain patients. I witnessed firsthand how biofeedback and relaxation training could enhance a patient's ability to step back, step away, from suffering. This was true even for those with the most challenging physical ailments.

Here is a little more foreshadowing of the chapters to come. For my doctoral dissertation, I conducted a relatively complex study on the patients of the Boston Pain Unit. I observed the differences between patients who complied with the required components of the treatment versus the patients who asked a staff member for additional treatment opportunities that were available to them, such as an extra counseling session or an additional biofeedback appointment. My hypothesis was that those patients who requested added services did so because they sensed the possibility of positive change, and they were ready to take responsibility for strengthening their minds and bodies. I predicted that that shift in their attitudes would indeed help them get stronger. They were no longer just complying with staff requests and attending the fixed schedule of activities. They were asserting themselves. They were actively engaged in the learning process and motivated to improve.

The results of my research indicated that this was true. Those who were more engaged had significantly less pain perception and a discernibly elevated mood by the end of their treatments. They were stronger and far less depressed. I didn't know it at the time, but this was the beginning of my belief in the richness of the "I want this" stance. *Want it* is the topic of the next three chapters.

My work as a clinical psychologist gradually shifted away from helping those with chronic pain and toward treating those with anxiety and panic attacks. In the mid-1980s I began writing about my work, and that became my first book, *Don't Panic: Taking Control of Anxiety Attacks*. Within those pages I defined the concept of the Observer, the part of each of us that can detach from our worried, self-critical, or hopeless judgments in order to simply notice what we are thinking and feeling.

The Observer bears similarities to what is now often referred to as *mindfulness*, a term first introduced in 1979 by Jon Kabat-Zinn, PhD, the exceedingly talented scientist and teacher who led a structured eight-week course in Mindfulness-Based Stress Reduction. If you have been paying attention to advice givers in the physical or mental health circles, you have no doubt heard encouraging words about the benefits of meditation, mindfulness, and formal relaxation. You'll find numerous studies showing that adding these practices to your skill set can augment treatment for issues as diverse as stress reduction, pain management, heart disease, high blood pressure, infertility, tension headaches, premenstrual syndrome, irritable bowel, insomnia, depression, and, of course, anxiety and panic attacks.

IS IT A SIGNAL, OR IS IT NOISE?

I'm not going to teach you all those formal practices (although you can learn about them in *Don't Panic* and plenty of other places). Instead, we are going to take all that has been discovered over the last forty years through research and treatment and cull it down to two sets of tasks, both having to do with your ability to mentally step back.

The first task is to activate what we've been talking about in these last four chapters. We are going to interrupt your worry to give you some choice in the worry process. You job will be to insert a pause in your worrying—a pause just long enough to declare that you are going to treat that worry as a signal or as noise. Remember, when worries are signals, your job is to problem solve. When they are noise . . . well, they are just repetitive, unproductive, anxiety-producing racket, and you can do anything you want with them other than take them seriously. But you have to declare how you're going to treat them—as signals or as noise—before you can respond to them. And you can make that decision only by stepping away from your worry long enough to choose.

The Observer
*The part of us that can detach from our
worried, self-critical, or hopeless judgments in
order to simply notice what we are
thinking and feeling.*

Ah, but there's a catch. If you are like most people with anxiety, you cannot always determine whether it is a signal or just noise. And if you wait and wait and wait to act until you are *certain* which it is, you will continue to stall and avoid. The truth is, there will be plenty of times when you will not know for sure whether it is a signal or noise, but you *can* recognize when you are tangled up in one of your typical noisy, anxious themes. In those instances, your best move is to say, "I don't know if it's a signal or just noise, so I am going to act as though it's noise." (I mentioned this "act as though" theme in Chapter 6, and I'll be talking about it several more times before we're done. Indeed, the concept is so important to our strategy that it will get its very own special attention in Chapter 18.)

A MOMENT-BY-MOMENT AWARENESS OF "I DON'T WANT THIS"

The second function of mentally stepping back is to help you become alert to all the ways you resist stepping toward your difficulties. Anytime we begin to reflect on an upcoming threatening situation, that resistant, I-don't-want-this part of us (which we spoke about in Chapter 3) will move quickly into one of two broad reactions. Each move seems like an extension of our limbic system's fight, flight, or freeze response. The first resistant move looks similar to our flight or freeze behaviors. When our urge to *flee* is kindled, we avoid facing the situation by procrastinating, stalling, or simply escaping to a safer place. We behave this way because we don't want to feel doubt or address the worries that pop up as we begin to move toward the things we fear. When we respond with *freeze* behaviors, we shut down our feelings, becoming numb or flat. Some people exhibit this freeze response in social situations. They might struggle to come up with the right words when they are called on in class, "blank out" during a test, or forget someone's name when they run into them.

The second way we tend to resist when we face difficulty or feel threatened is to adopt what might be considered fight strategies within the fight, flight, or freeze response, because we are working harder as opposed to backing away. To feel safe, we over-prepare, gathering more and more information we hope will guarantee that we take the right actions. We review our notes repeatedly. We call on those we think will know the right answers, believing they can reassure us and guard us from harm. We check, check, and recheck "just to be sure." We take all these actions in service of protecting ourselves from emotional or physical insult or injury. We firmly believe that a "right answer" exists, and if we keep trying to figure it out, we'll eventually discover that right answer—the answer that will keep us from risking pain or embarrassment or failure. Despite our belief that we are applying positive energy to the problem-solving process, fight strategies are avoidance, too. As long as we are planning, preparing, thinking through all the options, researching to determine the best choices, consulting the latest data, and trying to be smart about our decisions, we aren't being productive. We are actually stalling, just as we do with our flight or freeze responses. Our perfectionistic tendencies, driven by our need to avoid mistakes, are really procrastination in disguise. Ironically, the more we stall, the more time we have to worry.

When that resisting part of you is in charge, it devotes 100 percent of its attention to actively protecting you. That means it cannot simultaneously look for ways in which you can grow. In fact, it will stifle any potential you might have for creative exploring or learning.

If you want some choice in the direction of your future, it's essential that you learn to step back from such automatic responses. You have to detach yourself from them long enough to observe them, label them for what they are, and decide if you want to continue standing still in that way. As you anticipate an event, if you can notice a shift in your state of mind and body—a shift toward resistance—then you have the chance to step away from it if you want to. The key task here is *noticing*. Sometimes it takes a while before any of us can become consciously alert to what we're doing. But now we have some suspicious clues, based on our fight, flight, or freeze tendencies, as seen below.

Observing the Signs of Resistance

Practice stepping back to notice these tendencies:

- stalling or procrastinating
- becoming numb or feeling flat
- retreating to a safer place
- over-preparing
- continually researching
- continually seeking advice
- checking repeatedly
- seeking the "right answer"
- detailed thinking through of all possible options
- worrying!

A MOMENTARY STOP IN THE ACTION

Have you ever been caught in a tangle of briars? You *know* you have to back away to get unstuck; it's common sense. When you are caught in a tangle of negative thoughts and defensive actions, you have to back away from that tangle before you can move forward. Quieting skills are the cornerstone of this stepping back process. But, listen up, within our strategy you need to quiet down for only a few *moments*.

If we want to change an old response pattern, the first task in our strategy is to catch ourselves in that pattern. We have to know *when* to step back; we need to *cue* ourselves at that moment; and we have to know *how* to step back. The "when" is whenever we get tangled up with the old pattern that needs a new response. Cueing ourselves in the moment involves a simple statement such as, "Oh, I'm doing it again," or "I'm starting to freak out now, and I have an urge to [step away, avoid this, do a compulsion, etc.]."

Figure 3. Step BACK to gain perspective.

The "how" entails a separation from our automatic thoughts, feelings, and actions in order to find our observing self. Quieting down permits you to step away, even if for only a few seconds, so that you can find your Observer and notice what's going on. When you are worrying or think you might be engaged in some resistant behavior, all you have to do is cue yourself (e.g., "I think I might be stuck again") and then simply shift into a quiet pause. Loosen the grip of that automatic, negative reaction to the present moment. Let go a bit. If you'd like, you can do it with a breath: take a nice, long inhale and then a gentle, slow exhale. On that exhale you can even gently invite your mind to "quiet" or "let go." Allow your mind to respond to your invitation. Slacken your jaw. Loosen your shoulders. Relax your eyes. And give yourself even a mere five seconds to feel self-compassion, an added gift.

Allow your emotional and physical arousal to come forward into your arena of observation. When you can clear and quiet your mind, you can then hear these messages independent of your biases (like "get rid of pain immediately" or "don't approach if uncertain"). Observe them from an objective, supportive, accepting stance. They are not "bad." They are not "wrong." Very simply, they are the messages you have been using until this moment. You can now choose to continue in this frame of mind that comes with those messages, or you can offer yourself a new response.

The only thing we are paying attention to right now is how to get you to a place of choice. You need to be capable of pausing the current action if you want the option of changing directions. Mentally step back. Get a perspective on the current moment by disengaging enough to observe it and label it. That's it. Don't worry about anything else right now. Don't worry about your ability to change course right now. Develop this skill, and we will build on it soon enough.

All of this seems straightforward and perfectly feasible on paper, but it can feel pretty threatening during moments of, well, threat. Because when we feel vulnerable, we automatically seek to defend ourselves. We are certainly not inclined to drop our guard. That's why I want you to understand the logic behind this action. Our intention is to help you move from an automatic, rigid, almost unconscious response to one of choice, to a response based on conscious awareness. You cannot embrace a new point of view until you let go of your current stance. If you can loosen the grip that threat and worry have on you, you can then gather information more relevant to the present moment. You can become curious: "What have I just been thinking? What am I feeling? What is actually going on around me? What's the truth about this risk?" Answering these questions allows you to move to your next task: "How do I want to respond to what I am learning about my present moment?"

The Art and Gift of the Quiet Moment

- Cue yourself (for instance, "I think I'm stuck again")
- Shift into a pause of quiet. Loosen the grip of that automatic, negative reaction to the present moment. Let go a bit.
- If you'd like, do it with a breath: a nice long inhale and a slow exhale. On that exhale, gently invite your mind to "quiet" or "let go." Allow your mind to respond to your invitation.
- Slacken your jaw. Loosen your shoulders. Relax your eyes.
- Give yourself an added gift: a mere five seconds of self-compassion.

If you notice that you are scared or feeling threatened, you have a chance to determine whether or not this fear is a signal about *this specific situation*. If it is, you can decide how you want to respond to it rather than engaging in some knee-jerk reaction that pops up anytime you feel vulnerable. Perhaps it's a signal that you are not ready to engage in this activity, or that this activity is truly not safe. In that case, you can choose to back away so you can prepare for next time or so you can escape true danger. In many circumstances that involve the anxiety disorders, instead of defending and protecting yourself or backing up to better prepare, the decision should be to step forward into the situation to learn more. So the choice you need to make is whether to avoid and guard, to back away so you can prepare, or to step forward and explore. We're going to talk all about how to step forward in a later section of the book, surprisingly titled "Step Forward."

As you examine the situation, you might decide that all these feelings stem from noise. You're *not* about to humiliate yourself, and you *can* tolerate embarrassment when you stumble during your speech; the obsessive thought you just had *doesn't* mean you're a pedophile; you *don't* have to treat this panicky feeling as a heart attack. Despite the strength of your thoughts and the intensity of your distress, they are still not signals of danger, even though you have been treating them as such. In these moments, you need to thwart the power of that anxiety-provoking worry. When you choose to quiet your mind for a few moments so you can mentally step back, you are driving a little wedge of time into your anxious monologue. And within that little wedge of time, you are briefly shifting your focus of attention and giving yourself a different, concrete task. Up until that moment, you have been caught up in those negative thoughts and feelings. You have been marching to the beat of Anxiety's drum. And now you are taking only a few moments to step away and then absorb yourself in another assignment: to get quiet. You can afford those few moments, can you not? Especially if it might break the spell that Anxiety has over you.

And we're pausing not only to get quiet. Look how many tasks I'm asking you to accomplish in that brief little moment: cue yourself by subvocalizing a statement about how you've become stuck; maybe initiate a nice, long inhale and a gentle, slow exhale; invite yourself to let go of the other thoughts and feelings; invite your jaw to slacken and your shoulders to loosen; relax your eyes; and perhaps offer a little self-compassion. That's a lot of stuff to do!

And that's part of our strategy. The state of momentary dread and anxiety can be so all-consuming. If you want to break free of that pattern for a few moments, I think it's best to give yourself a task during those moments that requires a significant degree of focused, conscious attention. This is not distraction. You are not trying to block out anything. You are still engaged in the present moment. You are simply shifting the way in which you are engaged.

Oh, hey, before I forget, I need to clue you in on an important point. You can't do this stuff because I tell you to. The function of this task needs to make logical sense to you. And then you need to purposely and voluntarily *choose* to turn your attention away from a very compelling narrative of threat. Decide to let go because *you* decide. And then focus your attention on that process of letting go. Don't comply with my instructions. Activate your own intention. The only way I'm going to help you here is if my strategy ultimately becomes *your* strategy.

So when you create a mindful moment, what happens next? Instead of forging ahead with this anxious worrying or simultaneously fighting against it, you have come to a brief pause in the action by busying yourself with a series of small, quieting tasks. This momentary gap allows you the opportunity to start down a new path of thinking. It enables you a chance to take on a new point of view about what you are experiencing. It's like a "Choose Your Own Adventure" novel, where you assume the role of the protagonist and make choices that determine your actions and the plot's outcome. When you quiet your mind in these moments, you come to a fork in the road. Perhaps you have to decide, "Am I taking the path of believing that this is a signal? Or am I choosing to go down the path of treating it as noise?" Or maybe your two choices are between resuming your fight against distress and doubt, or taking the path that allows discomfort and doubt but leads to your positive future.

Figure 4. The mindful stance—stepping BACK with detachment.

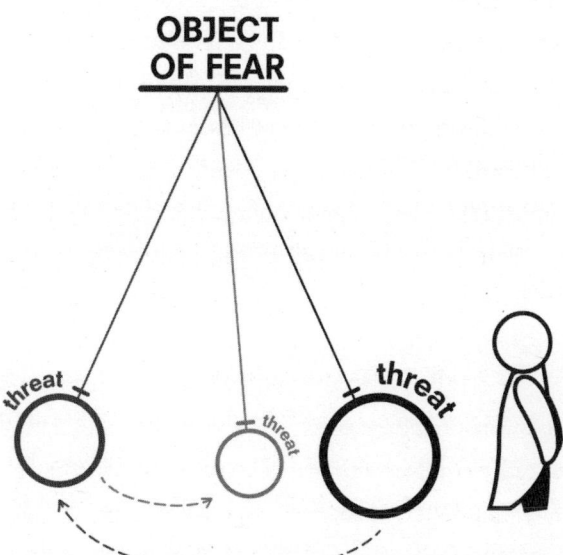

In Chapter 3, I illustrated how your resistance to feeling uncomfortable or uncertain—your I-don't-want-this response—has the potential to increase your symptoms, make you more afraid, and strengthen your urge to avoid. It's as though you are shoving on that pendulum, which adds energy, causing the pendulum to swing back with equal or greater force, and making you experience more discomfort and more uncertainty. Contributing to your own suffering is, of course, exactly what you don't want.

Now what might happen to that same pendulum if you decide to detach from your urge to push that threat away? Check out Figure 4. What if you do nothing? What if you step back, away from the drama of fear and resistance, and don't push the feelings of distress and uncertainty away? When you withdraw your energy from the pendulum, then gravity and air friction take over, putting a drag on that pendulum and slowing it down. Shall I say that again? When you do *nothing* to resist the present moment, it will dissipate. Anxiety *requires* your involvement. When you detach, you win. That's what we're looking for.

Listen, for some people (and you could be one of those people), all they need to do is to learn to step back into a mindful position, and that move alone will be enough to get them stronger. Even if they first need to apply all the other tactics of this book's strategy, in the end they may need only this simple process of mindful awareness of the moment and they will be set free.

At this point in our work, good reader, all we're looking for is the opportunity to make a conscious choice instead of running on Anxiety's autopilot. To give yourself that option, you *must* learn to step back when you are worrying, stalling, or avoiding. Without this skill, you will likely treat *all* your worries as signals when some of them are really just noise and can be dropped, ignored, and neglected. Sure, each of us knows how to get comfortable by backing up into a safe routine and avoiding anything new or threatening. But we also need the capacity to step into new territory. If we don't develop that skill and tolerance, we can never advance. Learn to find that mindfully quiet moment so you can access your Observer. It is a critical tool that will help you gain perspective on a problem and generate new, creative ideas. If you want help in mastering this ability to step back, you have a number of avenues. Look into courses in mindfulness or mindfulness-based stress reduction, meditation training, relaxation training, clinical hypnosis, yoga, and biofeedback.

Getting quiet in the moment is different from calming down and relaxing. You don't need to become mentally and physically calm. We are not looking for peace and tranquility here. In fact, calming down can be contraindicated during a difficult task. For our purposes, you need to be alert and focused. You need a means of detaching yourself from your ongoing negative interpretation so you can confirm it is called for (i.e., a signal). And you need a means of detaching yourself from your compulsive behaviors when they cause you to avoid the world instead of engage in it. Whether you are obsessing or acting defensively, if you pause long enough to mentally step back, you give yourself a chance to refresh your point of view so that you can step forward. But that doesn't require you to relax.

The Buddhists refer to the practice of meditation as a means of developing a finely tuned awareness of their own feelings. This awareness allows them to recognize the spark before the flame. And that's what we want to develop here. By stepping back you can begin to create a gap between the spark and the flame, between your *urge* to avoid and your avoidant action. And, like the Buddhists, you are going to find that this is an immensely helpful tactic.

WANT IT

CHAPTER 10

Taking the Paradoxical Point of View

O ur point of view is the window we look through to perceive an event. It's our unique perception of that event. In physics it describes the position from which an activity is identified or measured. Imagine you're on a moving train, throwing a tennis ball up in the air, tossing and catching in the same hand. A fellow passenger on the train might say the ball is traveling straight up and down, whereas a person viewing the activity from outside the passing train will probably describe the ball's trajectory as an arc. (Right? Because the train, with that ball on it, is moving forward.) Depending on your point of view—in this case, your position inside or outside of the train—your observation and description of the event could be drastically different from someone else's.

To put it more simply, let's say you're meeting a friend at a coffee shop "on the left side of Oak Avenue." You arrive at the destination and only then realize, "*My* left may not be *her* left." If you're traveling north on Oak, left is on the west side of the street; if you're traveling south, left is on the east side. The frame from which you view the world can mean the difference between a successful rendezvous and a frustrating series of texts:

A: "I'm on the left side of the street."
B: "So am I."
A: "But I don't see you!"
B: "Look to your *left!*"

If you are employed Monday through Friday, your view of the various weekdays—the name we've given to identical blocks of time measuring twenty-four hours each—is vastly different. Wednesdays are "hump days," Fridays are "TGIF" days, and Saturdays are the start of a forty-eight-hour taste of freedom.

If we were in a classroom together, I'd ask each student to come up to the board and jot down some synonyms for point of view. "What are the words we use on a daily basis to describe this phenomenon?" But since it's just me here alone at my computer and you there on your train or at your local coffee shop, we'll just have to pretend.

Synonyms for Point of View	
Frame of reference	Approach
Mind-set	Position
Orientation	Perception
Disposition	Belief
Attitude	Standpoint
Stance	Perspective
Frame of mind	Outlook

Not all your actions stem from your point of view. They can come from any combination of your genetics, past experiences, and current emotional state, as well as your free will, which can be directed by your interests, values, and goals.

But we all *do* create specific points of view, and they *do* have a powerful influence on our thoughts, feelings, and actions. They become shorthand for directing our next moves in the world. Activating the belief "Education will get me ahead" motivates a student to study instead of avoid. The attitude "I'm not worth it" stops someone from asserting her needs. The perspective "Life is short, eat dessert first" directs action toward pleasure before work. Our minds are built to make sense of our moment-by-moment experiences. It is a meaning-making machine. A chaotic, confused mind will race to find an interpretation so as to create logic. Our established points of view are its go-to guys, always available, always ready to help calm down that momentary, discomforting lost feeling. Each of us has thousands of these frames of reference, some that give us the Big Picture ("A merciful God loves us and watches over us"), and many more that pertain to the little nuisances of daily activity ("Cherry pie over key lime, always").

Some mind-sets appear to be loosely grabbed and relatively unstable. We relax into our confidence by leaving home to arrive at the airport in plenty of time for that flight and proudly reflect the belief "I'm in control of my life." Then we get to the accident that blocks the freeway with a mile-long mass of cars idling in place. "My life is ruined!" You see, points of view don't reflect reality. They either push an agenda forward ("Exercise is good for my heart"), or they create structure and meaning around a current set of thoughts and feelings ("Her lack of respect has me boiling mad").

Our perspective can change, just as our stance on any given political or social issue can change when perceived from a different angle. We actually get to *choose* how to perceive whatever event we might encounter.

SAME SCENE—
TWO VIEWPOINTS AND ONE PROPOSAL

Suppose you walk into the office on Monday morning thinking, *Ugh, I hate Mondays. I can't stand going back to work after the weekend. I wish it was Friday.* Like it or not, your interactions and experiences are reflected as well as influenced by that negative outlook. You will address your coworkers differently. You'll answer the phone differently. The day will feel longer, and tasks will seem more unbearable with every passing minute. Then when you step into the break room and discover that no more ground coffee is left, it'll further reinforce the idea that "Mondays totally suck."

When we are stuck, it is to our advantage to step back, choose to disengage from our current view, and look at our tasks from a different vantage point. What I'm suggesting, if you will, is that if we start think-ing of Mondays like Fridays, even though they are really Mondays, we might start having a Friday kind of Monday. And that's got to be more enjoyable than Mondays!

To do this is the essence of paradox, which is acting on a point of view that is the opposite of logic. Why would anyone want to look at life in an illogical manner? Because Anxiety has hijacked your reasoning process and now uses it against you. Consider what happens when you approach an intimidating situation with this mind-set: "This is going to go badly, just like it did last time. I don't want this. I can't handle it." That makes sense, right? But if you *continue* to maintain that stance, then you will either back away from such challenges or you will proceed with dread, worry, and distress. You already know how to do that. Let me help you learn a more clever way of handling Anxiety. By the way, acting cleverly is an important part of our strategy. Just you wait; I've got an entire section of chapters devoted to cleverness.

Let's say you and I are going out to eat at a newly opened restaurant (my treat). As we pull into the parking lot and see that it is full of cars, we might have two separate viewpoints. Your opinion is "Oh, great! This place is already popular. We're going to enjoy this." At that same moment, my stance could be "Oh, great. [Groan.] The parking lot is packed. That means the restaurant's going to be crowded. I can't tolerate crowds tonight. Or any night, for that matter. This is a bad idea. I can't do this."

Two viewpoints of the same scene. But each point of view comes with its own set of feelings and intentions. Yours will call up excitement and the desire to get a seat and start choosing from the menu. Mine pulls up threat and the desire to escape.

Here's my proposal: let's go after Anxiety at the level of your belief system. If we can alter your frame of mind about what it takes to win over Anxiety, then you will become clear about what you need to do in these moments of threat.

"THIS IS HARD,
AND I CAN HANDLE IT"

When we get caught up in our worries, we create a special point of view. Within that orientation, our behavior to resist and avoid makes perfectly good sense. This perspective is powerful. After all, it has guided us through the most distressing and threatening situations. But at the root of this point of view is the attitude that this situation is dire, that these worries are vital to our safety, and that the smartest decision is to become comfortable and certain by escaping as soon as possible. This is the position that leads us to avoid. If we can't avoid, then we will endure; we will suffer through. If I can be so bold, let me say that when any of us consistently operates within this attitude, we are making our lives smaller than necessary. If this is how you think, we need to fix that.

As I described in Chapter 4, anytime we adopt a stance that reflects the message "This shouldn't be happening!" we tap into the primitive and unconscious fight, flight, or freeze response of the limbic system's amygdala. We'll automatically have the urge to guardedly draw inward. Our next actions will become limited by a repertoire of highly restricted options related solely to struggling or escaping. This lower-level consciousness cares little about the nuances of the specific event. Its focus is on the most efficient end to the problem.

Now, I'll take that reaction any day of the week when I'm trapped in an elevator during a fire or skidding sideways on the highway. I'd even take it when I'm trying to grab that last seat in musical chairs. But not when I'm trying to manage the everyday trials and tribulations of my life. When we walk into most situations with that attitude, our chances of winning are greatly diminished.

We cannot focus on trying to fix each specific scene so you can forever feel safe and comfortable. I assume you've already attempted that, and it hasn't been enough to give you the freedom you want. So let's try a different angle, shall we? In these previous few chapters, I've been talking about the need to clarify whether your worries are signals or noise and then to find ways to handle the signals and let go of the noise. Your initial skill must be to mentally step back so you can make that determination. In Chapter 9 I described the mechanics of how to step back in any particular moment.

So what's next? It is to pay attention to the way you are judging your current experience. If you are making a mistake in your judgment, then we need to help you adopt a different opinion, one that empowers you. So let's ditch that "I can't stand this, and I gotta get away from it" point of view and experiment with this one: "This is hard, and that's okay. I'll handle it." (Of course, you have to *believe* you can handle it. We'll keep working on that one.) When you take on this perspective, you will stop resisting the present moment so much, and you will feel more motivated to move ahead with your task. If you are in a competition with Anxiety (and you had better believe you are), then this will be a much more powerful attitude. You're up at bat, and you're prepared to swing at any decent ball that comes across that plate, instead of adopting a more fearful, resistant mind-set like "This is serious. This is dangerous. I have to back away," which leaves you shuddering in the dugout.

Figure 5. Step BACK to gain perspective.

You can't look through the same pinhole and expect to see anything different. As Einstein said, "Problems cannot be solved by thinking within the framework in which they were created." That's why you and I are interacting right now. To solve your problems, we first have to change how you perceive your relationship to Anxiety. Let's create a point of view that motivates you to take new actions.

✧ ✧ ✧

In Chapter 6 you met Mary, who wants help with her fears of flying, parking garages, elevators, and tunnels. She's afraid of panic attacks and whatever harm they might cause her heart. She also fears becoming trapped and then suffocating, and the possibility of being crushed by a collapsing garage.

My goal with Mary is the same as my goal with you. I will be with her a brief two sessions, and in those ninety minutes, I'm going to offer her a new perspective on the strength of her heart, I'll give her a new point of view about her fear of suffocation, and I'll provide her the chance to reappraise her beliefs about being trapped.

More than anything else that she might need, Mary needs to change her mind. And if you're struggling, you need to change your mind, too.

I'm going to joke with her, give her facts, reassure her, and provoke some of her most uncomfortable feelings, whatever it takes to get her to see things from a different point of view. We both want the same outcome: to put those overwhelming threats behind her. We'd love to accomplish that in such a way that she can perceive those anxious worries as unnecessary, as irrational, irrelevant noise.

Let's see how we do.

In this first session, after she describes her past difficulties and states that her goal is to become a more comfortable flyer again, I turn our conversation toward her heart. She tells me that when she feels trapped on the plane, her racing, pounding heart scares her, especially because she's worried that it might cause her to have a heart attack. As soon as I hear her belief that a panic attack can lead to a heart attack, I know we must address it. Because if Mary continues to believe she's at risk of a heart attack when she panics, I'll have nothing to offer her, right? Why would she try out any self-help skills when they might put her at that degree of risk?

I ask if she has any family history of heart problems. Her mother has congestive heart failure, she says, but she's not concerned about that in herself. In fact, she doesn't think there's anything wrong with her heart. *Good*, I think to myself. *She believes her heart is okay.*

Instead, she explains that she's afraid she's putting intense strain on her heart when she gets scared on a plane, and *that* could cause her to have a heart attack. She thinks that could cause *anyone* to have a heart attack. "Because people do have heart attacks from shock and really strong duress, right? It feels like it's jumping out of my chest, almost like it's going to rip out."

So now I know the core of her heart fear. But I think she's got that information wrong, and I need to help her reappraise what's taking place in that panicky moment on the plane. "It sounds like your heart's working pretty well," I say. "To me, that's the sign of a healthy heart. It's what a heart is *supposed* to do in a threatening situation. If I were to open our door right now and a bear came charging to this room, your heart would feel like it was pounding out of your chest."

She challenges my logic. "And your heart pounds so hard because you're supposed to be able to run or something. But on a plane, it's pounding so hard, and I'm stuck in one little place."

She has it right. The function of the pounding heart is to prepare the body for fight or flight. However, she is scaring herself with that idea, and I want to correct her perception. "I think you're making an error when you say, 'If I'm standing still and my heart is pounding, it's more dangerous to my body than if I'm running.' That is a leap of logic that isn't based on science. But don't take my word for it. If you need to check that out with a physician, then you should. But you need to resolve that misunderstanding. When you are on the airplane and feeling anxious about not being able to escape, you will only compound your trouble when you also worry about having a heart attack."

"Fair enough," she says. "But it also makes me wonder how long the heart can take that before it does some kind of damage."

So here it is again. Mary's belief system about the fragility of the human heart is running the show. If we don't correct her perspective, we will be unable to help her get over her fear of flying. Nothing is more important than fixing this distorted view.

"What do you think about checking that out, too? Would a physician be able to reassure you? Or would you not care what they had to say?"

"Oh, yes, a physician's opinion would reassure me."

"So, if we were making a list of tasks for you, one item would be 'Let me gather a little more information about what is dangerous to my heart.' Because why compound a difficult problem with incorrect information? You've got enough issues already. You're on an airplane you can't get off of, and you're feeling claustrophobic! I think you're going to remove 50 percent of your problem if you are able to say, 'Boy, it *feels* as though my heart is going to burst, even though I know it's really fine.'"

I didn't think my challenge to her logic would have any immediate effect. I thought she really did need that medical consultation before she would change her mind. I was wrong, and I will tell you about that soon.

IT'S NEVER THE EVENT, IT'S ALWAYS THE INTERPRETATION

Mary's fear of suffocation is compounded by misinformation, too. She believes it's relatively *easy* for someone to suffocate in certain circumstances. I need to challenge that conviction. How will I do that? By conducting experiments in which she thinks she's going to suffocate.* Sure, I can correct her misinformation about her heart and suggest she talk to her physician for added reassurance. But this suffocation issue? I don't think I can effectively produce change simply by telling her she'll be okay and she won't suffocate. Mary has been traumatized by feeling

---

*This is a well-researched treatment procedure called interoceptive exposure.

like she was about to die. She literally felt she wasn't taking in enough oxygen. I believe we must recreate that sensation in a safe environment to see if she can learn something new about that sensation.

Mary seems to trust me so far. And it's clear she wants to take advantage of this opportunity to learn as much as she can. She's motivated. She wants her freedom back! I'm about to ask her to engage in some activities that will absolutely scare her. In order for her to continue, her goals must be more important than her momentary fears.

I recommend that you use Mary as a model, because you too must elevate your desire for change above your moment-to-moment doubt and distress. To be successful, you'll have three big tasks. First, you need a strong desire to take Anxiety down and win back your life. Then you must work hard to make logical sense of this approach I'm going to teach you. And, here's the biggest challenge: You have to step forward even while some part of you is yelling, "Stop! Don't do this! This is wrong!" Getting stronger requires that you step toward the threat while you purposely and courageously let yourself feel your fear. You can learn what you need to learn only by facing difficulty. Mary is going to illustrate all of this for you.

I ask her to put on a nose clip (the kind swimmers use) so she can breathe only through her mouth. Then I offer her three cocktail straws, those tiny straws used to stir a cocktail (thus the name), and ask her to breathe only through those three little straws for thirty seconds.

She has an easy time with it and doesn't feel much anxiety. However, I'm actually *looking* for her to have trouble breathing, since suffocation is about the fear of not getting enough air. We need to challenge her belief system *while* she's having difficulty breathing. I want you to understand this, too. Your best learnings will come when you re-create a safe, reasonable facsimile of your feared circumstance. If you can pair up your feelings of dread and fear with a new belief about your ability to tolerate those feelings, then you can change. People don't change by absorbing a new theory or studying new information. People change through experience.

Since my objective is to provoke her discomfort, I ask her to get rid of two straws so she will be breathing through only one. We agree on a scale of distress from 0 to 100, so she can easily report her degree of discomfort at any particular moment. I shorten the length of this experiment to ten seconds. Mary survives that trial and reports her highest number as fifty, indicating that she became moderately distressed. Let me take you into the scene as Mary and I debrief the experiment.

> **Mary:** *I thought this would be fine when I took a really deep breath through the straw. But then I realized that the exhale was going to take a long time, so it would be a long time until I could inhale again. That's when my distress went way up.*
>
> **Reid:** *Let me make sure I understand your message. You're saying, "I was having this experience, I made an interpretation about the experience, and then my anxiety went up. It wasn't the experience. It wasn't how I was breathing. It was that I said to myself, 'Oh, it's going to take a long time to exhale, and it's going to take a long time before I can inhale again' and immediately I noticed my anxiety going up." Am I saying it correctly?*
>
> **Mary:** *That's right.*

Notice in this passage that I labeled her awareness of that long exhale as "this experience." I do this purposely because I want her to learn a *general* principle, not something specifically related to breathing. I want her to move up one level of abstraction, away from breathing and up to "a difficulty." If she can extrapolate from this experience to a broad range of uncomfortable experiences, she is changing at the level of principle.

The work is not about your uncomfortable sensations; it is about your *response* to the sensations. Mary predicts that trouble will show up in seconds, as she imagines a restricted ability to inhale. *Then* she becomes more anxious. You and I cannot prevent you from having uncomfortable sensations. But we *can* do something about your interpretations when your discomfort shows up.

> **Reid:** *So does that give us any clue about where we need to focus? Do we have to focus on the behavior of breathing through the straw? Or do we have to focus on your interpretation of the experience?*
>
> **Mary:** *Well, the interpretation.*
>
> **Reid:** *So maybe breathing isn't the trouble. Maybe your interpretation is the problem, because that's what makes you anxious. Let's keep working on trying to change that interpretation.*

She is making that critical distinction here, which you need to make as well. The principle to remember is that when you are feeling threatened, it's *always* about your interpretation. There are plenty of reasons you would feel fear and physical distress. Most often it is because you have been traumatized in a similar way in the past. You don't need an interpretation to have that response, because that comes more unconsciously. But once you decide a threat is in front of you, once you say something like, "This is dangerous," or "This could go terribly wrong," you have made an interpretation. We're going to go after those!

The work is not about your uncomfortable sensations, it is about your response *to the sensations.*

When I'm feeling threatened, it is always about my interpretation. Early last Saturday morning, as I was driving down a country road, I hit a patch of black ice, and my tires lost traction for a moment. That gave me a zing! Of course, the zing was my amygdala instantly giving me a fight-or-flight response before I had time to think anything. (Thank you, amygdala.) Then I immediately made an interpretation, which went something like this: "It rained yesterday, it's below freezing now, and black ice could appear again anywhere on this road. So this is a threat, and I need to drive cautiously." I made a valid interpretation about the circumstance that led me to feel appropriately threatened as I continued driving. That's what was supposed to happen in such a circumstance.

This is exactly what Mary and I are working on now: Does she need to maintain her degree of threat about suffocation? She comes into the session believing that her interpretation is valid. We are generating experiences to learn if it's possible for her to invalidate that interpretation and grab on to a different interpretation that will progress her toward her goals.

I now increase her level of threat by asking Mary to breathe through a single straw for thirty seconds. I suggest that she let her mind be as quiet as possible and simply perform the task. She takes a deep breath before she begins, as though it might be her last for a good long time.

She begins the experiment, but within seconds she quickly pulls off the nose clip and removes the straw. She reports her rating in that moment as sixty.

> **Reid:** *So what happened? That was about eight seconds or so. Isn't that interesting, because you've already done it longer than that. Maybe when I said you were going to be doing it for thirty seconds, it flipped a little switch in your mind.*
>
> **Mary:** *Yeah, it scared me. I thought I wasn't getting enough air.*

EXPERIENCE—THE GREATEST TEACHER

There it is again. She became aroused in part because her amygdala was doing its job. Based on its past learnings, it sensed that the air in the straw was insufficient, and it put her on guard. I expected that would happen, because her amygdala has become sensitized due to her past traumatic experiences concerning suffocation. I want Mary to produce and then face that sensitivity in order to help her amygdala learn something new, so it will become less sensitive in the future. We're going to do that by continuing to study her interpretations and then modify her interpretations through learning from experience.

Reid: *So let's try ten seconds again. [I pause to reconsider.] Well, let's see if you can get to fifteen. [Another brief pause.] And if you can go beyond fifteen, then you can. But I'll let you know when fifteen seconds are up, and if you want to stop at that point and take it off, that's fine. But if we can go to thirty, which is our goal, let's do that.*

I just gave Mary a helping hand for this next experiment. If she can only last ten seconds, that's fine. If she can continue to fifteen seconds, great. If she happens to get to thirty seconds, that will be great, too. And I'm going to cue her as the seconds pass. These are all little crutches, and eventually Mary will want to work on removing many of her crutches so she will have a chance to face more of her insecurity. But right now, they serve the purpose to help her move into new territory, which holds the possibility of new learnings.

We conduct the third experiment, and she makes it all the way to thirty seconds. Her distress level reaches a high of fifty during that time, but as soon as she removes the straw, it drops down to a normal of about thirty. I ask her how she accomplished that, since just minutes ago she panicked at eight seconds.

Mary: *I think I felt like I knew how to regulate my breathing a little better, and also I kept in mind that I was in control of it.*

Mary engaged in an experiment in which she started to panic within eight seconds. Then, in less than two minutes, she adopted a new point of view—"I think I can regulate my breathing, and I'm in control here"—and immediately applied it to her next experiment. And that allowed her to go the full thirty seconds. She changed her point of view; that's the only thing she did. Now we are getting somewhere!

> **Reid:** *Oh. So here in this room you think, "I'm in control because I can take this nose clip off and take this straw out." And on the airplane, what do you think?*
>
> **Mary:** *I think something could happen with the oxygen supply. And then there wouldn't be enough air.*
>
> **Reid:** *Oh, yeah, I've read all the stories about airplanes running out of oxygen while they're sitting on the tarmac, and all those people dying. It's just awful. [Now Mary starts laughing.] You're laughing. Why are you laughing? You don't remember those stories? No?*
>
> **Mary:** *[Still laughing] No.*

Now, you're probably thinking that that's just a funny little exchange I threw in to lighten things up. But twenty-four hours later, when she's sitting on that plane for her scheduled flight and she begins to struggle with her anxiety, the memory of that moment of laughter pops into her mind and lets her shift her perspective away from her fear. Excellent!

But back to the session. I'm going to keep the pressure on. I want Mary to learn (and I want you to learn) that she keeps responding to her *interpretation* of the experience. If she maintains her preexisting point of view, she's going to remain stuck. So we *have* to dislodge that belief and then install a new one. If we can focus on her interpretation instead of the actual event, we can give her a new kind of control.

> **Reid:** *Okay, so, let me just get this straight. That's another interpretation you're making that ends up scaring you. "Oh, no, the air could run out!" This is like what you said about your heart, isn't it? "My belief is my heart is going to pound out of my chest and cause a heart attack if I'm standing still instead of running." So we might guess that*

that interpretation is adding, oh, maybe sixty percent to your distress. But think about this: You just did something within two minutes to change your experience. And it wasn't making the straw larger, was it?

Mary can't handle the realistic possibility of suffocation. Neither would you or I. No one could! When she's on the airplane, if she starts thinking, *I'm going to suffocate,* she'll move into full-blown panic and feel the urge to climb over the seats, push past the other passengers, and escape the plane. What if, instead, she can say, "Boy, it's stuffy in here. I'm starting to feel like I'm going to suffocate. I know this feeling. And I know I'm not about to suffocate, but I sure feel scared." Mary can tolerate a false sense of suffocation if she *interprets* it as false. She has to learn to step back in that moment, to separate her executive self from that part of her who was traumatized in the past and who is now really frightened. She needs to hear those messages of, "I'm going to suffocate," and then immediately reappraise the situation and tell herself, "No, wait, I actually *can* handle this." She'll probably continue to hear those fearful thoughts pop up, and she will still have to cope with her distress. But that will feel a lot easier than coping with impending death.

This is why I'm deliberately working on her content, on her beliefs about the capacity of the heart, and on the likelihood of suffocation. She and I need to settle any faulty interpretation so we can push her content out of the way. We need to get to the essential work of tolerating a *generic* sense of distressing doubt.

SURPRISE!
I'M MORE CAPABLE THAN I THOUGHT

We have time for one more experiment. I brought a scarf to the session. I explain that Mary's job is to tighten the scarf around her neck. Actually, I ask her not just to tighten the scarf but to tighten it a little more than she thinks she can tolerate. The experiment? To see if she can get past the momentary prediction of "I can't handle this."

Let me bring you into the scene. Mary has pulled that big, bulky white scarf around her neck and she is slowly tightening it. I tease her, "You look great. Truly." She responds with a wry smile, "Let's see how I look when I'm blue."

> **Reid:** *You want to get to that place where you go, "Uh-oh." Are you there yet?*
> **Mary:** *Yeah.*
> **Reid:** *I'm going to ask you to put the nose clip on now. And we'll do this for thirty seconds. Is that all right with you?*
> **Mary:** *Yeah.*
> **Reid:** *Okay. [I count the seconds] Five . . . ten . . . Tell me what you're thinking now. Speak to me. Talk out loud.*
> **Mary:** *This is fine.*
> **Reid:** *Where's your number?*
> **Mary:** *It's probably a fifty.*
> **Reid:** *And fifty is fine? You're at moderate distress, and it's fine? Tell me what you mean when you say "It's fine."*
> **Mary:** *Well, my heart is beating faster, but right now it's okay.*
> **Reid:** *How do you know?*
> **Mary:** *Well, I can't look it up yet, but you told me it's okay.*

That's an excellent surprise! I expected Mary would have to consult with a physician before she would change her mind-set about the strength and power of her heart. But she's changed her mind! She modified her belief about one of her major fears, and she did it within a brief thirty minutes. Now, in the middle of an experiment, she's already applying her new point of view in such a way that makes her more capable of tolerating her discomfort.

That's significant progress. She's willing to trust that her heart is not at risk when she gets panicky. But she has another huge belief that has also been in her way. Now that we're coming to the end of this first session, I ask her about it.

> **Reid:** *Our main task today and tomorrow morning is to modify your point of view about your fears and your uncomfortable feelings. What are we doing about your interpretation so far, would you say? What sentence would reflect your point of view right now?*
>
> **Mary:** *Well, just that some of the fears I have are unfounded, and that I can tolerate more than I thought I could.*

Excellent. If Mary can hold on to "I can handle more than I think I can *at this moment*," she'll be in great shape to continue her work here. Mary and I are not focusing on her getting *rid* of the symptoms and getting *rid* of being scared. We're working on changing the interpretation of what she's scared about. "I'm not scared because something is wrong in this moment. I'm scared because I've been traumatized in the past and therefore I *think* there is something dangerous happening now. I'm feeling scared, I'm having symptoms, and I can handle it."

This is what I want for you, too. If you are limiting yourself because you are worrying unnecessarily, I want you to discover that you are more capable than you think.

We have a few minutes left in the session, and it's time to plan some experiments for homework. Our second session comes tomorrow morning, so she has only tonight to practice her skills. My goal is for her to voluntarily choose to place herself in a threatening situation. Most of Mary's difficulties show up when she feels forced into tolerating discomfort. For instance, she loves to travel and needs to travel for work. So she's forced to take that claustrophobic airplane. In the past she also faced times when there was no available street parking and she was forced to use a parking garage. But what if she voluntarily and purposely *chooses* to put herself in one of those circumstances? And what if she voluntarily and purposely *chooses* to generate those typical feelings of doubt and distress? How does that attitude affect her response? That's the experiment.

Mary suggests that she travel to a nearby town so she can drive into a parking structure she typically avoids. Anytime she's forced to use a parking deck, she drives "really fast straight up to the roof" to get away from that closed-in feeling. "But I won't go up to the roof this time. I'll stay in the middle of it."

Stay tuned. In Chapter 16 you'll find out how eventful that experiment was.

✧   ✧   ✧

Here's what we have so far.

It's best for you and me to work directly on the way you look at your long-term relationship with Anxiety, because it has a way of messing with people throughout their lives. Finding a solution for one specific fear will not insulate you from future difficulties. But if you adopt a new perspective, you can apply it to a variety of circumstances over the years.

All of us seek comfort. We each want to feel relaxed when it's time for relaxation. And everybody wants to feel confident in the outcome of our projects. So it's no surprise that people who experience traumatic events—a near drowning, a panic that resembles a heart attack, blanking out in the middle of a conference presentation—will initially react by seeking comfort, safety, and reassurance. But as I described in Chapter 3, when we *continue* to use this approach to solving our difficulties, by avoiding and resisting and by seeking the comfort of certainty, we are inviting long-term problems. What we resist will persist.

This is a competition between two points of view within you. When your primary perspective in life is that you should remove all doubt and insecurity, your growth will be limited. When you believe you should focus on getting *rid* of symptoms and getting *rid* of being scared, that viewpoint will keep you stuck. If you want to take on any specific challenge, the best perspective is a paradoxical one: go *toward* uncertainty and distress and *away from* confidence and security. You must face difficulty. It's the only way any of us learns.

So in the previous section, Step Back, I talked about the need to shift your perspective from the typical way you perceive your problems and your usual ways of responding to them. In Chapter 9 I offered you a specific way to mentally step back during any challenging moment if you feel like you're getting tangled up and confused. When you can step back for a moment, you've created a little space. Great! Now what? This section, Want It, will answer that question. In the gap you create, you have an opportunity to step into a new point of view. I'm going to suggest that you don't simply call up a *different* viewpoint. I'd like you to call up an absolutely *opposite* viewpoint, one that can be reflected in two words, and you can already guess what they are: Want it. Want what you don't want. Want what you've been trying to get rid of. Want difficulty, confusion, and struggle.

And then take action based on that new mind-set. *Want* to step into the fray. And then step into the fray.

Welcoming such a sense of insecurity while you're attempting to solve a problem is quite unorthodox. But stay with me. You can always throw away this book when you've finished it. Until then, try to keep an open mind. I'm going to present some logical explanations for this illogical approach, starting with a profound experience I had a few years ago.

CHAPTER 11

A Profound Experience
with the Toilet

It's Monday morning. I have set aside most of the day to work on this writing project, and I'm committed to making the best of it. I've cleared my desk at my home office, turned off my e-mail, put a sign on the outside of the closed door—SERIOUS WRITING IN PROGRESS!—and I am now working, operating in high gear, with creative juices flowing. At my first break I visit the bathroom only to discover that the toilet is plugged up. I flush to clear it and then . . . a mass of filthy brown toilet water begins to rise, not gradually, mind you, edging toward the rim of the bowl. I rush to close the shut-off valve, frantically turning the knob, but it's futile! I turn and turn in vain as the water spills over the sides of the bowl onto my pristine white Berber carpet! I fumble for the plunger, and now I have a split-second decision to make, a decision with dire consequences. Do I stick the plunger into the toilet, thus displacing more water onto the no-longer-pristine, once-white Berber carpet, or do I hesitate and see if the water stops flowing?

Forget it! No time to hesitate! In goes the plunger as brown water splashes over the edge and onto the floor.

Finally I get results. The water has returned to its proper position at the bottom of the bowl, only now I am left with this disgusting mess and only six hours to address this before clients arrive. First order of business is to retrieve the wet-dry vacuum from the shed, suck up the spilled water, wash down the area with disinfectant and suck that up, too. Then I've got to pull up that end of the bathroom carpet to let it dry, hook the fans up to speed the drying process, and wash the throw rugs. My pants and shoes are soaked with soiled toilet water, so I've got to change those, too. Shucks. These are my favorite shoes. All of this is eating up my very precious writing time. Geez, I might as well march up the stairs and change the sign: Serious Cleaning in Progress!

I'm bent over beside the toilet, sound suppressor ear muffs in place, extracting the liquid with the almost deafening wet-dry vac, feeling appropriately irritated and grumbling to myself, "This is the *last* thing I need right now!"

A moment later I find myself subvocalizing, "This is *exactly* what I need right now." Huh. That was a weird thing to say. Where did that come from? And yet, almost instantaneously, all sound quiets in my mind. I am calm and clear. I continue working efficiently, just as efficiently as I was before, but without any mental suffering.

I didn't purposely call up that message. It was hanging out somewhere in my subconscious when it popped up at that very moment. One of several interesting aspects of this experience was that I didn't have to figure out *why* this mess of a task was exactly what I needed. I just had to get into that frame of mind, and for some reason that was impressively easy to do. With it came a miraculous "Aha!" that I have clung to ever since. I could still recognize how inconvenient and unpleasant the situation was, but by letting my body and mind respond to this new and refreshing perspective, delivered in a memo to self, I instantly changed my relationship with this (unpleasant and inconvenient) moment.

Now, whenever I can grab that perspective, it instantly lifts me from my suffering. If I can catch myself saying something that resembles *I don't like this, I don't want this, I'm unhappy with this outcome, I'm anxious about this,* or *I'm threatened by this,* and if I can then step back from that comment and shift into a welcoming mode—"This is exactly what I want right now"—I find myself in a much better place psychologically. It works like a charm, every single time I make that shift.

(Then again, I am a normal human being, so in most cases I don't *remember* to make the shift out of my resistant stance.)

During a difficult time, we have only two choices: either we accept, or we resist. If we fight the present moment, we are chewing up consciousness that could otherwise be used to cope with the circumstance. Whether you are a worrier or suffer from OCD, panic disorder, social anxiety, or a phobia, Anxiety thrives on your resistance to uncertainty and to discomfort. If you want to take territory back from Anxiety, you'll need to respond paradoxically to these troubling thoughts and feelings. How will you achieve that? Don't look to just tolerate those inner experiences. "I guess I can stomach this" isn't going to cut it. You have to find a way to honestly, purposely, and willingly *welcome* your uncertainty and distress. Invite them in when they show up, and be open to them unpacking their bags and sticking around if they so choose.

Here's how you might state this perspective to yourself: "As I consider facing a threatening situation, my worried thoughts are going to pop up automatically, as will my distress and my urge to remove all those negative thoughts and feelings. I am *not* in conscious control of my fears showing up, and I don't need to be. Therefore, I'm going to *accept* [as noise] those thoughts and feelings when they arrive. I'm not going to fight them or try to get rid of them."

The shorthand message-to-self might be "There's my phobia [or panic, or social anxiety, or OCD] giving me that worry again. I expected that. Of course it's going to show up now. I can handle this. I don't have to do anything." An even shorter message is "It's fine I just had that thought [or those feelings]." And the shortest? "I want this doubt and distress."

Crazy, right?

Why in the world would you say such a thing? If you take it at face value, this really does sound like a foolish response. But "I want this" is merely a *placeholder* for a new point of view. It's a *cue* to take actions based on this mind-set. When you're feeling scared and things are moving very quickly, you don't have time to go on some extended self-talk about how this new viewpoint is logically correct. Absorb that understanding now as you're reading this book and figuring out your strategy. Then in the moment, find a brief little message that reminds you to welcome the struggle.

All of us tend to resist anxiety-provoking experiences. We try to get rid of our fearful thoughts and feelings by escaping the threatening scene. But you can't accomplish your goals if you keep backing away. If you don't intentionally override that unconscious struggle against the threat and intimidation, you will remain stuck. Anxiety lives on that struggle. It dominates you through your resistance. What are you resisting? Well, if the present moment feels threatening, then you will probably resist the present moment! Unless you alter your perspective.

If you and I can work together to help you paradoxically *accept* the present moment and all its ugliness, and if you can embrace all of the dirty water and stained carpets that life has in store for you, then you can focus on what you want to do next.

So, how about some science to help us better understand this new concept?

YOUR EXECUTIVE AT WORK

In any particular moment, our conscious awareness can hold on to only approximately four chunks of information.* This is called our working memory. It allows us to store our immediate experience; it reaches back into our long-term memory to make sense of what we're experiencing; and it processes all of that information in light of our immediate goal. Take right now, for instance: What might your working memory be attending to? You are reading these sentences, trying to make sense of them based on your past experiences and your comprehension of the English language. And you are probably experiencing some kind of response to what you are reading, because you have an immediate goal to comprehend this idea of the working memory. So you might be thinking, "Where is this guy going with this line of thought? Who can make sense of what he's saying!" or "This idea is fascinating! This guy delivers such brilliance within a simple model. I can't wait to understand more." (Let's hope the latter, but I'm not judging.) Simultaneously, you may be registering the sounds around you (the ticking of a clock, the shuffling feet of fellow passengers on the subway), and you might be aware of how your body is feeling and whatever posture you're in. There's plenty to pay attention to at this moment.

RESIST IT	Two Responses to a Tough Moment	ACCEPT IT
"Why can't this be over now? I can't stand this. Why does this always happen to *me*?!"		"Obviously this is happening to me. I accept that, even though I don't like it. Now I'm going to decide what to do next."

*Nelson Cowan, *Attention and Memory: An Integrated Framework* (Oxford [Oxfordshire]: Oxford University Press, 1995).

If we can concentrate on only roughly four thoughts, images, or feelings at one time, then consider the cost when you actively resist the present moment. "Why can't this be over now? I can't stand this! Why does this always happen to *me*?!" When you have these thoughts, you are actively resisting, and that resistance can use up 25 percent of your available resources. Don't do that! That's like trying to write someone a sentimental note on his birthday card while simultaneously singing "The Star-Spangled Banner." Who would do that? All of these messages about resisting the present moment will chew up consciousness that could otherwise be devoted to *handling* the present moment. In fact, they do the opposite: They turn you *away* from the task.

Acceptance might sound like this: "Oh no, this is terrible. I can't stand this!" [Now mentally stepping back.] "Hey, wait. Obviously this is happening to me. I accept that fact, even though I don't like it. Now I'm going to decide what to do next." Does this make sense to you? Your automatic response will most likely be resistance, just as mine was when the toilet overflowed. Step back, notice your resistance, and then choose to stop fighting *in that way*. What might you gain if, rather than resisting, you move toward a position of acceptance? When you drop your resistance, you free up space in your present awareness, so you gain greater capacity to focus on your skills.

Within your working memory, the guiding light is your powerful central executive. It can push away irrelevant information and distractions while simultaneously directing your attention to where you want it to go in the next moment.* Not only that, but some of the newest research tells us that your central executive helps you concentrate so you can narrow your focus of attention from those four chunks down to one

---

*T. P. Zanto and A. Gazzaley, "Neural suppression of irrelevant information underlies optimal working memory performance," *The Journal of Neuroscience* 29 (10) (March 2009): 3059–66.

chunk of information.* An astounding feat! If it has the ability to push out unhelpful thoughts so you can attend to what's important, let's use your working memory to help you become stronger.

As you start to grasp how our working memory operates, some of these crazy ideas I've been spouting may seem slightly less crazy. In those moments when Anxiety is counting on you to resist, if you can then change your point of view so you accept instead of resist, you will immediately free up space in your working memory. That gives you more mental power to help you take back control from Anxiety. Wanting what you are already experiencing will bring you a newfound freedom.

Remember that both your fear and your desire to get rid of any threat will pop up automatically. So even if you give yourself the opposite message, "I actually *want* this," don't expect that message to remain stable and dominant. Moments later you can expect that resisting message to return front and center. What do you do then? Mentally step back again.

Anxiety needs you to hold this perspective: "I've got to back away from any threat so that I can get rid of my fearful thoughts and feelings." Instead, if you apply the skills of your working memory, you can focus your attention on accepting those anxious thoughts and feelings by literally saying to yourself, "It's fine that they just showed up. I can handle these feelings. I don't have to do anything with them." Or if you want to exercise the power of paradox, you can up the ante and respond with a seemingly absurd point of view: "These are exactly the thoughts [or feelings] I want to have." It's to your advantage to profoundly accept that the thoughts have popped up. (Note: You are *not* saying, "I hope these thoughts continue.") Why profoundly accept the thoughts? Because you are already having them! And because if you don't wake up, become alert, and accept those thoughts in a firm and clear way, you will spontaneously start resisting them again.

---

*K. Oberauer, "Access to information in working memory: exploring the focus of attention," *Journal of Experimental Psychology: Learning, Memory, and Cognition* 28 (3) (May 2002): 411–21.

Changing Your Response to a Tough Moment
You experience something unpleasant
⇩
You mentally resist: "I don't want this!"
⇩
You step back and notice your resistance
⇩
You choose to drop your resistance and move to acceptance
⇩
So you can focus on how to handle the moment

But wait a minute. Remember that bit about the central executive being able to narrow your focus to a single thought? Well, when you are really scared, it narrows your focus down to one thought, too: *Get me out of this!* So here is yet another reason to actively subvocalize a profound acceptance: you will have to insert a pretty strong message into your consciousness at that fearful moment to jar yourself free of your negative pattern. How? By doing the best you can to step back, which we covered in the previous section. You need to train yourself to mentally step back so you can hear when you make these anxious, worried statements. Your task is to notice them and decide either to respond to them as though they are a signal or respond as though they are noise.

Are you still following me? Because this can be a helpful concept. When you make a *comment* about what you just thought or felt, when you have an *opinion* about that experience, you have just stepped up one level of abstraction, up to a point of view. You've stepped away from the tangle of your worries, and you've put a little mental distance between you and your anxious thought or feeling. This will momentarily release you from the domination of Anxiety. Anytime you catch yourself getting worked up, you can then say to yourself, "Oh, I'm doing it now. I'm doing what I was just reading about. Good, I noticed it!" When you say that, you will have just separated yourself from your anxious reactions by going *up* one level to a place where you comment on them. You may be able to hold on to that point of view for only twenty seconds before those anxious thoughts pop up again. That doesn't matter. What matters is that you did it! For a few moments you were no longer a victim of Anxiety. You can build on that.

Here is the other valuable news for us about the working memory. It's able to reach back into your long-term memory and pull up resources you need in the moment. What will it pull up? It will go looking for whatever assets you might need *in service of your current, immediate goal.* Your working memory knows nothing about your long-term goals. It's not aware that you eventually want to change jobs or travel more. It's not considering your desire to meet a partner someday and get married. The working memory pays attention only to what you want right now. Awesome! Let's use your working memory to its greatest capacity! It's built to help you get whatever you believe you want in the next few moments.

Therefore . . .

When you're anxious, change what you want *in the moment*. When you're scared, change what you are asking for *right now*. If you will do that, then your incredibly powerful working memory will be working for you.

In case the thought crossed your mind, don't think you can just ask your working memory to end all of your suffering. That doesn't fit into our set of tactics. I suggest you ask for exactly what you're experiencing in the moment: "I don't need to get rid of these feelings. I want to accept that these feelings are here." If you will do that, you will no longer be fighting the present moment, and the present moment will be *much* more bearable. *But you have to ask for it,* because that becomes the signal for your working memory to retrieve the resource of acceptance from your past experiences.

Figure 6. Step BACK, notice you are resisting, and then step UP to embracing the moment.

Here's more great news. Once you have repeated this process enough times, your long-term working memory (yes, you have that, too) will link together all that you have learned.* That means your work becomes easier over time. Once you've established one of these messages as your own, like, "I can handle these feelings," then anytime you call up that message in the future, you will be cueing your working memory to retrieve any helpful internal resources associated with that message.†

It doesn't matter what difficult thought or feeling pops up spontaneously. Let me repeat that. It doesn't matter what the thought or feeling is! Neither you nor I can consciously control activities that are generated from our unconscious, so let's not bother trying. Let Anxiety win that move. What matters is how we *respond* to them.

---

*A. S. Berry et al., "Practice-related improvement in working memory is modulated by changes in processing external interference," *Journal of Neurophysiology* 102 (3) (2009): 1779–89.

† K. A. Ericsson and W. Kintsch, "Long-term working memory," *Psychological Review* 102 (2) (1995): 211–245.

I WANT EXACTLY THIS

Now that we have covered the science a bit, perhaps this "crazy" notion is appearing more and more rational. Confronting our fears can stir up a slew of feelings, among them insecurity, embarrassment, terror, doubt, and worry. Attempting to prevent that swelling emotional response (because we can really only *attempt* to prevent all of those feelings from surfacing) is irrational.

If instead you subvocalize that seemingly absurd message of "This is exactly what I want right now" and simultaneously understand *why* you are saying that, you become stronger because you are dropping your resistance. You are disciplining yourself to stay in the present moment. You're not wishing for a different feeling or for a different circumstance or that your life were unfolding differently than it is at this moment. You are accepting that this moment is all you have *at the moment*. This attitude will offer you newfound power as you face what the moment demands.

Anxiety isn't expecting us to welcome and accept these experiences. It counts on us to resist and block and avoid, to say *I can't tolerate it* and *I can't continue* and *Please, let this be over!* So when you paradoxically permit what is happening, who's in control now? The answer: you are.

But what if you go even further? What if you adjust your attitude as you start thinking about *approaching* difficulties? This is a good time to introduce Cousin Don.

PLAYING CHARADES WITH ATTITUDE

I'm visiting my relatives in Wisconsin for the weekend. We're playing charades, and my team is in the kitchen creating our next set of stumpers. Cousin Julie, as a joke, decides to jot down Aleksandr Solzhenitsyn's book *The Gulag Archipelago*, a memoir about the Soviet labor camp system. As the game proceeds, I watch Julie's husband, Don, pull this particular title out of the bowl. Now, if I had grabbed this one, I'd promptly roll my eyes and scold the other team. "Guys! This isn't fair! How am I supposed to do this one?!" Don, on the other hand, just stares at the slip of paper, his face completely void of expression. He does this for a good ten seconds, and then he goes to work. He gestures with his hands to indicate a "book." On his right hand he indicates "third word." After some charading about, his team produces "arch" and then "leg." On to the second word. His teammates yell out "log" and then "gooey." (Honestly, they got "gooey.") They're probably seconds from naming the title before the time is up.

What's the key difference between Don and me? Don is aroused by the challenge, which keeps him focused, active, and engaged. The moment his eyes land on that title, Don says to himself, "Yes, this is for me," or, "I can do this," or more simply, "Go!" His working memory is busy conjuring up internal resources to help him find a solution and provide clues to his team. It's giving him precisely what he's asking for.

I, on the other hand, would have added a completely different set of variables to my reaction: self-doubt, pessimism, and distress. I would have kicked things off with this dance of self-depreciation and *then* begun the task, without much hope that I would achieve it. If that is my orientation in the moment, what am I requesting from my working memory? I'm asking it to pull forward from my unconscious any memories of feeling pessimistic or incompetent. Can you see how that would weaken my ability to perform and problem solve? I'd "go negative," and so I'd become less creative and more inhibited. I'd surrender the round before it even began.

I want what Don's got—that ready-for-anything competitive spirit. When we create a sense that we are prepared for whatever comes next, we are bringing our best game to our actions. We do this with a point of view that says, "I have the skills needed to take on this challenge. I have a chance here." If we're not yet ready to believe we have what it takes, then our stance can become, "I choose to take this on. I'm going to *act as though* I can handle this challenge." (I'll tell you more about how to act as though in Chapter 18.) This stance seems to make a lot more sense than continuing to say, "It's terrible this has happened," or, "There's no way I can handle this."

EMBRACING THE PRESENT

My wife and I are touring southwest England, in the county of Cornwall. The farther we travel toward the small coves on the coast, the narrower the roads become. Often we end up on paths so narrow that we can reach out of the car windows and touch the five-foot-high stone walls that line the road. The flowering vines that emerge from the walls repeatedly rap our side mirrors.

As I'm driving (too carefully, mind you), a car comes up behind us, and I imagine the driver is impatient with me. My body becomes tense, responding to the clear thought in my mind: *I don't want this situation.* My inner voice is expressing my larger frame of reference: *I want to end any circumstance that generates bad feelings.* Obviously, I have options here. I can pull over at first opportunity, or I can speed up, or I can move the mirrors to eliminate my distressing view. But I do none of these things. Instead, I've allowed a not-so-comfortable strategy to assert itself into my course of action. I've decided to resist this experience, to get tense, to want to get out of my predicament as quickly as possible, and to worry about it until release finally comes.

Then I remember to consciously go to my newfound friend and say, "This is just what I want right now." My intimidation promptly lessens. All my same choices are still available to me, and yet I'm no longer suffering. This state has a shelf life of about twelve seconds. Then I must repeat the note to self, "This is precisely what I want right now."

How easily that message comes, how long it sustains me, and how often I remember it vary over time. But I absolutely want this perspective influencing my state of mind. I'd like you to experience its benefits, too. You don't have to push, push, push into all of your intimidating territories. But when you choose to approach situations of doubt and discomfort, if you can then alter your frame of reference to some derivative of "I'm willing to experience this at this moment" and sit with that for as long as you can, then you will have an advantage over Anxiety. Accepting whatever unpleasantness arrives at your doorstep gets you to stop resisting, and then you can be alert to the world around you and focused on your next move. You are not saying that you accept that this state of affairs will *continue*, not even for another moment. But if you are ready to change your relationship with Anxiety, then *begin* by accepting exactly what is already happening in the present (difficult) moment.

Why take this stand in the face of distress? I can think of four reasons, starting with the most important one.

You are accepting a situation that *already exists*. Resisting the present has no redeeming value. Your heart is already racing. Your cheeks are already red. That water has already flooded over and onto the (did I mention it was a) pristine white Berber carpet.

Becoming upset about a difficult state of affairs is like moving into shock. In terms of problem-solving energy, any one of us will become temporarily paralyzed if we focus on our upset. We can burn a great deal of energy in that paralysis: "Oh, no! I can't believe this has happened to me! *Again*!" We are essentially spinning in place. Agitated paralysis is a common and automatic response to such stressors. We tend to experience it in our most uncomfortable situations. But when we notice this response, we need to instruct ourselves to "Wake up! Shake out of it!" and then pick a new attitude, an attitude like "It's okay that this is hard. I'll cope with it." That will give you more power.

It's best to accept the present *before* we attempt to change it. Psychoanalyst Donald Winnicott has been quoted as saying, "The first step toward change is the complete, albeit temporary, acceptance of the status quo." Remember, the working memory can pay attention to only about four chunks of information at any given moment. If you allow yourself to focus on the "I've got to get rid of this (bad) experience" message, you are chewing up consciousness you could be using to figure out what to do next.

When you stop fighting the present moment, you can turn all of your attention to ways to influence the *next* moment. The essence of this paradox is to strive for change and simultaneously accept that there may be no change. Why take that stance? Because it is the most pragmatic mental shift to make if your goal is to move forward unencumbered by your fear of loss. If I'm feeling anxious, I can attempt to cool out by a variety of means. For instance, I can take a couple of calming breaths, or I can sit quietly and mindfully for a few minutes. But as I'm doing that, the best stance to take is "Let me see if I can cool out these anxious feelings. If this works, great. If it doesn't work and I'm still feeling nervous, that's okay, too. I can handle feeling anxious." Why in the world would I want to say that? Because the alternative is "I'm feeling quite anxious. I need to do something to cool out these feelings. This had better work, because if I still feel nervous, that will be awful." That message is hardwired into my amygdala as a signal of danger. "He's telling me that this *has* to work! If it doesn't, that will be awful!" With that cue, my amygdala jumps into action, secretes even more epinephrine in my brain and throughout my body (like I described in Chapter 4), and now I feel even more wired. When I'm feeling anxious, the last thing I want is to unknowingly cause myself to become even *more* anxious.

I'm Willing to Experience This at This Moment

- You are accepting a situation that *already exists*.
- Becoming upset about a difficult state of affairs is like moving into shock.
- It's best to accept the present *before* we attempt to change it.
- When you stop fighting the present moment, you can turn all of your attention to ways to influence the next moment.

It will be exactly the same for you. If your heart is racing, it's fine for you to decide to quiet it by taking some calming breaths. But if you take those calming breaths with the point of view that it's now or never—"This is wrong. I can't let my heart race like this. I've got to slow it down!"—you'll be working against yourself. (Anxiety *loves* it when you resist the present moment.) As soon as you decide "This shouldn't be happening," you send a simple, direct message to your limbic system, a message your amygdala perceives as "Protect me from danger!" The amygdala responds, "Yes, boss, I'm right here! I'll save you!" and signals your body to secrete more epinephrine, causing your heart instantly to beat *faster*.

Our goal is to take territory back from Anxiety. Since Anxiety thrives on your resistance to insecurity and discomfort, your job is to act in the opposite manner. When you step toward what you fear, you will feel doubt and distress. Mentally step back so you can notice those feelings. And then in that mindful gap you have just created, change your strategy. Change your point of view. Shift away from believing that you need to fight to get rid of those feelings. Swing over to accepting that you are feeling threatened. Find a message-to-self you can deliver quickly and easily, reminding you of your intention. That's what these three chapters in this section, Want It, are all about.

CHAPTER 12

Message to Self: I *Want* This

I called my son Patrick the evening of his Junior Olympics Tae Kwon Do competition (he was thirteen at the time, and I couldn't attend due to a prior commitment). When I asked him how it went, flatly he said, "I lost."

In the sparring portion of the competition, two competitors wearing their dobok (Tae Kwon Do uniform) and various pads and protective gear get into the ring. The goal is to score as many points as possible in the timed round. It's very much like a regular boxing match.

"Well, what happened?" I asked. "Was he bigger than you?"

"No, not really."

"Was he stronger than you?"

"Not really. I don't know."

These kids hop around on the mat for a bit, circling and sizing up each other (again, like a regular boxing match) before one charges the other, and the two begin kicking and punching at each other's bodies. While some bouts are tame, others can get pretty aggressive, even in a junior competition setting. In fact, USA Tae Kwon Do felt the need to include the following clause in their 2009 rulebook: "Inability to continue because of fright, crying or loss of will following a kick to the head which did not cause injury does not constitute grounds for disqualification of the attacker."

Patrick finally opened up about the event and explained that as soon as the bell rang, his competitor ran toward him and delivered a roundhouse kick to Patrick's side, knocking him onto the mat. In essence, his opponent startled him within a matter of seconds. And after that moment, he didn't want *that* experience again: to suddenly take a stinging kick from his challenger and get knocked to the mat. In his remaining time, he became 100 percent defensive, making it his goal to remain standing for the rest of the fight. No matter what, he would not end up on the mat again. He did a lot more backing up than stepping forward during those minutes.

At the end of the two rounds, the score was one to seven. His opponent managed to score seven points on him, primarily because Patrick wasn't focused on his offensive tactics. He was fixated on the defensive. Scoring points was the last thing on his mind.

This seemingly negative experience taught Patrick a valuable lesson about stepping forward. He became an outstanding student of the martial arts and completed the arduous journey to black belt in Tae Kwon Do.

LOVE THE MAT

It's no surprise that one of the mottos trainers and instructors in various martial art forms all over the world pass on to their students is *love the mat*. In some cases, they've expanded the motto to "Love the mat and the view of the ceiling." I can appreciate that visual of lying on your back on the cold cushioned surface, even for a second, staring at the distant lighting grid above you, just enjoying the view.

If you're training and competing on a regular basis, it's a given that you're going to end up on the mat over and over and over again. If you hate the mat—if you step into the ring thinking, "Don't get hit, don't get knocked down, don't lose"—then you're chewing up consciousness that could be attending to your skills. You're devoting your attention and energy to bracing against the mat.

You'll hear the same or similar mottos in core work and abdominal exercises ("Let's do another round of planks. Come on, love the mat!") and in yoga studios, where a common thread is that the mat is your very own island and a place of comfort. Koré Grate, executive director of the Five Elements Martial Arts and Healing Center, is a renowned women's self-defense and empowerment instructor and is famous for her "Learn to Love the Mat" classes. Whatever the arena, this paradoxical strategy works because a large chunk of your consciousness is no longer consumed by your fear of the mat. Your concentration is no longer on not falling, not failing, or not taking the hit. Your new position is "Fine, I may end up on the mat. So what? I can handle it." This allows you to move forward. You can focus more of your consciousness on handling the competitor in front of you (or your skill set, or your core exercises, or your self-defense mantras), thus diminishing the chance you'll end up on the mat.

Let me rephrase that. We are going to end up on the mat repeatedly. If we are busy protecting ourselves against hitting the mat, if we are working to guarantee a certain designated comfort level, our consciousness is in an internal battle that weakens our performance. The less we worry about being thrown to the mat, the less likely we are to end up on the mat. I'm promoting a paradoxical strategy that says to go after what threatens you, welcome discomfort, and allow the occasional punch in the gut from Anxiety. *When you're in the jungle, run toward the roar.*

You *cannot* keep backing up into a place of safety and expect to gain control. You must step into the chaos and fight for control *there*. When you figure out how to do this, you will begin living out in the world again. To be fully engaged in life, you must give up control as you now know it. Only then will you gain a whole new level of control.

THE NEUROLOGY OF "I WANT THIS"

Your prefrontal cortex is the part of your brain that makes interpretations about what you are experiencing. It can work in your favor, or it can work against you. When Anxiety is in charge, your prefrontal cortex will scare you by exaggerating danger and telling you that you don't have what it takes to handle the threat. Your major task is to find ways to compete with the prefrontal cortex telling your amygdala, "This experience is dangerous, and I'm afraid I can't handle it." One way is to allow those fearful thoughts to pop up (because they're *going* to pop up, whether we like it or not). Don't try to get rid of them. When they arrive, step back and notice them. Once you create that mental gap, give yourself a new message similar to "I actually *want* this feeling." In essence, our goal is to get your prefrontal cortex focused on generating these paradoxical statements so they will take priority over your fearful thoughts.

When you have been traumatized in the past, how do we help your amygdala figure out that it doesn't have to *keep* juicing you up with epinephrine? Actually, your amygdala will learn on its own when you purposely and voluntarily choose to place it in a safe, reasonable facsimile of the fearful situation and let it hang out. This requires that you also start detaching from those dramatic thoughts you have generated in the past in *response* to threat. (*Oh, no. I can't stand this. I've got to get rid of these feelings. Now!*) Yet to get stronger, you will still need those uncomfortable thoughts and feelings to show up. In neurology we use the expression "You have to activate to generate." This means you have to activate the neurocircuitry of fear, and you have to activate it specifically *during the event that is scaring you* in order to generate a new response to that specific event when you encounter it again in the future. Be willing to put yourself in those scenes repeatedly, but make sure you are stepping onto the platform of acceptance while doing it. It's possible you won't have to repeat it a number of times in order to change. But the best attitude to have is "No matter how many times I have to repeat this, I'm willing to keep doing it until I get strong." That stance needs to trump the attitude of "Oh, gosh, am I better yet? Because I don't really want to do this anymore."

Choose to Become Distressed and Afraid

- You have to voluntarily and purposely choose to *generate* distress if you want to learn to manage distress.
- Go after what threatens you, welcome the discomfort, and allow the occasional punch in the gut from Anxiety.
- Give yourself a paradoxical message similar to "I actually WANT this feeling."
- Choose to feel clumsy, awkward, unsure, and afraid.
- Act on the mottos "Love the mat" and "Run toward the roar."

Unfortunately, you can't simply put yourself in the threatening situation and then distract yourself when you get scared. Your amygdala needs to sense that this experience is similar enough to the original one that traumatized you. At the same time, however, your amygdala needs to become aware that this is different, because this time it notices that you're scared but not terrified, and you have an urge to run but you're not acting on it. So you need to perceive yourself as safe enough and then choose to experience those uncomfortable feelings instead of escape them. Your amygdala has to hang out, unencumbered by your resistance. *That's* how it learns.

If you got trapped in an elevator once in the past and now you feel phobic of elevators, but want to get over your phobia, you need to get on an elevator, let yourself get scared, and ride up and down the elevator, welcoming those fearful sensations instead of fighting them. And then do it again. And again. If you will repeat that action, then instead of remaining on autopilot, secreting all that epinephrine your amygdala always gives you, it will begin a new learning process to determine just how much epinephrine it really needs to secrete. If you keep riding that elevator (assuming you don't get trapped again) while you actively maintain the stance of "This is really what I want to be doing right now," your amygdala will begin to make new decisions as it faces elevators. At the same time, these experiences allow your long-term working memory to build internal resources and make them available to you more rapidly in the future. This is all good strategy.

Giving Your Amygdala a Chance to Learn

1) Step into a safe, reasonable facsimile of the traumatic scene
2) Let yourself feel threatened and get scared
3) Welcome the fearful sensations: "This is what I want right now"
4) Hang out

Change what you say to yourself and believe in what you say. That's how you will prevail over all those negative comments your prefrontal cortex has been generating. If you can embrace whatever you are experiencing in the (uncomfortable) moment, your amygdala will do its job and learn not to secrete more epinephrine than necessary. Over time you will become less afraid and better able to tolerate your fear.

How do you refocus your prefrontal cortex? By creating that momentary gap in your negative diatribe so that you can say, and believe, such messages as these:

✧ I want this distress. Sitting with and accepting this distress is going to make me stronger.
✧ I can handle this uncertainty.
✧ I'm willing to feel this.
✧ That's content. I'm not paying attention to content.

You can even learn to say this one, "Come on, Anxiety, gimme me your best shot." I'll tell you all about that one when we get to the section Be Cunning.

Once you respond with a message of willingness, expect that within moments you will hear yourself resisting and feel that urge to get away from the distress. That pendulum is just going to swing back and forth for a while. If you told yourself, "I'm willing to feel this," and then your discomfort magically disappeared, that's not going to help our project. Your amygdala needs to have the chance to linger in the distress while you aren't busy enflaming it through your prefrontal cortex. Let those thoughts and feelings come, then detach from your resistant stance and swing back over to your accepting stance. Do it again and again and again. Don't get frustrated with your rebound over to resistance again. If that happens, tell yourself it's just what you're looking for.

Let me say again. You have to voluntarily and purposely choose to step into the distressing event if you want to learn to manage your distress. You must step forward, into the threat, and *let* yourself become afraid. That gives you a chance to master your fear. If you permit yourself to feel afraid, you have already begun to walk down the path to mastering these skills. When you *choose* to become distressed and afraid, you are now taking back ownership of your life from Anxiety.

Figure 7. Expect that you will resist, and then practice detaching, again and again.

THE SCIENCE OF HABITUATION— THIS IS HARD, AND I WANT IT

How can I possibly suggest that you should *ask for* doubt and discomfort? I can explain. But first, let me remind you that ever since Chapter 7, we have been addressing worries that are noise, not signals. You might be having a hard time paying your bills these days, and that's something to be concerned about. But when Anxiety takes over, it convinces you to worry throughout the day. When you worry at inappropriate times (like when you're trying to sleep), or when worry only makes you feel bad instead of also activating a problem-solving session, then we are working on that kind of worry now. When your fears and worries have led you to avoid activities you really want to engage in again, we are working on those topics now. All the tactics in these chapters are designed for noisy worries, not signals.

In behavioral therapy we have a term called *habituation*, which has been a long-standing principle in the treatment of phobias and other irrational fears. Habituation means gradually learning to tolerate a relatively safe situation that has been scaring you. It requires three variables: frequency, intensity, and duration. Applying this principle means that you face the feared situation frequently, all within a short few weeks. As you face your fear, you should generate at least moderate distress. (On a scale of 0 to 100, imagine getting your distress to fifty or above.) And you should linger in that difficult scene for an extended period of time. Lately we've been refining some of the concepts behind habituation, and these changes make a great deal of sense. (I'll tell you about that work by Drs. Barlow and Craske in Chapter 24.) But that's not our concern right now. For our purposes, these definitions will work perfectly.

But wait a minute. I've had plenty of hard-working clients who challenge me when I described this approach. If they have panic disorder, they might say, "Dr. Wilson, I *go* to the grocery store. At least three times a week! And I *stay* there, sometimes for forty-five minutes to an hour, while I'm feeling *so* anxious. But I'm still no better!" They seem to be actively engaging in what we call exposure practice. They are meeting the basic criteria for habituation: they're exposing themselves to the fearful situation frequently enough; they feel quite distressed; and they are staying forty-five minutes to an hour, which fits the definition of an extended period of time.

Yet it's not helping them. Why not? Because as they stand in the threatening situation, their self-talk includes, "Jeez, I hope I don't have a panic attack. I wish I could get out of here right now, but I *have* to do my shopping. I *hate* this feeling. How much longer? How much longer!?!" This is just what we were talking about in the previous chapter. As they remain in the threatening environment, their opinion of the present circumstance—"This is bad. I want to escape."—is working against them. The statements of their prefrontal cortexes are now an active part of their working memory, which accesses past experiences that went poorly. All this resistance is using up chunks of their working memory, crowding out thoughts of any positive coping skills.

And the same can happen with you. Your negative judgment is always going to override any *techniques* you might use to get stronger. That's why you and I are not relying on techniques. Your resisting mind, just like mine and everyone else's, can push aside techniques. So we are building from the top down. We started with solid principles. We are now constructing a point of view that leads to a broad strategy that will then direct your actions. Technique is overrated. Acting on principles is the long-term solution.

Imagine you have social anxiety and you are working on your fear of being criticized by others during your departmental meetings at work. You attend these meetings every week—there's your frequency. Each of those meetings lasts a solid hour. Add to that the length of time you are anxiously worried both before and after the meeting. All of that counts as your duration. And, of course, you get pretty darn distressed during that time, so there's the intensity. Now we've got the frequency, intensity, and duration of the habituation model. And yet you aren't getting stronger. What's missing here? If before each meeting you predict that things will go badly, and if before you speak up you keep generating worried thoughts about what you're going to say, and if as you leave the meeting you start worrying about how you expressed yourself, then you are standing in your own way of getting stronger. The messages of fear and worry generated by your prefrontal cortex won't let you gain any ground. That's why we must make some modifications in this habituation model.

Imagine you have a fear of elevators and you try to get over it by riding up and down the sixteen floors of your office building repeatedly. That's pretty good strategy, right? But what's the chance of your mastering that elevator phobia if during each ride you scare yourself with, "Boy, I've been lucky so far. I wonder how many strands of that cable are still left. Could it snap at any moment? Of course, it's never happened to me yet. That means I must be due for a tragic fall!" You are actively generating interpretations that this elevator riding is dangerous while you are actively attempting to overcome your fear. That's *never* going to work. When your negative interpretations run wild, completely unrestrained, they will always trump your courageous action, and you will stay stuck. I believe this is the top reason why people in behavioral treatment for their anxiety disorders are not able to recover. It makes sense to me that if you do work on your elevator phobia in this way, you'll try these attempts only a few more times before you conclude, "It's no use. I can't get better. The stairs are best for somebody like me."

You and I are not taking a behavioral therapy approach to your problems. We are leading with the cognitive: your thoughts and your attitude. Your prefrontal cortex is going to supersede any chance for habituation if it continues to reflect the point of view that says, "It is best to get back to where I feel safe and comfortable again." To compete with such a perspective, you need to take on an attitude that stems from habituation. Consider this logic: "I *need* to frequently generate distress and sit with it for a while in order to get stronger. I *want* to get stronger. So I actually *want* frequency, intensity, and duration."

But don't just step into your threatening environment. *Seek out* frequent exposures to your threat. And if you then feel distressed and insecure, *welcome* those feelings. And if your doubt and discomfort seem to be lasting a long time, then *want* them to last. The change we are looking for is a shift in your *attitude* toward your threat, your doubt, and your distress. That means you must courageously step toward what scares you. But you *don't* do it in order to habituate. You do it as a means to practice this change in your point of view.

To build your strength, you will need to move into territory that is now under Anxiety's control. You are going to feel clumsy, awkward, unsure, and afraid. Your job is to willingly choose to have those feelings when they show up. The truly unfamiliar territory you will be aggressing into is the psychological terrain in which you purposely scare yourself. I know all this continues to sound absurd, because it's paradoxical. And it will be hard for you. It's *supposed* to be hard. That's why we call it work. But it's not complex. I will coach you on how to face your fears with a simple frame of mind that no longer feeds Anxiety.

ONLY DO WHAT YOU WANT TO DO

Speaking of nonsensical, here is certainly an unorthodox suggestion: only take actions that you *want* to take. Don't push into fearful situations simply because you think, *I have to do this in order to get better.* If you don't want to face the difficulty, back away. If you don't want to take an action, don't take it. If you don't want to practice these skills, don't practice. If you approach a challenging circumstance and then decide you don't want to step any closer, stop.

Don't take any action only because you *should* take it. Take it because you see the logic (twisted as it is) in taking it, you purposely decide to take it, and you willingly choose to take it. When you *want* to do the hard work that is required to get stronger, then push on.

You and I both know that a part of you will *not* want to step forward. Everyone has that experience because it's universal. When we contemplate taking a challenging step, some part of us doesn't want to struggle and would rather back away. So expect that part of you to show up. Your task is not to let it become your executive voice. You can hear it, you can understand why you'd have that thought, but you can't allow that voice to be in charge of your actions. You need to act based on an executive message of "I choose to step forward. This is hard, and I still want to do this."

Let's say you often become intimidated and anxious when a car comes up behind you "too closely" on the highway. Now you're driving down the highway in order to practice tolerating that intimidating feeling. A car pulls up behind you, and you begin feeling all that typical distress. At this point you have a choice. You can say, "I don't like this. And yet I'm going to continue to allow myself to feel anxious right now." Or you can say, "I don't like this. I'm going to pull over until they go past." Either choice you make is fine. Anytime you choose to stay with and welcome your distress or your insecurity, you're practicing your skills. In those moments, you are scoring points against Anxiety. But that doesn't mean you *always* have to score points against Anxiety. As soon as you make an executive decision to stop practicing, then stop practicing. When you're ready to practice again, go ahead.

I know you're going to be surprised to hear me say this, but there is a paradox that's associated with this only-do-what-you-want-to-do theme. (You're not surprised? Oh, you know me too well.) The paradox goes like this: Only do what you want to do, and want to do the hard stuff.

Another Paradox
Only do what you want to do.
And keep finding ways to want to do the hard stuff.

To get stronger, you need to want to take actions that intimidate you. Keep stringing together moments in which you choose to feel scared and step forward anyway. But *start* this process by developing the skill of wanting to do whatever you decide to do. If you believe an action is worth taking, then genuinely want to take it. Here's the message-to-self: "Things might get dicey here, and I'm going to stay the course anyway." Generate activities related to your theme that could get you feeling apprehensive and insecure. That's your challenge. And when those feelings do show up, your challenge is to willingly stay with them.

If you are afraid of being embarrassed, then your work is to learn how to embrace embarrassment. When you become embarrassed, your job is to tell yourself something like, "This is hard for me. And I can handle these feelings." (You can't just mouth the words. You need to mean it.) Then let yourself linger in the feeling of being embarrassed. You don't need to get rid of that feeling. As soon as you take the stance that you have to get *rid* of that feeling, you have put Anxiety back in the dominant position.

A Paradoxical Twist to Habituation

- *Want* to step into your feared situation.
- If your doubt or distress shows up, then *want* it to show up.
- If your doubt or distress gets stronger, then *want* it to be strong.
- If your doubt or distress sticks around, then *want* it to stick around.

Your job is to handle any present moment in such a way as to stop fighting it. Let's return to that habituation model of frequency, intensity, and duration. Choose to step into your feared situation so you can hang out with a sense of insecurity or distress. Do that frequently. While you're there, if your anxiety gets stronger or you start feeling even more uncertain about how things are going, then embrace *that* experience. That's the intensity part. Why do that? Because you are feeling stronger anxiety or doubt at this moment. Accept what is currently present. You have only two possible responses to any moment: either you embrace it or you fight against it. As soon as you fight against it, Anxiety is dominating the moment again.

In that same way, if your anxiety doesn't diminish or your uncertainty spontaneously sticks around, embrace *that* experience, since that's the duration part of habituation. Remember, a more timid or insecure part of you will be thinking, *I do not want this experience. I want to get rid of this experience.* There's no problem with those kinds of thoughts popping up. In fact, you should expect them. Just don't put that intimidated part of you in charge.

DOMINATE OR BE DOMINATED

Yes, you're right. Once again I am offering you responses that seem patently absurd. Nobody in their right mind (myself included) is truly excited by the experience of doubt and discomfort, and certainly no one wants to literally hunt down those feelings. Yet choosing to seek them out is the opposite of the disposition that maintains the dominance of Anxiety. Anxiety *needs* you to back away when you feel intimidated. Do you get that? It is *not* looking to give you an uncomfortable sensation. It's looking to give you an uncomfortable sensation *that you resist.* Your job is to find *any other way* to respond besides resisting. The most important principle here is that when you stop resisting and you stop avoiding, you start getting stronger. In other words, it's not just what you do, it's what you *stop* doing.

Anxiety *needs* you to play your role of shrinking back, of trying to get rid of these feelings that intimidate you. Instead, if you can stay open and willing to take on this absurd stance, even if it is tongue-in-cheek, you will generate a new frame of reference that is incompatible with what Anxiety so desperately needs to survive. Once you stop backing up and start moving toward Anxiety, Anxiety becomes subservient to you. No matter how clumsy you are at attempting to welcome Anxiety, to the degree you will pay attention to mastering that tactic, you will detach from your tendency to resist. And that's a winning strategy.

WHAT'S AUTOMATIC VERSUS WHAT YOU CAN CHANGE

Here's how you might experience this shift in the moment. When the provoking threat shows up, it produces two automatic responses within you. The first will be your sense of intimidation. It could be an image or a worried thought, a sense of danger, or some sudden impulse. If it's a thought, it can take any form that implies something bad could happen. *I could fail this test. I could suffer in Hell from this blasphemous thought. I could look foolish. I could get trapped. I could freak out. I could get rejected. I could lose.*

Your second automatic response will be a compulsive urge: your insistence on removing the threat and reducing your distress by something you do or say. The driving stance is "I can't let that happen!" So you will feel this strong impulse to leave the scene or to seek some reassurance by asking for help, taking a medication, checking for safety, or repeating some thought or action. Consider this initial sense of intimidation and your immediate urge to get rid of it as within Anxiety's domain. We're going to let those go, because we are not trying to fix such automatic and spontaneous reactions. Our work begins immediately *after* those thoughts, feelings, urges, and drives. Our focus will be on what you do next.

These Come Automatically, So Accept Them!

The Intimidation—a thought, image, or impulse that makes you feel uncertain, anxious, and at risk

THEN

The Urge—your insistence on removing the threat by something you do or say. It will take the form of "I can't let that happen!"

This is the moment to intervene. Your first task is to mentally step back from the moment, separating yourself from the part of you that is worrying, just like I talked about at the end of Chapter 9. Put a label on your current experience so you can gain some perspective about what's going on: "Oh, here's my worry about money again," or, "Oh, I can feel my urge to check the faucet again." You're not making a negative judgment about the negative thought popping up. It's not, "Oh, no! There's that worry again!" In fact *don't* be angry, upset, self-critical, or disappointed by the thought. Simply step back objectively to observe it and name it.

Stepping Back and Wanting It

Notice the threatening thought, image, or impulse.

⇩

Name what you notice. "Oh, I'm worrying about that again."

⇩

Want that. "Good! I want this doubt."

⇩

Notice that you feel scared.

⇩

Want that. "Good! I want to feel scared, too."

⇩

Hang out while feeling uncertain and frightened.

Now what? Anxiety expects you to struggle to get rid of this uncomfortable doubt. Instead, take a stance that is opposite of what Anxiety needs. That's going to be a reasonable facsimile of "*Good.* There's my worry. Right now I want not to know [*about how to solve my money problems or whether or not the faucet is dripping*]. Because that gives me a chance to feel uncertain. And that's what I want, too." Doesn't that sound absurd? But that's what we're looking for: to *want* to be unsure, because tolerating a sense of insecurity is how you get stronger.

Next will come another automatic response: you'll feel *more* scared. Why? Because seeking to feel certain about safety is a defensive strategy. Anytime we drop a defense at a time of threat, we will feel more vulnerable and more scared. (If you don't believe me, then the next time you are driving seventy miles an hour down the highway, pop off your seatbelt for a while.) This is the moment for your second therapeutic intervention: mentally step back again and name what's going on: "Oh, I'm more afraid right now [*about my money situation/about the house flooding*]. *Good*. I'm looking to feel scared, too."

Now what? Hang out as long as you can with these feelings as you continue to engage in your chosen activities. Every time you can engage in this paradoxical response and then turn your attention back to your chosen activity, you score a point against Anxiety. If you don't want to tolerate the doubt or discomfort anymore, do whatever you have to. You don't need to practice your skills all day every day. Practice them moment-by-moment. And then start stringing together as many moments as you can. Assume that the more moments in a row you can practice, the stronger you will get. *Eventually* you will have to do it for a longer period of time, but you don't have to do that now.

COBBLESTONES AND UNCERTAINTY

It seems like we humans are continually on the lookout for the quickest, easiest, or most predictable path to any given end. Convenience stores and fast food. Escalators. Faster download time. Text messages. And there's nothing wrong with any of that, I suppose. Google Maps provides us with the most direct route from A to B, and if the traffic indicators glare red, we can adjust that route to avoid the hassle. For many of us, a good day is one that is hassle-free.

The trouble with our smooth, well-ironed environment is that the real world has bumps in it. *Life* has bumps in it. The world is not a paved street. It's characteristically flawed and full of surprises.

I suppose we have a choice in that we can continue to take a detour with every approaching pothole, or we can accept and eventually embrace the uncertainty that comes with daily life, training and retraining our brains to deal with the ever-changing path we walk on. It turns out that the latter approach is not only better for us mentally; it has a significant effect on our physical health. Ask the residents of Acorn Street in historic Beacon Hill, Boston, or the residents of the "Dumbo" neighborhood in the Brooklyn borough of New York City. After all, research suggests that people who live and walk on cobblestone streets have an improved sense of balance, an improved cardiovascular system, and all-around improved health, and we can attribute these positive health conditions to the "poor" (as in "not smooth and even") conditions of the streets on which they live.* The bumpy, rocky, coarse, uneven, unpaved streets outside their front doors are actually doing them more good than harm.

Imagine you and I are now walking together down Acorn Street. Each time we take a step on that unpredictable cobblestone street, our brains are engaged in the task, giving both mental and physical instructions. Our minds are alert, constantly adjusting to the erratic ground beneath our feet. Our cardiovascular system is making similar adjustments, changing the way it pumps blood through our bodies.

If you still don't believe me, take a trip to China and be on the lookout for black stone mats laid out next to the streets. Passersby remove their shoes and step across the black cobbles, sending information through the feet, signaling the vestibular network to engage in a

---

*William McCall, "The path to better health and lower blood pressure may be paved with cobblestones," *Associated Press* report, July 12, 2005.

workout, improving their overall equilibrium. They're literally thrusting themselves into uncertainty for the sake of better balance.

I can't imagine a purer, more pleasant, or more appropriate paradox for us to consider.

When you work with trainers or fitness coaches, they do not put you on the elliptical machine on a steady incline at a constant pace. No, they put you on the BOSU ball and do their best to make you *just unstable enough*. They'll pull you off the weight machines and put free weights in your hands because they want your muscles to feel awkward. When muscles are awkward, they start firing off more, and that in itself builds strength. When you're in a spin class, the best instructors will have you in and out of the bike's saddle, at both high and low resistance, so your body never acclimates to the workout. *Why?* Because the purpose of any well-conceived physical exercise is to promote disruptive change. That's how you build strength, build muscles, increase stamina, improve balance, and improve performance.

This is exactly what you and I need to do. We need to create a well-conceived strategy to build your ego strength and your mental muscles and to increase your grit and resilience so you can handle distress and rebound after a loss. By doing all that, we will improve your performance.

How do we do that? We disrupt your pattern and get you out of balance, out of your set routine, and out of your comfort zone. You need to seek out opportunities to feel clumsy, awkward, embarrassed, insecure, and self-conscious. That is such a crazy thing to do. And it works so well. But there is no way for you to *know* that until you *experience* it. All my talking here will have zero benefit unless you translate this strategy into action.

IN DEFENSE OF AWKWARDNESS

The *Wright Flyer* was the first successful heavier-than-air powered aircraft. The Wright brothers designed their plane to be *unstable*. It was *so* unstable they could barely control it, even with a great deal of practice. The pilot had to continually make adjustments to maintain pitch.

All previous designers assumed the plane had to be inherently stable. So why in the world would the Wrights purposely construct an unstable plane? Because then they could *control* it. If they wanted to influence the plane's takeoff, direction of travel, and landing, they had to exert control, and that required an airplane that needed control in order to be stabilized.

When you attempt to live within a continually stable routine so you can feel safe and in control, you have it backward. If nothing in your circumstances is allowed to change, your world is very small and you have no control.

If we're truly interested in living in the real world—the world of cracks and crevices and cobblestones, the world of instability and accidents and unexpected incidents—then we must train ourselves to cope with the insecurity of not knowing and the sensations that come with awkwardness. That leads to resilience: our ability to spring back from troubled times. We must learn to deal with variability in our environment, unpredictability in our lives, and changes in the nature of our circumstances. We must, first and foremost, learn to step on the cracks rather than stepping around, over, and in between them.

As you move toward the activities you've been backing away from, be willing not to know for certain how things are going to turn out. I encourage you to adopt the principle of expecting the unexpected and welcoming the discomfort of awkwardness and uncertainty that comes with facing any challenge.

Our doubt and discomfort are not the foe. They can be greeted at the door as welcome visitors. Why? Because if we fight to keep them out, we give control over to Anxiety. If we welcome them (they are coming anyway), we become the subject of the interaction, not the victim. The point of view to strive for is "I notice that I'm feeling awkward, and I'm doubtful of the outcome here. I want *exactly these feelings*, because they are required during this learning process. If I don't master this step of welcoming, I don't get to the next step. I want the next step."

The other reason to take on this stance is that it's the most efficient way to get to the next step. Here is paradox in action: Welcome the present moment in order to move into the future.

By the way, I have no interest in your "wanting" all of these experiences because some psychologist said it would work. "I want this" and friends (friends being "This is hard, but I can handle it," "I can tolerate this," "I'm willing . . . ," etc.) work only if they're truly earnest. You can't fake it and expect results. The message "I want this" is no "open sesame."

I received a note from a former client who had moved away to attend law school. We had been working on her social anxieties because she had been quite timid about speaking to others for most of her life. Since her preteen years, she had done all she could to keep anyone from noticing her, fearing she would come across as weird or different and then be judged harshly and rejected. She had not wanted to take any action that might even remotely draw negative attention from others, and she had always exaggerated the likelihood that she would do or say something weird. One important lesson she absorbed in treatment was that being socially anxious, the risk she is taking when she speaks up, is much more about the terrible feeling of humiliation *inside* herself and has very little to do with getting harshly judged by others. After a good, long while in treatment, she began to understand that her job is to take actions socially that will generate that internal state of humiliation. And then she needs to tolerate that feeling. It's a terribly uncomfortable feeling to withstand. But it's much different from her faulty belief that at any moment she could say or do something that caused others to judge her as a social misfit and outcast. No one in their right mind would take actions that would immediately lead to being an outcast. But every adult has to withstand moments of embarrassment and even shame.

Yes, her comments in this note may be tongue-in-cheek, but she has the right attitude! (Italics below are mine.) You don't know this woman (if you did, you'd really like her), but I knew her well. With all her incredible insecurities, if she can adopt this stance and put herself at risk of feeling humiliated in order to have the chance to get stronger, then you can, too.

Dear Reid,

I get a gold star for the day. I was curious about something in one of my classes (of 60+ people), so I raised my hand and asked. *Unfortunately no one laughed at me . . .*

I have oral arguments in about a week. I have to get up in front of a (pretend) judge and argue one side for 15 MINUTES!!!! I'm very nervous about it, but at least it's not graded. And the humiliation can only last so long, or perhaps it will actually go smoothly. *Although what I really want is to trip on my way up to the podium, stutter the entire time, blush excessively, and have an extremely bad case of the hiccups.*

STEP FORWARD

CHAPTER 13

Dangling by Fingertips

The idea of stepping toward the challenge, with the possibility of freaking out, or harming someone, being humiliated, getting fired, having a heart attack sounds daunting, doesn't it? But wait a minute. That's way too threatening. Let's tone it down some. What about a challenge that's thrilling, one so invigorating that we are eager to compete again? Competitions should involve applying strategy in such a way that we can win, not just keep from losing. How about an uplifting, feel-good analogy for what it takes to succeed at beating Anxiety? I've got just the story! Welcome to Chris Sharma's world.

If Chris Sharma is worried about anything at this very moment, it's not the height at which he's climbing or the three-story free fall into the water below. It's the water itself, which the locals describe as *totalmente congelada*. This time of year, the Mediterranean is "freezing cold," and as much as you might mentally prepare for that moment, you feel it the second your body slaps the surface.

Regardless, Chris Sharma is shirtless (customary work attire) in blood red shorts and signature yellow shoes that, no surprise, he designed himself. He looks down only for a moment, if anything to reassess his line (his own unique path to the top). Beneath him the sea swells. The foam surges on the rocks. He reaches back with his free hand and dips calloused fingers into a mesh bag of chalk hanging from his belt and resumes the DWS (deep-water soloing) up the face of the cliff.

DWS is a relatively new addition to the sport of climbing. It involves ground-up free soloing (i.e., climbing without ropes) above water, and Chris Sharma is one of its most notable pioneers. Right now he is dangling several dozen feet above the raging Mediterranean Sea, mounting an arch known as *Es Pontàs*, which stands majestic at the southeastern edge of the Spanish island of Majorca.

Clearly the sport requires Herculean strength and agility, but there's something acrobatic and ape-like about Sharma's movements. He tucks his left leg up close to his waist to propel himself upward to a seemingly out-of-reach hold high above him. His footwork is loose and effortless but nonetheless calculated. Looking up, yes, the ascent appears impossible, but Sharma is almost reckless as he scrambles up the arch, tackling a line that has never been accomplished before. The chalky fingerprints at the base of the cliff have all been washed away by the sea.

He clutches thin ridges on the limestone surface, some of them less than a quarter of an inch thick. He spots a slab of stone emerging from the cliff face above him and grips it between white, calcified fingertips, grunting, his legs flailing over the void as they struggle to find anything that might pass for a foothold. For a moment his knees hug the façade, but it's not where he wants to be. His tendons strain to maintain the hold. The muscles in his back ripple as he swings left and right. He's been preparing for this moment his entire life.

He eyes his salvation: a clean rock edge about two arms' length to the right. He recalibrates in an instant. Sharma thrusts himself in that direction but misses the intended mark and, without warning, plummets forty feet into the turbulent sea surging beneath him.

Sharma knows a great deal about falling down and getting back up. At the age of thirty-three, a self-proclaimed "old man" in his sport, Sharma is one of the most renowned and envied rock climbers in the world. A veteran in the industry, Sharma is a modern-day nomad, hopping from one rock to the next, flying from Santa Cruz to Maryland to the Mojave Desert, often living out of a backpack and always in search of the next big challenge.

For Sharma, the enjoyment comes not so much from reaching the peak as it does from discovery, exploration, and the unknown: "There [are] a lot of people that maybe focus too much on getting to the top," he says. "They just want to get to the top and have that success, which is too bad, because so much of it takes place in the process of working on it. That's the whole life of it."

Once Sharma has taken on a new project, one that is sure to test and push his limits as a climber, he doesn't plan his course and train elsewhere. He trains on the rock itself. "I'm not the type who can train, be doing something now so that in three months I'll be strong enough to try a route. I just go try a line a million times. The training occurs on the route." For Sharma, a crucial part of the experience is the falling down, learning from his falls, and returning to the rock face after each fall with new information and a reinforced motivation. You can almost hear it in his voice—in his screams, as a he plunges into the icy Mediterranean—the exquisite joy of falling.

You don't have to emulate his joy of falling. But please consider Sharma's words as guidance: the training occurs on the route. Get as close as you can, as soon as you can, to the event you fear. Practice your skills there.

It's not surprising that Sharma at one time took a profound interest in Eastern philosophy and meditation. His technique requires as much mental footwork as it does sheer physical strength. "When you first try [the climb], you can't do all the movements, but then you start piecing it together and figuring it out." His projects are psychological, he says, demanding not only his physical best but also supreme focus and motivation. His attitude and adaptability permit the "experience of exploration" and his willingness to confront the unknown. He sets goals but allows for change, finding his line only once he's on the rock itself. He tolerates being awkward and clumsy. He's able to fall and revisit and fall again.

The training occurs on the route.
Get as close as you can, as soon as you can, to the
event you fear. Practice your skills there.

And, occasionally, Sharma's yelps on the rock face are not out of pleasure but pain. After all, he is a world-class competitive athlete tackling what are considered by his contemporaries the most difficult climbs on the planet, and as with any physically aggressive sport, you're bound to suffer some injuries. One might say it comes with the territory.

Granted, Sharma can't make certain moves now that he could do when he was sixteen, the age when he began climbing professionally. But his mind is stronger than ever, and he has twenty-one years of experience under his belt, experience he carries with him at the start of each new endeavor. "When you actually do it, at the end, maybe it even feels easy, because you have it so wired, you're not even really thinking. You're just relying on the muscle memory, because you know it so well by that point."

And it's that muscle memory that allows him to reemerge from the water, shake off the freezing cold wetness, and tackle *Es Pontàs* again and again and again. It's the failures and the repetition that make Sharma the athlete that he is.

"I WANT TO TAKE ON THIS CHALLENGE"

Chris Sharma is engaged in a challenge that requires great tactical skill. He's one of a kind, and none of us needs to excel to his level of play. But he is winning because his overall strategy includes principles you should embrace (I'll help you).

1) He steps forward and takes on the challenge. "That's my job," he says. He *wants* the challenge. He *seeks out* the challenge.

2) He believes he has the *ability* to master the rock. He does not *know* that he can master it. (If he knew he could master it, it wouldn't be a challenge to him, and he would feel relatively uninterested.)

3) He is willing to be awkward and clumsy as he learns. "When you first try [the climb], you can't do all the movements."

4) He expects he will be uncomfortable. He's willing to be "bitten" by the rock. He knows it comes with the territory.

5) He's willing to experience dramatic failure on his way to success. He perseveres. He keeps going in the face of all those failures.

6) Even though he could lose something of great value (his health, his life), once he has decided on a climb, he doesn't attend to that worry while he's engaged in the work. He focuses on his skills.

I am hard-pressed to imagine that Anxiety will continue to dominate you if you learn to respond to your worry and fear in the same manner Sharma responds to the rock. Of course, you don't have to be physically accomplished like Sharma to win this challenge. But you do have to take on an attitude that is quite similar to his. So consider these five responsibilities as you face the challenges ahead:

1) **Step toward, not away from, your challenges.** Take them on with the attitude and commitment of "This is my job." *Want* to take on the challenges. *Seek out* the tough encounters. Move *toward* what's difficult. Think of the aphorism "When you're in the jungle, run toward the roar." What you'll discover over time is that when you run toward rather than away from what is difficult for you, you'll arrive on the other side of your challenges because you're not resisting them anymore.

2) **Have faith that you have the *ability* to master your anxious worry.** You don't have to know (yet) that you *will* master it, only that you can.

3) **Willingly and voluntarily *choose* to feel clumsy, awkward, unsure, embarrassed, insecure, and afraid** as you learn these tactics of facing what you fear. You cannot engage in a major new project while seeking comfort and certainty at the same time. Any threat worth facing is worth getting uncomfortable, uncertain, and distressed over. It comes with the territory, and it's a sign that you are working on the right stuff. You might need to give yourself a motivating message like "I'm scared, and I'm doing it anyway!"

4) **Permit yourself to fail on your way to success.** Then persist in the face of your failures. You *must* risk losing something, just like everyone else who is taking on a challenge. You won't step forward if your message-to-self is "I can't handle failing." The ideal outlook is "I might fail this time, and here's how I'll handle that." That way, once you commit to a task, you can focus on developing your skills instead of worrying about losing. Michael Jordan, arguably the greatest basketball player of all

time, says this about failure: "I've missed more than nine thousand shots in my career. I've lost almost three hundred games. Twenty-six times I've been trusted to take the game-winning shot and missed. I've failed over and over and over again in my life. And that is why I succeed."*

5) **Invest energy into this work.** You cannot take on the challenge if you withhold your energy. Your energy needs to match the energy of the threat. Don't be afraid to take an even more aggressive stance—"I'm taking back my territory!"—because a good challenge is worth getting angry about.

What's shorthand for all these five responsibilities? Well, it's not "I don't *want* to take on this challenge. But I'll do it if you're telling me I *have* to in order to get rid of all this doubt and distress." Try this one instead: "I *want* to take this on. It sounds hard, but I think I can handle it." You can operationalize that message by the same route Sharma accomplishes his highest goals. Step toward the challenge. Scare yourself by engaging with Anxiety, who has the potential to beat you.

Facing the Challenges Ahead

1) Step toward, not away from, your challenges.

2) Have faith that you have the *ability* to master your anxious worry.

3) Willingly and voluntarily *choose* to feel clumsy, awkward, unsure, embarrassed, insecure, and afraid.

4) Permit yourself to fail on your way to success.

5) Invest energy into this work.

---

*Robert Goldman and Stephen Papson, *Nike Culture: The Sign of the Swoosh* (Thousand Oaks, CA: Sage Publications, 1998), 49.

If you adopt our strategy and then repeat the tactics you learn in this book—and I mean if you repeat them over and over again, through all those awkward, clumsy, insecure phases, right on into the last phase, which is competence—you will develop your own muscle memory. You will have it wired. And that's our goal here.

What's the reward if you master these abilities? You get your life back. That's what we're playing for, right? Your goal cannot be focused on *getting rid of* something (although you can consider that symptoms will go away spontaneously as you master your skills). We are in this to give you all the rewards (and all the struggles) of living life to your fullest.

CHAPTER 14

An Olympic Attitude

L ike so many Americans at the time, I spent the evening of August 18, 2004, glued to the television during the gymnastics portion of the Olympic Games. The men were competing in the all-around, and I'm passionately rooting for this kid from Wisconsin named Paul Hamm. After three of six rotations, he is in first place, and now he's sprinting toward the vault. He has never missed a vault landing in competition. He executes two and a half twists in a split second. Then he doesn't just miss the landing, he falls into the judges' table!

I am devastated. I'm thinking, *This is going to be too painful to watch. How can anyone bring his attention back after such a disappointment?* And I turn off the TV. I didn't wait for the three or four replays of the event, the analysis of the imperfect landing, or the explanation of how he subsequently tumbled off the mat and onto the judges themselves. I didn't even stick around for the scoring, the 9.137 that plummeted him from his first place position to twelfth.

I drummed up the willingness to turn on the TV twenty minutes later, and at that moment Hamm sticks his landing after the high bar, and with that he wins the gold medal in the all-around. Now I am shocked and amazed. "How in the world . . . ?" What could have occurred in those twenty minutes, not only on the floor, but also in his mind? How could he physically and mentally recover from such a devastating blow—a blow so disturbing to *me* that my only response was to walk away from the television?

Thankfully, David Letterman posed that very question when Paul appeared on *The Late Show* after returning from Athens.

"How do you put something like that out of your mind?" he asked.

Now Paul reveals a tactic that shows him to be the masterful athlete he is, and I am in awe of his presence of mind in this most stressfully competitive environment. "It was tough," Paul said modestly. "At that point in time I was kind of upset. I thought I had cost myself any chance at a medal. And I just said to myself, 'I'm gonna go after the bronze.'" Hamm, who had been training for this specific competition for a decade and who was on the road to gold or at the very least a silver medal, chose to lower his expectations to what he believed was a more realistic goal. Had he maintained his original mind-set, he probably would have been too distraught to perform. Entering the fifth and sixth events in the all-around and setting his sights now on the bronze, Paul performed to his utmost and made what Letterman heralded "an unheard-of recovery."

"I had one of the best parallel bar performances in my life right after that, and I saw myself in fourth place," Hamm recalls, "and I was like, 'Well, I'm in fourth place now, why don't I go after the gold?' And I came up with the best high bar performance of my life." Paul nailed the landing on both events, scoring 9.837 on both the parallel bars and the high bar, surpassing the silver medalist by twelve-*thousandths* of a point. "What a star he's been since that fall on the vault," the announcer said, moments after Hamm aced the high bar and minutes before he became the first American man ever to win a gold in the all-around gymnastics competition.

I can still see Hamm's coach hugging him jubilantly on the sidelines of the gym floor, looking him square in the eyes and saying, almost to himself, "Never give up!"

Just as memorable as Hamm's individual all-around gold are the events surrounding the same vault exercise at the 1996 Summer Olympics in Atlanta, eight years prior. Eighteen-year-old Kerri Strug was the last woman on the USA gymnastics team to compete in the vault, only moments after teammate Dominique Moceanu received a poor score after falling on her first and second landings. Strug needed to score a 9.493 in the event to secure a gold medal for the USA gymnastics team. Then, on her first attempt, she sprained her ankle.

Actually, it wasn't simply a sprain. She managed to stand up on what turned out to be two torn ligaments and a left ankle with a third-degree sprain. She limped from the landing mat to the starting position, wincing with every step. She looked over at her coach, Bela Karolyi, who could only think of one thing to say, which he called out to her five times: "You can do this. You can do this."

Despite the sudden severe and painful injury, Strug executed her second vault beautifully. Upon landing she promptly dropped to her knees, crawled toward the corner of the mat, and beckoned her coaches, who rushed to her aid and carefully helped her off the floor. "Probably the last thing she should have done was vault again," the announcer says, "but she did," scoring a 9.712 on that famed second attempt. Minutes later, Bela Karolyi carried Strug to the medal platform to accept the gold with the rest of her teammates, forever known as the Magnificent 7.

Beware of generating unrealistic expectations, like *conquering* all anxiety. Maybe by employing all of the tactics we'll be talking about in this book and really putting forth the effort, you'll rid yourself of worry once and for all. But the trouble with "conquering" anything is that it's an absolute, and it's almost always unrealistic, in the same way Paul Hamm knew that aiming for the gold while in the twelfth place position is unrealistic. Knowing the unlikelihood of a comeback, Hamm's goal in that fifth event was to score high enough with his parallel bar routine to secure a third place finish.

Kerri Strug's focus in that second attempt was to get through it. Her coaches may have been calculating the mathematical possibilities of success, since this was the most critical moment ever in U.S. women's gymnastics history at the Olympic Games. But if Kerri had stood at the starting position, telling herself that she must score a near-perfect vault, and that the whole team was counting on her, she would not be concentrating on her skills, and the performance she faced would require every bit of her concentration. And so, as she waited for the signal to begin her second attempt, Kerri cleaned away any disrupting thoughts and then repeated Bela's message inside her mind: *Yes, I can do this.* But once she began running toward the vault, she thought of nothing but her task. "I really was just focused on the technique of the vault, like for the twisting to be tight."*

Yes, I want you to be inspired by both Paul's story and Kerri's story. More important, though, I want you to learn from them, because they are masters of mental control, just like Chris Sharma. Bring your attention to the task in front of you. As you do that, let go of your perfectionistic expectations. The function of lowering your expectations is to allow you to believe you have what it takes to achieve the goals you set. And *that* makes it much easier to step forward. You can certainly give yourself motivational messages, like, "Yes, I can do this." But once you step into your task, shift your concentration to whatever skills you want to apply to the immediate circumstance. Don't get ahead of yourself. Focus on the present moment.

FAIL? I CAN DO THAT!

I remember taking my first group therapy course in graduate school, more than thirty-five years ago. I still see the syllabus in my mind's eye,

---

*Team USA, "Gold Medal Moments: Kerri Strug Lands on Her Feet at the 1996 Summer Games in Atlanta," *YouTube*, July 10, 2012. *www.youtube.com/watch?V=7ZRYiOa5IM8*

listing the dates when each of us would lead a simulated therapy group in class. We all dreaded it. We dreaded messing up and looking stupid and incompetent in front of our peers. Not surprising, on the day when we began (I was in the first round of sacrificial lambs), I was in a cold sweat, almost panting with anxiety. I was facing a situation that not only could spiral out of my control but could make me look like a bumbler. What a catastrophe that would be! Then, as we situated ourselves in a circle of chairs, our professor, Dr. John Gladfelter, introduced the task. "Here's the assignment: I want you to be the worst group therapist you can be. Just be as bad, as incompetent as you can possibly manage." What?! I was stunned for a minute. Then I realized he meant it, and I thought, *I can do that!* I could feel the tension draining away like dirty water from a sink.

How did it turn out? No one actually tried to be a buffoon. But with the pressure off, and with no need to follow some still vague and ill-defined rules, we all witnessed moments of creativity and intuitive wisdom shining through. More than anything, we *relaxed* by receiving a reprieve from having to do everything perfectly. As we took our attention off our fear of failing, we stopped focusing inward. We had more outward attention available. We could actually connect with the others sitting in that circle, to see and hear them as they really were. Since we didn't have to funnel all our energy and attention into squelching or hiding our own fears, we got a taste of the healing power of real human contact. We no longer felt under the gun to predict and control everything that happened in our tiny little worlds, and that allowed us to experience the freedom of spontaneity.

I started playing soccer later in life, around my mid-thirties. I never excelled at it, but I loved it. After playing in some community leagues for two years, I could no longer give up my late afternoons for the practices. All that was left for me was a Saturday morning pick-up game at Lincoln Field in our little town of Carrboro. Let me set the stage for you.

This is a game that had been played just about every Saturday for fifteen years. A couple of older guys show up, but most are these young hotshots who have played soccer since childhood.

Then there's me. I'm a poor dribbler, a wild shot, and I can't get my speed into fourth gear anymore. This is definitely a situation where I have every reason to back away and go home. But I fervently want the joy of playing, and here is how I make it work. I know that often they don't have a full complement of twenty-two players, so they *need* bodies on Saturday morning. I always volunteer to play the unattractive position of defensive fullback. That way I don't have to run or dribble much, embarrass myself, and gain the imagined wrath of my teammates.

Most important, I have a point of view that works. I lightheartedly accept my role as the worst player on the team, more like the team mascot getting a chance to take the field. My skill level matches my expectations and those of the other players. With that in place, I won't be blackmailed by my embarrassment about a poor play, or some new guy's criticism of my skill. I create a safe zone for myself, and then I have a blast. I can't imagine a more enjoyable way to spend my Saturday morning.

Be an incompetent therapist? Piece of cake. Succeed at being the worst player on either soccer team? I can do that with my eyes closed. When the performance pressure is gone, I'm ready to play!

I know it won't be so simple for you to apply these specific tactics to your situations, but I want you to consider the theme I'm addressing. You *must* step forward in order to get stronger. You must respond to your fears in such a way that you start taking actions instead of avoiding. That's what this conversation is about: deciding to act and then figuring out how to support yourself in that action.

In any challenging event, when we adjust our goals to match our capabilities, we create a winning strategy. If you expect that complete mastery of a task is out of reach, then create a personal challenge that *is* within reach. It is the smartest thing you could possibly do to enhance your performance. The less threatened you are by loss, and the more you can perceive the encounter as a challenge worth taking, the more powerful you will become. It is a winning point of view. When all I have to do is be the worst group therapist or the least skilled guy on the soccer team, then I'm ready to go. When Paul Hamm reaches for the bronze instead of the seemingly inaccessible gold, and when cousin Don thinks it will be fun to take on *The Gulag Archipelago*, whether he wins or loses, then they are alive, awake, engaged in the moment.

Here's a secret that might come in handy: The biggest challenge you will face is your own personal high standards. Lower your standards and then act. If you are socially anxious, you probably need to work on speaking up more. And why don't you? Because you add a clause to your expectations that makes you too anxious. You don't just say, "I need to speak up." You say, "I need to speak up and *look good* while I do it." You see the problem here? There's no way for you to know in advance how you're going to come across to others when you speak up. If you don't talk that much, there's a chance that when you do, you might come across awkwardly. In any situation, if your stance is "I'm going to take this action, and *it has to turn out the way I want it to*," then I completely understand why you back away instead of step forward. You really want to get stronger? Then take actions. Do you want to view your actions as successful? Then lower your standards.

Here's a secret that might come in handy:
The biggest challenge you will face is your
own personal high standards.
Lower your standards and then act.

You can't expect to walk into a threatening situation with the stance "I'm going to make that sweating issue go away for good." No amount of therapeutic coaching or meditation or technique can support you when you establish such a demanding expectation. But what if you shifted your commitment to "I'm going to get through a meeting at work with sweaty armpits"? You have a chance to accomplish *that* goal. In the same way, no matter how hard you wish for it, you can't magically get rid of your fear of a shaky signature. If you're waiting for your fear to go away before you practice signing your name in public, you're going to wait a long time. Have you noticed? But you *can* decide to tolerate your signature as messy and contorted and illegible if that's how it turns out. That's a realistic goal, although an uncomfortable one for some.

Set some beneficial goals for yourself, like tolerating your mistakes, or coping with the possibility that you might sound boring, or get rejected, or feel uncomfortable.

YOU MUST COMPETE TO WIN

It's important to lower your expectations so that you can actually step toward the threat. But, look out, here comes another paradox. To compete is to risk. When you step up to any challenge, you have to be willing to lose something of value. Let's return to the game of chess for a moment. If you lose your king in checkmate, you lose the game. Yet in one of the best tactics during the endgame, you centralize all your pieces to gain as much center power as possible. And then you aggress. Your king, which you can't afford to lose, becomes an *attacking* piece and moves to the center of the board, picking fights for every single center square.

It will be no different for us here. Once you decide not to believe those noisy worries when they show up, you must be willing to tolerate the outcome of your battles, to bolster your sense of your ability to manage any potential negative consequences. You must show up ready to engage in the challenge even though you feel intimidated. If you can't put up with losing, then you are not going to bring your best self forward for the challenge.

Anxiety manipulates you by assuming that you will not step forward if certain risks are at play: the wrong decision, a full-blown panic attack, some illness that the doctors haven't identified yet, and so forth. It will dominate you through your unwillingness to experience even a small chance of these occurrences. When you can perceive this as a *ploy* by your challenger, then you have a chance to win. If you decide to step forward, a part of you will be scared. Allow that scared part of you to show up during the challenge. Don't try to get rid of it. Just make sure you don't appoint it as the team captain.

To accomplish our goals here, you will need to feel uncertain, uncomfortable, awkward, insecure, intimidated, or any other feeling of insecurity. And then you need to step forward anyway. When you decide to take on a challenge, I promise you that you're going to feel like you have just moved your king into a very vulnerable spot in the middle of the board.

No, that's not dramatic enough. You may actually feel like you're taking your first parachute jump and you are leaning out of the plane's door, seeing those tiny little dots on the ground that represent big old houses 10,000 feet below. It can *feel* terrifying. But you need to *act* as though it's not that risky. How else are you going to get yourself out the door?

Since it's not helpful to focus on your fear of these dire consequences, what *do* you pay attention to moment-by-moment? If you want to win, bring your total focus and commitment to the competition. Anxiety needs you to consider the possibility that you might pay some price for stepping forward and then decide to back away because you don't want to handle those consequences. Your task at that moment is to step forward anyway. Think of the challenge involved in a swim meet. You can't capably compete in a 200-meter freestyle race while simultaneously allowing your mind to wander to how crushed you will feel if you lose. Long before you dive into the water, decide that you will tolerate losing and drop that topic of conversation. Then focus on what it takes to win. Remember the discussion about working memory back in Chapter 11? If you start thinking, *I hope I don't lose,* your working memory is going to call up all the wrong information from your past. When you name your current chosen task as "I want to take my most powerful and efficient strokes," you're giving your working memory its best opportunity to help you.

None of us will perform up to par if our orientation is that we are putting our reputations at stake, or that there's a high likelihood of humiliating ourselves or seriously harming someone. If we attribute too much importance to the outcome of the event, or if we take on a challenge while fearing we will cause more harm than good, then we will tighten up, hold back, lose our focus, and put ourselves at a significant disadvantage. We can't perform well if we are focused on our dread of losing. We have to compete with our attention on *winning,* not on our fear of losing, despite the fact that we *could* lose. We must believe that, regardless of the outcome, when the event is over, we will be able to soothe any of our wounds, take our lessons with us, and get ready for the next match.

Listen to these words written 2500 years ago by the Chinese philosopher Chuang-Tzu: "In an archery contest, when the stakes are earthenware tiles, a contestant shoots with skill. When the stakes are belt buckles, he becomes hesitant. And if the stakes are pure gold, he becomes nervous and confused. There is no difference as to his skill but, because here is something he prizes, he allows outward considerations to weigh on his mind." If you are like everyone else who currently struggles with worries, you are engaging the threat as though you are going to lose something of great value. And as Chuang-Tzu says, when you think you're playing a high-stakes game, you become frightened and confused. Your perspective *must* change, or you will focus too much on *not losing* instead of on *winning*. (Don't worry; I'll help you apply this principle.)

Your perspective must *change, or you will focus too much on* not losing *instead of on* winning.

Do you still think this is a foolish idea, to fight the battle against anxious worry as though you were in a competition? Let's think of the role of firefighters for a moment. Firefighters must risk their lives to save their fellow citizens, as well as their animals and property. To secure their *own* safety to the best of their abilities, they will study, test, and drill in both strategy and tactics. Over and over. Then when they race into the dwelling fire, they are ready to take on the competition of the runaway flames and collapsing structure. They *are* in a competition with this fire, and they are focused on winning. What's their goal? To preserve lives and property without accidentally placing any of their team in danger. They can't *afford* to dwell only on worries about whether they are going to die. So they are competing against Anxiety as well. Their safety depends upon their ability to focus on the best-known strategies for survival, applying tactics they have rehearsed again and again. Take a look at a few of their rules of engagement.*

When you arrive, size up your tactical area of operation. Pause for a moment, look over the area of operation, and evaluate your risk. Determine a safe approach to completing your task.

---

*Adapted from "Rules of Engagement for Structural Firefighting: Increasing Firefighter Survival," developed by the Safety, Health and Survival Section, International Association of Fire Chiefs, February 2012.

DO NOT risk your life for lives or property that cannot be saved. Assess fire conditions and possible occupant survival of a rescue event. Don't engage in high-risk search and rescue when fire conditions prevent occupant survival or when total destruction of the building is inevitable.

Go in together, stay together, come out together. Always enter a burning building as a team of two or more. No firefighter is allowed to be alone at any time while entering, operating in, or exiting the building.

Maintain continuous awareness of your air supply, situation, location, and fire conditions. Stay focused on the present moment. Continually assess your needed resources and the immediate threats.

Stop, evaluate, and decide. Think before you expose yourself to unsafe conditions. Raise an alert about a safety concern without any concern about penalty.

Firefighters apply these strategies and tactics moment-by-moment. They must doggedly maintain their attention on these tasks. Allowing their minds to wander could cost them serious consequences.

HOW DO YOU WIN?

Lest you take the wrong message here, I'm not using firefighters as an example of the importance of always remaining vigilant and always worrying about dangerous outcomes. Firefighters need to do that, not you. And they *do* step forward, even knowing that they may face unexpected, serious consequences. The message I want you to receive is that firefighters are a great illustration of how you should operate out there in the world based on your own set of principles. If you don't solidify the principles that will best help you step forward and take action, Anxiety will step in and fill the void, like it's already done.

We are going to build those principles together, and you should only adopt ones that make sense to you. With them, you can face your threats, whether real or imagined. The tactics you engage will stem from those principles. Once you are ready to act, the only "win" you need to pay attention to is winning the moment. Focus on the little skirmishes. Anxiety has been beating up on you, and it's not going to stop simply because you've decided to adopt a new approach. When you step forward, assume that Anxiety will attempt to distract you, to throw you off your game. Sometimes it will win, and sometimes you'll win. So start by being willing to lose. (Odd, isn't it?) Then every time Anxiety says "back up" but you step forward, you've just won that skirmish.

If you discover your house is on fire, do you know the skills that home safety authorities recommend? When the smoke alarm sounds, the objective is to find the best way to escape the house as quickly as possible. This strategy has tactics. For instance, if we are in the bedroom with the door closed, we are to follow these guidelines:

- ✧ Stand close to the door and feel the door with the back of your hand, not your palm.
- ✧ If it's cool, open it slowly with your back facing the door.
- ✧ If you see an escape, crawl down on the floor away from the fire and leave the house.
- ✧ If the door is hot, dial 911.
- ✧ If no phone is available, go to the window, and with a flashlight or light-colored material, wave to signal for help.

Expert guidelines should direct our actions. Becoming so panicky that you can't think clearly can have dire consequences. That's why you need to prepare. You cannot simply read these house-fire guidelines one time. Review them several times, quiz yourself, and then literally rehearse the skills in your bedroom. Because—have you noticed?—when we become threatened, our minds can turn to mush. But if we have rehearsed our skills enough, our actions will be guided by our procedural memory, which resides just below our conscious awareness. During a threat, we will feel afraid; however, the last thing we want in an emergency is to allow the *emotions* of fear to make decisions for us. In a house fire, we put ourselves at risk if fear overtakes training, leading us to race to the door and fling it open without regard to what's on the other side. During threat, we need to operate with a clear strategy and well-rehearsed tactics. And the first of those, what I'm describing in this chapter, is to commit yourself to handling your exaggerated worries, your potential losses, and your fear.

Oh, wait, what is all this "rehearsal" business? Hold on to your hat for this one. I think it's best to consider that *every* time you step forward, it's a rehearsal. I'm recommending you hold a point of view that says that every activity is a practice; there are no tests. Win or lose, every encounter with Anxiety gives you a chance to become stronger.

We are about to progress into some of the most important tactics within our game plan. Please recognize that you must set down some of your old maneuvers that are not only limiting your success but contributing to your problems. As you continue to learn here, one of the best ways to set down those old schemes is to simply redirect your attention to the new ones. You don't need to keep reminding yourself *not* to engage in your old practices. Instead, remind yourself to focus your attention on the new tactics. The old will fade away by default.

CHAPTER 15

How to Talk like a First Responder

I t's a cold Saturday morning and we are coming toward the end of our workout, so we are about to practice two 3000-meter races. I'm sitting in the three-seat of the *Australia*, our beautiful new quadruple scull, a narrow, sleek, and fast racing boat with four rowers, each with two oars. We are racing against an identical boat. We are evenly matched in strength and skill, and in the first race we finish within half a boat length of each other. We spin the boats and get ready for the second race. We are the crew of CHAOS Rowing; our ages range from about thirty years on up to me, the elder, in my early sixties. All of us love to row and are always happy to be on the water.

But when we are racing, it's all business. There's no such thing as "perfect" in this sport, but we all strive in that direction. And today in each boat, it is four rowing as one, every action the same. Our objective is to move the boat as far as possible with each stroke in the most efficient manner. The rowing stroke is a constant movement, applying power with the whole body and then recovering. A full stroke begins as we are coiled forward in the sliding seats, with knees bent and arms outstretched. We raise our hands slightly, dropping the blade vertically into the water. At the beginning of the drive, all the work is done by the legs as they push back against the foot stretchers, pulling the blades forward and moving the boat in the water. Now our upper bodies begin to uncoil, then the arms begin their work, pulling the handles toward our chests, drawing the oar blades through the water. By the end of the stroke, we are leaning back about 10 degrees, and the abdominal muscles are fully engaged. Now the drive is over and we release the pressure on the handle and push it down slightly, releasing the oar from the water. Next, we push our arms forward to a full extension. The body follows the hands and the sliding seat moves forward until the knees are bent and we are ready for the next catch. When we take thirty strokes a minute, we do all of that in two seconds. Over and over and over.

Rowing is physically and rhythmically intense, in a very precise way. And when all the rowers and the boat can row as one, it's a thrilling experience. I still remember a brief thirty seconds of a row seven months ago in which I was in an all-out peak experience: totally present in this forceful and challenging physical action and at the same time observing what is going on while simultaneously absolutely exhilarated. Thirty seconds isn't very long, but I'll remember those moments forever. And I plan to have many more of them.

All our continued work on technique comes down to crossing the finish line ahead of all other boats. The second race begins. We row steady and clean. At about 500 meters, our bowman yells out a new command. "Up two, in two." (Increase the stroke rate per minute by two strokes after the next two strokes.) Then shouting enough to be heard over the sounds of two boats and sixteen oars, "One!" Another stroke. "Two!" We're rowing at twenty-six strokes per minute, and we are focusing our minds and bodies on the efficiency and power needed to propel our boat into the lead. From behind us we hear Richard's voice again from the bow seat. "In two, power-ten." (After these two strokes, exert all the power you can muster into driving your legs back, and the boat forward in these next ten strokes.) "One . . . two! Give me legs!" Rapid. Intense. Power. All as one. I now make an audible "huh" at the end of each exhale, a sound that shows up on its own as I engage the oar with full exertion.

And then . . .

I can't breathe! My force has exceeded my lung capacity, and now I am in a panic state.

It's 35 degrees, and both my shirts are zipped up to cover my neck. What was outside of my awareness only moments before is now quite clear: these zippered shirts are also restricting my airway as my muscles are now demanding more oxygen. But there's nothing I can do about that. Each of my hands must remain wrapped around the handle of its own nine-and-a-half-foot oar.

I'm freaked. We're rowing at a furious intensity, and my inner dialogue is a terse yet mentally loud two-way altercation that sounds like this: "I can't go on. I've got to call 'way enough.'" (That's a command that signals all rowers to immediately stop rowing in mid-stroke.)

Followed by an opposing voice: "Keep going. Keep going."

But at this moment, I'm afraid that if I continue rowing . . . Well, I don't quite know what will happen, but it will be something like I will blackout and just fall forward in my seat. I'm screaming in my head, "Now. Say it now. 'Way enough' now. Before it's too late!"

But, geez, I *really* don't want to do that. No one has ever, in any boat I've been in or around, called "way enough" because they couldn't catch their breath. I don't want to be the first. I'd be so embarrassed. More important, I don't want to disappoint my fellow rowers. We have committed ourselves as a boat to win this race. Our job is to win this race. Just like the four in the other boat are committed to winning. We row as though this is the biggest race of our lives. That's just how you do it.

One does not stop a boat mid-race because of some discomfort. I don't want to be the one that spoils this. But I might have to be.

One voice: "Keep going. Keep going." The other voice: "I've got to stop. I've got to stop NOW. I can't do this. I'm in trouble. I can't breathe! I can't go on!"

I hear the bowman call out, "Thirty more strokes!" I'm phoning it in now. I give zero power to my legs, because any more exertion will put me further into an anaerobic state. I'm contributing nothing to our effort now except doing my best to maintain proper form. I'm solely trying to move my legs, my back, and my arms in sync with the other three in the boat. "Twenty more strokes!" the bowman calls.

I can't go on. I can't breathe. I have to stop.

Keep going.

"Ten more strokes!" I'm silently counting each stroke. Talking to myself, "I can take nine more strokes . . . Eight more strokes . . . It's five more seconds . . . I can get there . . ."

We just edge out the other boat as the race ends. Now we shift to paddle mode, slowing the stroke rate and taking the pressure off our legs. Now that it's over, I'm happy that my executive voice won the day, because I did get through it, and I didn't let down the others in my boat, and I didn't have to sheepishly admit that I'm not as aerobically fit as I would like to be.

Here's the irony. Despite my sense that I was losing control, our boat set the club record for the fastest 3000-meter row. Then another boat broke our record the next morning. What fun!

This story illustrates what any of us goes through when we're really afraid. We are totally alert to our present experience and simultaneously predicting a dreadful future. I had struggled because moment-by-moment I wasn't sure if I could make it. I wasn't even sure that promoting the "keep going" message was the smart decision. If I had passed out, it would have been the wrong decision. Yes, I was part of a competition. But the biggest competition was the battle inside my mind.

As I'm sure you already know, negative self-talk can paralyze any of us. That's what you and I need to work on: how to win those internal battles.

TALKING YOURSELF INTO ACTION

Let's take a step back and study this territory of self-talk. It will be one of your strongest assets, so we need to know how best to take advantage of it.

We tend to talk to ourselves throughout the day. Ninety-six percent of adults report some kind of inner dialogue.* (Really? You thought you were the only one?) One-quarter of all our waking hours include some form of self-talk.† Perhaps we are not all masters of mindfulness, but neither do we move through the day mindlessly. Setting the alarm clock, packing the gym bag, designing new marketing materials, caretaking a toddler—most of our calls-to-action are directed by a message that is at least one level higher in abstraction. "Seize the day." "If I stay in shape, I'll remain healthier." "Our numbers are slumping, and I need to take some action." "Better childproof this room!"

Some people approach everyday life with a mantra that is a manifestation of their larger frame of reference. Even a simple phrase can dictate how you respond in any given moment or situation. For some, *Let go and let God*—from 1 Peter 5:7: "Cast all your anxiety on him because he cares for you"—is a conviction they can relate to and obey. For others, the Golden Rule is the message they carry with them always: *Do unto others as you would have them do unto you.*

---

*A. Winsler et al., "Maternal beliefs concerning young children's private speech," *Infant and Child Development*, 15 (2006): 403–420.

† C. L. Heavey and R. T. Hurlburt, "The phenomena of inner experience," *Consciousness and Cognition*, 17 (2008): 798–810.

Outside of biblical passages, some will adopt John F. Kennedy's exhortation, "Ask not what your country can do for you . . . ," urging the common man to act, to participate, and to instigate the change they seek. What about William Shakespeare's "All the world's a stage/And all the men and women merely players"? The best advice the bard has ever given us might be this reminder not to take oneself and the world around us too seriously.

We have preprogrammed built-in messages for almost all our activities, whether routine or significant. If you're heading to an important job interview, you've probably formed a mental list of simple instructions: "Don't be late. Be polite. Shake hands. Maintain eye contact. Enunciate." These commands help you move toward the desired goal, which is *I'm going to get this job.*

Positive self-talk has long been studied in sports performance. Athletes don't just engage in superstitious rituals moments before they perform. They motivate themselves ("I can do this"; "Give it your all"), and during the action they give themselves specific instructions to maintain their focus ("See the target") or execute proper technique ("Follow through"). Researchers have shown that both motivational and instructional self-talk can enhance performance and improve outcome.[*,†] And both types work best for beginners.

And this is why when you watch shows like *The Biggest Loser*, if you're a fan of reality television, you'll hear the trainers repeatedly ask the contestants what they hope to get out of this journey and why they've decided to put themselves through this torture. Mid-lunge or mid-pushup, the contestants will grunt, "I'm doing it for my family," or "I'm doing it because I want to be happy." The trainers ask these

---

[*]J. L. Van Raalte et al., "Cork! The effects of positive and negative self-talk on dart throwing performance," *Journal of Sport Behavior*, 18 (1995): 50–57; and [†] C. J. Mallett and S. J. Hanrahan, "Race modeling: An effective cognitive strategy for the 100 m sprinter?" *The Sport Psychologist*, 11 (1997): 72–85.

questions in moments of stress because that outcome picture provides motivation when we need it most. In an episode of *Extreme Makeover: Weight Loss Edition,* in which super obese individuals are selected for a year-long transformation, Chris Powell offered this insight while training a 355-pound woman who had lost her sense of direction and self-worth: "It's in these pivotal moments when she's terrified—that's when fight or flight happens. And that's when I get to see what she's got. It's in these moments you can see if she wants to run, or I can challenge her to fight. I need to build her self-confidence, I need to build her self-worth, and she needs to know that she can fight. Fighting is what makes you strong, and fighting is what you need to do for the rest of your life. That's how we survive."

We've been using self-talk in treatment for all kinds of health and mental health problems—pain patients, students with emotional disorders, even children with anxiety or depression—ever since famed psychologist Don Meichenbaum in 1977 began studying his treatment approach for behavior change.* So it's safe to say we can apply it to your tasks.

RUN HILLS HARD

My brother Phill was a track star in high school. Then in college he continued his achievements, running both cross-country and track all four years for Duke University. One of his relay races set a conference record that stood for twenty-nine years, which, in case you don't know, is an extraordinary feat.

As I mentioned in Chapter 9, I was at the University of North Carolina, two years behind him and just eight miles down the road. (Don't get me started on our basketball rivalry.) As I began to take up running

---

*D. Meichenbaum, "Cognitive behaviour modification," *Scandinavian Journal of Behaviour Therapy,* 6 (1977): 185–192.

for exercise, Phill taught me the tactics for efficiently running up a hill, the same tactics taught by his coach, Al Bueller, one of the greatest college track and cross-country coaches in the history of the sport. Coach Bueller's job was first to explain the physics involved in using efficiency and power to quickly ascend a hill. There were four principles of action. Get the body forward by dropping your head and raising your arms. Apply energy to the task. Push forward and up. Generate faster turnover of your legs.

Yes, this task of quickly and efficiently running up hills is based on the principles of physics and physiology. Yet when you're in a race, you have no time to think through any broad principles. Each of these college athletes needed to translate those principles into a simple set of moment-by-moment instructions that directed their actions. For Phill, they became these self-instructions:

- ✧ Raise the arms
- ✧ Swing the arms
- ✧ Look five to six feet ahead
- ✧ Shorten the stride
- ✧ Pick up the tempo

I have shared this story in probably forty workshops over the years. I stop at this point in the story and ask the audience of mental health professionals the following question, and I ask it of you now. As he's running up the hill in a cross-country meet, why would my brother tell himself, "Look five to six feet ahead"?

What's your guess? Take a moment to think about it.

I'll wait . . .

The most common responses I receive are "He wants to make sure he doesn't stumble over any rocks" and "He wants to keep his eyes from looking up to the top of the hill, because that would be intimidating."

That gives me the opportunity to say, "These are all good common-sense answers. But, nooooo, they're not quite right."

Let me say again. As you face a difficult task, all self-instructions should extend from your strategy, and that strategy will be a set of principles. Look back at the four principles Coach Bueller presented. What part of the strategy was Phill applying through the message, "Look five to six feet ahead"? I assume the answer will now become quite clear. The first task in the strategy is to get the body forward by *dropping your head* and raising your arms. By looking five to six feet in front of him, Phill gets his head down, and, based on physics, gravity now will work in his favor instead of against him.

I'm not suggesting that you talk supportively to yourself when you have a difficult task, although that's a nice idea. I'm telling you to start with a master plan. Develop a point of view that will enable you to generate your strategy. Then translate that strategy into simple, brief directives you deliver within self-talk. Speaking of a master plan . . .

FOCUS, FOCUS, FOCUS

Since 1988, Freeman Hrabowski, now president of the University of Maryland, Baltimore County (UMBC), has helped turn a little-known commuter school on the outskirts of Baltimore into a midsize state university with a reputation as one of the most innovative schools in the country, graduating outstanding scientists, engineers, and mathematicians, many of whom are minorities. Forty-one percent of the bachelor's degrees earned there in 2010 were in those fields, well above the national average of 25 percent. Students at UMBC follow a demanding schedule and strict rules designed to instill a sense of discipline and build community.

In 2011, *60 Minutes* profiled the accomplishments of Hrabowski and his students. At the close of the segment, he is shown giving a talk to one of the classes in the school. He finishes by saying, "Nothing takes the place of hard work, attitude, and getting support from each other. And that's what this is all about. 'Focus, focus, focus.' Give yourselves a hand. Keep working hard."

Now that sounds quite motivational. But you're missing the visuals. Each time Hrabowski repeats the word *focus*, he speaks quite deliberately, as though he is reminding them of an important instruction. He holds his hands on either side of his face and then brings them forward and back about ten inches each time he repeats that word. Three times he says "focus" and three times he moves his hands in that fashion. And every single college student in that classroom repeats that message simultaneously with him, like a Greek chorus, with those same gestures. What does that mean? All students at that university are trained to express that message and to use that message to help keep themselves on track. They have a master plan! Repeating those words is a cue to institute their master plan. When they get distracted at the library from the two students whispering behind them, they can repeat that mantra to help pull their attention back to their studies. When they're taking an exam and begin to worry that they don't know the subject matter well enough, they can repeat that mantra to help them focus back on the next question.

What's going on here? Detachment and absorption. "Focus, focus, focus" becomes a cue to detach themselves from what they're currently attending to and absorb themselves back on their desired task. If they're responding to its intention, these students don't start thinking, *Hmmm, I wonder if I really should continue to play Angry Birds*. In other words, they don't analyze the decision to refocus their attention. They operate on automatic pilot. When they hear that "focus" message, they let it be their cue to stop, turn away, and begin to absorb themselves in their studies. A skill like this will be of great benefit to you. Anxiety will distract you with doubts and worries and insecurities. You need to turn away from those distractions and refocus your attention back to the task at hand, whatever it may be.

But lest you think that the idea behind "focus, focus, focus" is the domain of a single university, let me set the record straight.

You may not know this, but if you were to ever spend any time working with a personal trainer at the gym, he or she is well aware that your emotions, and even your body, will tell you to stop working out. The voice in your head will convey that you will feel *better* if you will just stop. One of the ways your trainer will combat that message is to help you focus on the numbers: counting down the number of repetitions left in any particular exercise. Detachment and absorption.

Your spin class instructor knows it's easy for you to get winded in any class and then begin to lose your form or slow your pace. The best instructors will shift your focus of attention. For instance, Tommy Woelfel,* at Crunch Fitness LA, continually reminds those in his class to focus on the three components that are within their control: form, pace, and resistance. Every time he teaches a class, he will repeat this message: "Focus on keeping your body in the proper position; focus on keeping the pace that is set at the start of each jog or hill or run; focus on upping the resistance to a level that is challenging to you." Proper form makes for a better ride. Keeping your chest up and your neck aligned, for instance, allow you to have better breath control. So you have to trust the form despite your fatigue. Tommy teaches this technique because he knows that when riders become fatigued, their tendency is to put their entire bodies into pushing those pedals. They bend over toward the handlebar, collapse their necks down, and sway heavily from side to side with each pedal push.

Imagine you are one of Tommy's regular students. Now you're at the gym, working out by yourself on a stationary bike. How do you reduce the likelihood of falling into these bad habits? What if you periodically

---

*http://www.ridewithtommy.com/

called up those ready-made instructions from Tommy? You could then cue yourself with any one of three simple mantras, like, "Maintain form," "Pick up the pace," and "Up the resistance." While you're spinning, from time to time you're certainly going to space out or get caught up in one of the songs you're listening to and then start bending over the handlebar and unknowingly slow your pace. Of course! But if you train yourself to keep returning to subvocalizing one of those mantras, and if you use it as a cue to absorb yourself in the mechanics of proper spinning technique, you can get yourself back to good form and pace.

To break a board in the martial art of Tae Kwon Do, you need to kick or punch *through* the board, so the sensei will instruct you to aim for a spot that is *past* the board. You can't stop or slow down when you hit the board. To override your fear ("I can't break a piece of wood!"), the sensei will tell beginning students to focus on accuracy, focus on proper technique and the correct positioning of the foot, and focus on that spot "beyond the board." If you are receptive to your sensei's message, when you hear yourself get distracted by "I can't do this," you will use that as a cue to refocus your attention on accuracy, technique, stance, and that spot beyond the board. How do you refocus? By telling yourself to. And by responding to your own request.

When first learning to play guitar, you need to play through the pain. Moreover, a student with delicate fingers may have to develop calluses to be able to tolerate playing. Therefore, you need to practice every day (working through the pain) and focus on the steps presented to you by your teacher (e.g., learning the chords, strumming, the pressure of the strum, the rhythm, etc.). You put your focus on a number of places: Are my fingers on the right strings? Is my thumb in the proper place? Is my wrist relaxed? Arm muscles loose? Shoulders down? Am I holding the pick properly? Do I have a proper stance? So when you hear yourself saying, "I can't do this. It hurts too much," cue yourself to detach your focus from "This is too hard." Then move your attention over to your skills.

A wonderful example of changing your focus is the way swimming instructors teach children how to dive. The brain perceives water as a solid object. This is why children pick up their head just prior to diving. They don't want their heads to hit the hard surface. So they end up smacking the chest or belly on the water's surface, and that hurts. Therefore, young diving students face a predicament: the only way they will learn to perform the dive correctly is to override their urge to protect themselves!

Chris Bergere, the men's and women's diving coach at Yale University, says, "Children have a conditioned reflex to pick their heads up and put their hands out when they feel like they're falling. As children start walking, they learn that if they don't keep their head up and their hands out, they get hurt." Bergere suggests that instructors talk through the process of diving when the child is nowhere near the pool. "Explain to your child that the water is soft and that they should never lift their chin up."* But children are no different from us adults. They need something else to focus on so they don't revert back to unhelpful behavior. So the diving instructor trains them to focus on the physicality rather than the fear of falling. They will repeat these messages again and again, and they want the child to take them on as messages to self: chin tucked; hands flat, one on top of the other; and so forth. They will take the action in stages, beginning with a sitting dive, advancing to a kneeling dive, and eventually to a standing dive all the while repeating those directives. And all the while the children are building their working memory to master diving for their lifetime.

TALKING FROM ABOVE

So let's review. We all talk to ourselves, and we do it all day long. If you are awake sixteen hours a day, you will accumulate about four

---

*Chris Bergere, personal communication to author, November 2014.

hours' worth of self-talk, spread out over the whole day. That's four hours of commenting to yourself about your experience! Now you've read numerous examples of using this self-talk as an essential skill in learning anything new. I've told you about training to efficiently race up a hill, Freeman Hrabowski's "focus, focus, focus" to help students concentrate, the personal trainers and the spin class instructors at the gym, the sensei who teaches students where to focus their attention, and how one learns to play guitar or to dive into a pool. If you want to enhance your performance and improve your outcome, why not act like so many successful performers do? What we say to ourselves will either compound our problems or be part of the solution to our problems. You and I would be quite foolish indeed if we built a self-help program while ignoring self-talk. So we will return to this topic in Chapter 23, where we'll work together to generate specific moment-by-moment messages for you. If you can commit to the task, and if you can practice over time, then after a while, things will start to come together. Let me explain.

My brother had a third phase of skill development as he learned to run those hills. (The first two were to comprehend the strategy his coach taught him and then to translate it into moment-by-moment self-in-structions.) After his first couple of months as a freshman cross-country runner, he no longer needed to subvocalize his five messages (raise and swing the arms, look five to six feet ahead, shorten the stride, pick up the tempo). They became part of his muscle memory, as long as he cued himself. He just needed one big message to help him apply his strategy, and he picked "Run hills hard." As he saw a steep incline coming during a workout or race, all he had to subvocalize was "Run hills hard," and he then routinely engaged in his efficient actions.

When you think about it, in just about every common task, we can give ourselves a simple message that is a cue for a more complex process.

"Proof the paper before you turn it in" can generate a sophisticated set of grammatical corrections. "Be polite here" will engage a different variety of actions depending on whether a police officer has just pulled you over, you are having your first dinner with your future in-laws, or you are asking for a refund past the thirty-day guarantee.

Our work here will be similar. Once you've given yourself specific instructions a number of times, you'll develop some shorthand message that will represent the action you need to take. After working on the skills in this book, perhaps one day you will be standing in front of a task that seems daunting to you. You hesitate. It seems like a pretty risky action. If you said, "Whatever it takes, I'm going to finish this," that message doesn't instruct you on the task; it encourages you to push through resistance and continue on. Or you could even say to yourself, "I want my life back" as a cue to step forward into the struggle. That message doesn't tell you what to do. There's no explicit instruction. You will use it as a reminder, since you will already know the basics of what to do in these situations.

As you're sitting in your car, about to merge onto the highway to do a driving practice, I suppose you could go into a long subvocalized monologue, like, "My fear of the highways makes me have to drive on all the back roads to bring the kids to school and pick them up every day. I can't even visit my mom, because then I would have to get on the interstate, and I can't do that yet. I feel embarrassed and inadequate. Getting onto the highway right now feels oh so very scary. But I understand that, hard as it is, I have to practice this in order to get stronger. I'm going to have to tolerate feeling awkward, clumsy, insecure, and scared before I'm going to get stronger. And this is the practice I've designed for myself today. I need to get on this highway. I'm *going* to get on this highway." But that sure is a lot of talking, and the time for action is now. It's possible that you could allow the message "I want my life back" to represent that entire communication, and then let it motivate you to merge onto the highway. Otherwise, of course, it's not going to be much help.

FIRST RESPONDER

You can't let yourself be the only intimidated one anymore. You need to consider yourself as both the one who is feeling threatened and as the First Responder. You have to find a way to take care of yourself when you're scared, just as a first responder is trained to care for those at the scene of an emergency. But you also need to move into action if you want to reach your goals. When you get caught up in your obsessiveness or your panicky worry, that's your cue to step back mentally, just like we've been talking about in the previous chapters, and then to talk to yourself in a simple way that helps you manage the scene and move toward your positive goals. You need to elevate that voice of the First Responder above your panicky worry. Arguing with yourself isn't going to help. You can't allow these two sides of you, these two voices in you, to stand on equal footing. If you do that, you will end up standing still. Your First Responder voice needs to be the executive voice, in charge.

You also can't just give yourself a message. In the midst of feeling intimidated, your more insecure side will then need to *act* on the instructions, despite all the uncomfortable doubts that are sounding off. You need to persuade your scared self to step forward anyway. When you tell yourself, "Go ahead and step forward," your whole body and mind need to be ready to take that action. Mouthing the words will do you no good. Repeating a message you read in this chapter won't help. You have to buy into the protocol represented by the message. And whatever you say to yourself should get you to *act*, not to sit still and keep thinking.

✧   ✧   ✧

Do you remember Mary, who had been struggling with panic attacks and claustrophobia? In our second session, I described how she might use a strong executive voice to help herself when she's feeling the urge to escape. Here's the rest of that conversation:

> **Mary:** *I'm not the type of personality that responds really well to strong commands.*
>
> **Reid:** *Okay. Well, is there a way to modify what I'm saying that might be more helpful to you in those moments?*
>
> **Mary:** *I'd probably say, "You're stronger than that. You're stronger than that. Just stay." It's a different tone of voice, I guess.*
>
> **Reid:** *Okay, that seems fine. Here's another way to think of it. Imagine one of your kids in high school is in the pool, and all of a sudden, in the relatively shallow water, he starts flailing, and he looks like he's going under at any moment. You're going to reach out and ask him to grab your hand, but he's still flailing. What would you yell to him at that moment? Your hand is within reach, but he's failing to grab it. What would you say to him, and how would you say it?*
>
> **Mary:** *[speaking strongly] I would say, "Stop. Here it is." Right? "Here's my hand. Calm down."*
>
> **Reid:** *Okay. "Reach out. Find my hand." Right? So that's what we're talking about here.*
>
> **Mary:** *Okay.*
>
> **Reid:** *It doesn't have to be angry. It just needs to be firm.*
>
> **Mary:** *Okay, firm is better.*

Mary needs to find her own voice that will work effectively in those moments. But I did want to influence her choice, because most of the time the first responder voice needs to speak briefly, simply, and firmly. When you're flailing, you might very well need to hear that instruction in the form of a command. When I set the scene of her student struggling to stay above water, Mary didn't speak gently and quietly. She spontaneously used a First Responder voice, which was stronger and louder. But listen carefully to this; that was a *compassionate* gesture on Mary's part. She wanted to take *care* of the student. And she did it by using a commanding voice. When a part of you is flailing and scared and confused, to give yourself at that moment a clear, strong directive is a caring gesture. Find the voice inside you who wants to take care of you during times when you are acting courageously.

Speaking of Mary, we left off at the end of the first session. She decided to practice some of the skills we talked about by driving through a parking garage that evening. Keep in mind that she's been too intimidated even to enter most parking garages the previous several years. Let's see how she did.

CHAPTER 16

"I Made It as Unpleasant as I Could and Then I Waited"

A s she settles into her chair to begin our second session, Mary has that look—a look she's no doubt seen on the faces of her students when they are confident in their performance on an exam or waiting eagerly to share a piece of writing. It's a look of pride in the work. It's a feeling of self-satisfaction in the face of a particularly formidable challenge. Already certain of the answer, I ask Mary if she had a chance to practice her skills the night before.

"I did," she says with a smile. "I went to a parking garage in Scottsdale. It's three stories. Unfortunately for the practice, it was sunset and there was a fair amount of light coming through."

Did you catch that? Mary says "unfortunately for the practice" there was still light coming into the parking garage. That statement reflects an excellent attitude. When the parking garage has light, her practice is "unfortunately" *easier*. Mary's not looking for easy; she's looking for difficult, because difficult is going to move her closer to her positive goals. She's giving herself greater control by *wanting* to practice the difficult. Yes, she's uncomfortable, and she's anxious. That's good, because her governing stance is "I'm going toward what scares me."

This is what you should strive for. When you do an experiment, when you decide to practice one of these new skills, take ownership of that event. Don't do it because you should. Do it because you *want* to do the hard stuff so you can get stronger.

She continues. "But still, the ceiling was quite low, and it's a garage I avoid normally. I really didn't feel quite as panicky as I usually do, so I went into the middle—"

I interrupted her because I was curious why this typically difficult garage wasn't giving her so much trouble last night. Was it the available sunlight?

"No, the session yesterday really did help. I had already thought about my plan quite a bit before I went there. I just kept running the logic through my mind of how and why I was going to do the practice."

This is what courage sounds like. Yes, we can call this a practice session, because Mary intended to check out the value of some newly acquired skills. But this was also a courageous experiment because she had no personal experience to tell her that that plan was going to work, and she was stepping into an environment she has long perceived as life-threatening. In yesterday's session, Mary explained in no uncertain terms that parking garages were dangerous, you could suffocate in them, and they could collapse at any moment and take your life.

Those judgments have not disappeared. But she courageously quiets the voice that generates those opinions and pushes it to the back of her mind. Then she pulls up to the front of her mind a brand-new point of view and makes it her dominant voice. Why take such a risk? Because the logic of that strategy makes sense to her, and she can see how it will help her advance toward her positive goals.

Instead of permitting her fear to control the conversation in her head, she focuses on the purpose of this experiment. She's not passively complying with my instructions. She's not saying, "I know I need to do this practice, but I really don't want to . . . but he tells me I should." Instead, she takes ownership in the protocol. It's hers now. She talks to herself in a voice of leadership, and she states the actions she's going to take. In essence, she tells herself, "Here are the reasons why I'm going to do this. And here's what I'm going to do." She doesn't tell herself just once. She maintains her momentum by mentally reviewing both the reasoning and the plan again and again. Mary is serving as an excellent role model for you right now. She's showing you how to orient your mind prior to a practice.

But how is that logic helping her moment-by-moment?

"I knew what I was going to tell myself once I got in there: 'It's not going to collapse, there's plenty of air. And, yes, the ceilings are low, and you're not going to like it, but it's going to be fine.' It was such a nice summer night, so I thought maybe the garage would be full, with people wanting to be in town. That kind of waiting has been a problem for me. If I'm on the ramp, and I'm waiting to get out, and I'm stuck there as people are trying to exit the garage . . . I don't like that at all. But I said to myself, 'So what if it's crowded and you have to wait? It'll be fine. It's not going to be pleasant, but there *is* enough air, and I'm *not* going to suffocate.'"

Mary has already accomplished a central task in dealing with an anxiety disorder. She has pushed the content away, and this gives her a tremendous advantage. She will *never* learn to tolerate the possibility of suffocating in the garage. And it's impossible for her to tolerate a high likelihood of the ceiling collapsing on her. By correcting her misunderstanding about those fears, she can now attend to coping with her discomfort. What did she tell herself? "You're not going to like it. It's not going to be pleasant." She knows it won't be *easy*, but tolerating discomfort is within her reach. Tolerating imminent death is not.

Just so we're clear, she also has to cope with a sense of insecurity. She doesn't know how well this plan is going to help her in the garage. And even though she has downgraded the degree of real threat to her, she will still have a sense of doubt, at least in her unconscious. That's what's generating her anxiety. The exact work she needs to be doing is to learn to tolerate distress and intimidation in her threatening environments. What is the strategy she's going to use? As you are about to hear, she will *seek them out*. She wants to generate those feelings, and she will look for opportunities to sit with them. She has a chance to learn from this experiment because she doesn't have to fight with her content.

That's why I emphatically encourage you to do whatever work necessary to make it *not* about your content. When you accomplish that, you will have reduced your tasks down to two: feeling uncertain and feeling uncomfortable. Those aren't easy tasks, but both are within your reach.

I had a few of my own worries after we ended that first session, because I didn't talk to Mary about the ways people tend to protect themselves from their insecurities or discomfort by using what I call safety crutches (as discussed in Chapter 3). Struggling with claustrophobia, Mary can make her practice easier by going to a place within the garage where there is more light, or by rolling down the car windows to get fresh air, or by turning on the radio to distract herself from her fearful thoughts.

But no, not Mary. Once she arrived at the five-story garage, she drove up to the third floor. She assumed that would be sufficient: a low ceiling, with two floors below, two floors above. But it was just before sunset, and all that light passing into garage was making her task easier. Was she relieved? Nope. She immediately maneuvered her car to the darkest place she could find on that floor, parking diagonal to a corner, facing two cinderblock walls. I asked her why she picked the darkest place. "Well, because I was trying to get that panicky feeling going so I could just stay with it for a few minutes."

Did you hear that? She was looking for an *opportunity* to get panicky so she could practice a new way of responding to it. Excellent! Is this how *you* think when you approach one of your threatening situations? If you're like most people, you don't. Mary is your model. Go get your anxiety. Go get it! Look for the feeling of doubt. Go find it! Seek out doubt and distress. What Mary doesn't realize yet is that simply accessing that disposition of "looking for an opportunity" will strengthen her.

"I turned the radio off, and I left the windows up, which I never do. Then there was still quite a bit of light coming through the open sides of the garage, so I went like this [she forms blinders around her eyes with her hands] and just concentrated on that really low, concrete ceiling."

Listen to what she says next: "My heart was starting to beat faster. But I just tried to make it as unpleasant as I could so I could sit with that for a little bit. And I waited."

What?! Are you hearing this? She's feeling her physical anxiety rising, which in the past would signal to her that danger is present. This is the most difficult time of her practice. The car is stuffy with the windows rolled up, there's nothing to distract her, the darkness is making her uncomfortable, and so is focusing her attention on that low concrete ceiling. How does she cope? Does she tell herself that this has been enough practice and it's time to go? Does she roll down her window a little to get a bit of fresh air?

Nope. She's not even waiting for discomfort to show up. She's *making* it show up. At this moment, she's no longer the victim of Anxiety; she is now the dominant one. She tries to *increase* that distress so that she can linger with it. A part of her is absolutely scared of the dangers right now. But she has another role available to her. She wants that voice to stay in control, and so she talks to her fearful side in a reassuring voice. "I just kept saying, 'The ceiling is low, but it's not going to collapse. I'm a few minutes from the entrance, and there's plenty of air in here, and it's not going to run out. Even if the cars were all exiting, it still wouldn't run out of air. There's enough permeability to the building.' And I said to myself, 'Any moment that you want to, you can roll the window down and you can walk out of here. But you don't need to. Stick it out; this is fine.'"

Mary wanted *helpful* practice, not easy practice. When she noticed she wasn't anxious enough, she tried something more difficult. That's the point of view I want you to take on: looking for opportunities to purposely, voluntarily choose to step toward what frightens you.

For Mary, it immediately paid big dividends. She summed up her practice with this comment: "As I drove out, I felt more empowered. I felt really happy."

She got more than good feelings. Through this powerful experience she adopted a new strategy that made sense to her, and she acquired a new point of view that will lead her toward her positive goals. Feelings like happiness are quite pleasurable, but they are short-lived. A workable strategy, based on a simple logical system, that makes sense and helps you feel empowered . . . *that* can last a lifetime.

And listen to the next reward she got. After sharing her story of the previous night's practice, Mary continues by saying, "On the way here this morning, I was thinking of other situations that were really, really scary to me." She tells her story of feeling trapped on the streets of Boston and then another occasion of feeling trapped while driving through a tunnel in a national park. "I started imagining myself in those situations. And I thought, 'Well, I guess it would be just like the parking garage.' I would say, 'You're going to get out of here. This tunnel's not going to collapse. There is enough air. And even if you take a wrong turn, you'll eventually take a right turn, and you'll get out.'"

Twelve hours prior she declared she was so traumatized by her last trip to Boston that she would never return there. Now she is envisioning how she could handle any of those tunnels. She can see herself taking back territory in her life! I'm feeling so happy for her.

But I'm not going to let Mary rest on her laurels. She has a flight coming up in five hours, and I want her to be ready for her fear of suffocation and restriction to crop up. As the session continues, she experiments with putting two pillowcases over her head. By doing so she provokes and then tolerates the fearful discomfort that comes with the sense of suffocation. But I still want to work directly on her fear of restriction. So I ask her if she would be willing to again put a pillowcase over her head and then allow me to bind it around her neck with packing tape. That seemed kind of creepy to her, but . . . Hey, wait, I'll just take you into that scene.

Mary understands the function of this experiment is to help her better prepare for the moments when she starts feeling trapped on a plane, in a tunnel, or in any other enclosed space. But she says she's feeling a little creeped-out by the thought of someone binding her up in such a fashion. After only a brief hesitation, though, she agrees. "Okay. Let's do it. [pause.] But obviously you're going to take it off when I tell you, right?"

I say that I will, of course, but I request a little negotiation. "Before asking me to take it off, would you allow yourself to sit for little bit with that urge to have it come off?" Mary needs to learn this skill of noticing the urge but not acting on it. And you need to learn it. That's why I wrote Chapter 9, on developing your Observer. You need to catch the flicker before the flame. You need to catch the urge before the action. You can't win this competition if you act on every impulse to escape. You must learn to step back and hear that message to run. And then you need to practice standing there anyway. You have to take the heat.

She agrees to my request. "And when you notice that urge," I ask, "what do you want to say to yourself?"

"I'd like to say, 'I can handle this. Just hang with this for a while.'"

That's a great message. She wants to reassure herself and then encourage herself to stay with her fearful sensations instead of acting on the urgent demand ("Get me out of here!") from her frightened side.

She puts the pillowcase down over her head and then permits me to bind it loosely around her neck with the packing tape.

Then her numbers begin to climb. Sixty. Then seventy. Up goes her heart rate. Now seventy-five. Really pounding now. Eighty-five.

This is the highest anxiety she's experienced in the two days we've worked together. She sits forward in her chair. I ask her how changing her posture serves her. "I'm in action mode," she says. Her body is ready to run. "It's going really high. Can you take it off?" I remove the tape and then the pillowcase.

Mary: *Ooh. It was really restrictive in there. I kept saying "It's okay," but then the anxiety just got too high. My feelings overran my thoughts.*

Reid: *It's your body's instinctual response to the sense that you're trapped. It's anticipating your being unable to escape, and it's working impeccably for you. What you just experienced is completely understandable and normal. Right?*

Mary: *Right.*

Reid: *We're going to do it again, if it's okay with you.*

Mary: *Okay.*

Even though Mary had a normal response to a new sense of restriction, she and I both know that she needs to toughen herself up. On the airplane this afternoon, she is probably going to feel a sense of suffocation and restriction of movement. She's not going to have the opportunity to get off the plane at that moment, nor does she need to. In a tunnel, we can expect she's going to experience those same feelings again, too. If she doesn't think she can handle those feelings, then she's going to continue to get anxious when she flies, and she's going to avoid those tunnels whenever possible. To reach her goals, she needs to ride out those momentary sensations of panic. If she can learn how to get past those temporary urges here today, she'll take home a new skill that gives her the upper hand.

I want that same outcome for you. Don't let impulses to escape dominate your actions and restrict your life. You must take back this territory. It's hard, but it's not complex.

Let's get back to the session. Did you notice how quickly Mary's anxiety spiraled upward? It's ironic, but I think it's true, that if Mary can take some of these big principles she's learning and manifest them at a moment's notice, she can take back her life. Therefore, Mary needs to handle these threatening events with a moment-by-moment strategy. We're going to work on that now. First, I ask her what caused her anxiety to rise up to an eighty-five.

> **Mary:** *I felt like I was going to suffocate.*
> **Reid:** *And how was the availability of air through that pillowcase? Did you think there was less air?*
> **Mary:** *It felt very different than when it was a pillowcase without the tape. The space was quite a lot smaller.*

I'm going to challenge two of her points of view. When she becomes increasingly anxious, she tells herself that she could now suffocate. And she *believes* that message. She thinks she *could* suffocate. She thinks she may be *about to* suffocate. That's why she ended the practice. So, first, I challenge that belief with some new information.

> **Reid:** *Would you be willing to press this pillowcase up against your mouth and breathe through it just like this? [I demonstrate.] Find out what you experience when it's completely pressed up against your mouth. [She puts her mouth directly on the pillowcase and takes a few breaths, in and out, seemingly without difficulty.] What do you notice? How restrictive is the airflow? How's your ability to get air?*
> **Mary:** *Oh, I guess I can get air.*

> **Reid:** *[in mock surprise] Oh, really? Isn't that interesting! [Now more curious] So, is there something you can tell yourself when we do this again, if you choose to do it again? What would you say?*
> **Mary:** *"There's enough air. This is fine. Be quiet."*

There it is. Mary willingly takes the information I just gave her and converts it into a new tactic. "In these circumstances (safe but closed-in places), when I suddenly start thinking I might suffocate, I can call that stance into question. I can reassure myself." Then she translates that tactic into a message she can give herself at the *moment* of threat. This executive voice can talk to the part of her who is threatened, the part of her who yells inside her mind, "Take this off! You're suffocating!" Her goal is to reassure her frightened side in such a way that it stops governing her actions.

To correct her understanding about suffocation is helpful. And it's necessary for her to find a reassuring voice to manage her panicky feelings. But these changes are not enough. The second viewpoint I need to challenge is her belief about how much she is able to tolerate. This is a critical task, not just for Mary but for you and everyone else who struggles with anxious worries. You can expect that there will be times in which "I can't do this" is the dominant voice. You have to take a leap of faith by *acting as though* you can handle a task that in the moment you don't believe you can handle. In case I haven't gotten through to you yet, let me say it a different way. To get stronger, you gotta do stuff you don't think you can do, and you gotta do that stuff while you *simultaneously* doubt you can do it. You're not going to do it by getting rid of the voice of doubt. You're going to do it by adding a voice that says, "Stay."

For any of us to grow, we must learn to tolerate more than we think we can tolerate. We need to defy our limited beliefs about what our capabilities are. When we choose to engage in challenging activities and follow them through to their conclusions, we expand our sense of our capacity. We will feel intimidated beforehand. Our insecurities will show up while we're smack in the middle of these activities. And sometimes they'll show up afterward, telling us how that was too much and that we shouldn't try to do it again. We're *not* going to extinguish those doubts. They come with the territory, and we need to take them with us on our adventures. Just try not to put them in the driver's seat.

To get stronger, you gotta do stuff
you don't think you can do, and you gotta do
that stuff while you simultaneously
doubt you can do it.

Before yesterday, whenever her anxiety started to spiral upward or when she heard those impulsive messages of danger, Mary had the urge to escape, and if she could escape at that moment, she did. She needs to be able to tolerate strong anxiety and tolerate those intense impulses to avoid, and yet not avoid. She can handle those thoughts and feelings by engaging an executive voice that reassures her about safety and about her abilities. But when she *suddenly* gets *highly* threatened, she needs to give herself commands that can override the insistent message of "run."

Now we're going to try on her plan to cope with these feelings of suffocation and restriction and her urge to run: "There's enough air. This is fine. Be quiet." Mary puts the pillowcase back over her head, and her anxiety starts to shoot up quickly. I ask her to take the pillowcase off and to give herself a little time to regroup. After a brief half-minute she puts it back on.

Reid: *Talk to me. What's your number?*

Mary: *It's sixty-five. I'm really having to tell myself that I can do this right now.*

> **Reid:** *Okay. You're in control, so you let me know if you want me to do the next step and when.*
>
> **Mary:** *[moments later] Yeah, do the next step.*
>
> **Reid:** *[I place the packing tape around the pillowcase at her neck.] Okay, what's your number at this moment?*
>
> **Mary:** *I'm managing to keep it at about a sixty, sixty-five.*
>
> **Reid:** *By doing what?*
>
> **Mary:** *By breathing and by telling myself I can breathe.*

Now something interesting happens. Within thirty seconds, Mary sits back in her chair, a sign of settling in to the experience. She's not leaning forward in "action mode" anymore. I ask her what allows her to sit back.

"Well, I want to get better."

Oh, my. I think she's got it!

She sits back in her chair and takes the heat because she *wants* something valuable for her future, and she wants it right at this moment. She has two competing agendas in the same moment. She elevates one ("I want to get better"), and by default the other one is diminished ("I've got to get out of here!"). Gaining her positive future is more important than escaping her current discomfort.

This is the lesson I want you to absorb. The way you can learn to take the heat in the moment—the unavoidable chance of something going wrong, or getting embarrassed, or losing something you value, or panicking—is to *want* something, right then, you think you might gain by staying in the moment. After she tells me that, here is her very next sentence.

> **Mary:** *It's funny. Just now I was thinking about sitting on an airplane, and I thought that this feeling is very much the way I feel when I'm on the airplane and the door is closing. And, yeah, I can*

breathe. It's not something I like, but I can breathe. And I can switch that little air on if I need to.

Whoa! How about that? Less than ten minutes ago, she panicked with suffocation fears after I put the packing tape around her neck, and we had to stop the practice. Three minutes ago she pulled the pillowcase over her head and that immediately sent her into high anxiety. Now she's pulled that same pillowcase over her head, and I've taped it down around her neck. Same event but totally different response. She's not gritting her teeth, trying to bear up. She's not counting the seconds until she can escape. She isn't a victim of claustrophobia at this moment. Not only is she sitting back in her chair, but while she's simultaneously feeling moderately distressed, breathing, and telling herself she can breathe, she now has enough freedom in her mind that she can drift forward to a future flight where she reassures and comforts herself in the moment when she's coping with a closed-in feeling. Remarkable!

> **Mary:** *And I had my eyes closed before, because I didn't want to see how close the sheet was. But now I've opened them.*
> **Reid:** *Did that do something to the numbers?*
> **Mary:** *Yeah, it actually did. It made them probably go up five or seven notches.*

Look how quickly she is learning about what she can tolerate. She's at the highest level of anxiety she's been able to sustain in any of the practices these two days. And then she voluntarily, purposely opens her eyes. Why? In order to give herself more work to do. Can you see how committed Mary is to taking back her life?

I let her linger there another half a minute or so. I remove the tape so she can lift the pillowcase off of her head. She takes a deep, full breath, straightening misplaced strands of hair with a brush of her hand, and the very next thing she says is, "Wow. I never thought I'd get that far today."

Not surprisingly, Mary had great success on her flight that same day. I e-mailed her again about a year later, and she told me that she was managing tunnels and parking garages well. She'd had only one panic attack on a flight in the past twelve months. When she became apprehensive in one long, unexpected tunnel, "I remembered those horrible things you put me through," she said, "and I got through those!"

BE CUNNING

CHAPTER 17

The Art of Cunning: Rope-a-Dope and the Brer Rabbit Offense

B ecause of a boxing match's physical aggression, many people get little pleasure imagining one. So I ask your brief indulgence in a description of what ABC-TV declared as the greatest event in the forty-five-year history of its *Wide World of Sports*.

By 1974, Mohammed Ali had established himself as one of the best heavyweight boxers of all time. In 1964, at twenty-two years old and still known as Cassius Clay, he won the world heavyweight championship in a stunning upset of Sonny Liston and then defended his title against former heavyweight champion Floyd Patterson in 1965. He lost his boxing license in 1967 for refusing to enter the armed forces during the Vietnam War and did not fight again until 1970. A series of wins placed Ali as the top contender against heavyweight champion Joe Frazier, and their March 1971 fight in Madison Square Garden was nicknamed "The Fight of the Century." Ali lost his first professional fight that night. He won his next ten fights and lost again in 1973 to Ken Norton. He beat Norton later that year and finally took down Joe Frazier in January 1974.

A bout was set for October 30, 1974, between Ali and heavyweight champion George Foreman in Zaire, Africa, called the "Rumble in the Jungle." Ali was his usual cocky and colorful self before the fight.

"I've done something new for this fight. I done wrestled with an alligator, I done tussled with a whale; handcuffed lightning, thrown thunder in jail; only last week, I murdered a rock, injured a stone, hospitalized a brick; I'm so mean I make medicine sick."

But exuding confidence and taunting his opponent before the fight would not be enough to win this one. While Ali had struggled against Joe Frazier and Ken Norton, and lost two of those four fights, Foreman had beaten Frazier and Norton easily in second-round knockouts. Plus, Ali was an ancient thirty-two years old, while twenty-four-year-old Foreman was in his prime and considered an awesome and dangerous boxer who throws some of the hardest punches in heavyweight history. No one gave the former champion a chance of winning.

Against all odds, Ali won that fight, and here's how he did it.

For months before the fight, both men lived in Zaire as they trained. While Foreman worked out in isolation, Ali built a visible relationship with the people of Zaire with his strong pro-African beliefs and his flamboyant charm. By the time the two boxers entered the ring, Ali had the cheering crowd firmly on his side.

Ali's prefight boasting and taunting included how he was too fast for Foreman to keep up with. And he opened the first round of the fight with a flurry of punches to reinforce that message. Coming out of his corner in the second round, Foreman expected to step forward in a toe-to-toe battle. Instead, Ali retreated to the ropes and taunted one of the hardest hitters in boxing to hit him repeatedly while he only protected his face. Foreman became angry and continued to give his best shots to

Ali's midsection. Ali responded, "Is that all you got, George? They told me you could hit." Many of Foreman's punches were deflected or didn't land squarely. Ali allowed the ropes to absorb some of the energy of the blows so as to reduce their damage. Occasionally Ali would counter with a flurry of punches to Foreman's face, which electrified the crowd. Then right back to defensive mode, protecting his face and body leaning against the ropes. The move would later become known as rope-a-dope.

By the seventh round, Foreman began tiring and occasionally dropped his arms to his side. Late in the fight, Foreman smashed Ali with a thundering blow to the body, and Ali whispered to him, "Is that all you got, George?" And Foreman thought to himself, *Yep, that's about it.*

Ali started dominating Foreman with his speed and energy. At the closing thirty seconds of the eighth round, Ali dropped Foreman at center ring and won the fight.

As I opened this chapter, I asked that you indulge my story of the Ali-Foreman fight, since their sport is so physically aggressive. Feel free to entertain a less violent imagery. Maybe a triathlon. Field hockey. Duplicate bridge, even. But I want you to know that you need to engage in this process as though it is an aggressive sport. This work is hard, and you won't be comfortable. The good news is that it's not complex and these tactics *will* help you.

Ali did not win because he was stronger or because he was a fighter in his prime. It was his challenger who was in his prime. Foreman was a three-to-one favorite. Ali was cunning, and he serves as a good example of "know your challenger," just as champion poker player Annette Obrestad from Chapter 2 studied her competitors. That's why Ali bragged ahead of time that he was going to be too fast for George. That's why Ali whispered in Foreman's ear at the same time George was pounding away on him. He was trying to get him mad. He was trying to get him to punch with all his strength. Ali set up Foreman, and then he took him down.

You and I are going to use the same tactic for Anxiety. We will create an offensive strategy that will set it up. And then we're going to take it down. But you need to be willing to absorb some blows. You may not *experience* any blows, but you need to have the attitude of "I'm willing."

And you will need a good dose of craftiness. I have just the model for you.

THE BRER RABBIT OFFENSE

Brer Rabbit is a likeable enough character in the canon of American folktales . . . but I wouldn't want him to date my daughter. I wouldn't ask him to housesit when I leave town. In fact, I don't want to have any negotiations with Brer Rabbit. He's a trickster.

But his wit and his wiles are a model for us. So let's not discount him quite yet.

The tales of Uncle Remus as compiled by Joel Chandler Harris are older than any of us on this planet, featuring a rotating cast of characters—Brer Rabbit, Brer Bear, Brer Fox, among other Brer creatures—going about their merry lives in the woods, bogs, and cornfields of the postbellum South. Looking past the archaic language (the text was written in the dialect of the Southern plantation folk who shared these tales with Harris), the plots of the various stories center around some form of mischief, with Brer Rabbit being the most mischievous of the group. Often he will want something someone else has, or he'll get caught in a trap and need to outwit his captor. Whatever the scenario, because he is the wittiest and wiliest of the creatures, Brer Rabbit uses the art of manipulation to get what he wants.

In *Brer Fox an de Stolen Goobers*, a thieving Brer Rabbit picks Fox's goober patch clean despite the wooden fence that Fox has built around his little plot. Brer Fox is furious, of course, and finds the gap in the fence where that scoundrel (whoever he might be) managed to sneak in. So he fastens a rope to a tree and sets a spring trap just outside that gap in the fence. Sure enough, the next morning, as Brer Rabbit slips into Brer Fox's goober patch, he steps right into the trap, the rope tightens around his hind legs, and he's propelled into the air and left dangling over the goobers with no chance of escape.

When Brer Bear happens by the goober patch, Brer Rabbit makes no mention of his predicament. He doesn't plead with the bear to release him. Rather, he tells the gullible bear that he's working a job for the fox. "Skeer-crow sorter work," he tells him, and Brer Fox is giving him a dollar a minute to hang there and do nothing. Brer Bear is intrigued—he's never made a dollar a minute in his life! And Brer Rabbit reminds him that he could use the cash. If he doesn't take this job, "Den how you goin' ter buy your fambly der Christmas presents?" asks the rabbit. "Ain't you gon' ter have no turkey?" Moments before Brer Fox arrives to catch his culprit, Brer Rabbit convinces Brer Bear to assume his skeer-crow responsibility, so the bear frees the rabbit and climbs up there to willingly take his place. "Looks like Brer Bear's been stealin' your goobers," Brer Rabbit tells the fox. "I see you got him ketched here in your trap!"

In the same vein, the cunning rabbit deceives a susceptible fox in *Brer Fox, Brer Rabbit, and de Well*. Brer Rabbit gets caught down in the well behind his home. Brer Fox hears the commotion and peers down into the well to investigate. Brer Rabbit, knowing full well that outsmarting the fox is his one-way ticket out of this pickle, tells the fox that he's down in the water scooping out the fishes: the *fitsy-fotsy-figgaloo fishes* that sell for fifty dollars a pound. There are scores of them, he tells the fox. "De water is just natchally alive wid um!" Not one to turn down the chance to make a quick buck, Brer Fox jumps into the bucket at the top of the well, sending him down toward the dark, fish-less water, and sending Brer Rabbit, who's sitting in the lower bucket, back up to freedom.

The various tales include some that are more outlandish than others (as in the one where Brer Rabbit convinces Brer Bear that the wheels on the wagon produce silver coins) and others that are more malicious (convincing bear and fox to stick their heads into a beehive), but what is consistent through all of them is Brer Rabbit's *craftiness*.

Whenever Brer Rabbit is in a pickle, it is this craftiness that helps him escape. In *De Tar Baby*, Brer Bear and Brer Fox have created a trap to capture and kill Brer Rabbit once and for all (this would be one of the more malicious tales). Through a rather simple ruse, bear and fox snare the rabbit in a wad of tar, rendering him helpless and immobile. "We sure ketched you dis time." They celebrate and cook up plans on how they intend to make the rabbit suffer. When Brer Fox threatens to roast the rabbit, Brer Rabbit fires back, "Roast me just ez hot ez you please, but don't fling me in dat brier-patch." When Brer Fox reconsiders and threatens to drown the rabbit, Brer Rabbit replies, "Drown me just ez deep ez you please . . . but please, *please* don't fling me in dat brier-patch!" In his guile, Brer Rabbit plants the seed that the worst possible punishment, the most heinous death he can imagine, is getting tossed into that brier-patch. "It ain't goin' ter be much fun ter skin Brer Rabbit, cause he ain't skeered of bein' skinned," surmises the bear. "But he sure *is* skeered of dat brier-patch!" declares the fox, and with that he tosses the rabbit right into the thorn bushes. Of course, this is what Brer Rabbit wanted all along. He "wuz born" in the brier-patch, and he can navigate around the thicket without a single scrape.

Through this paradoxical manipulation, Brer Rabbit manages to get precisely what he wanted. Notice that Brer Rabbit is never candid and is rarely sincere. He could very well *ask* the bear and the fox to let him go, to forgive all of his transgressions, and free him from the tar out of the goodness of their hearts, but that's not his style. It's much craftier (and far more enjoyable) to toy with their expectations, let them believe they have the upper hand, and then ultimately come out on top.

More significant (and even more appropriate for our work here) is Brer Rabbit's tenacity. He knows what he wants and sets about to get it, by hook or by crook, because there is, in each of Uncle Remus's tales, some desirable outcome, whether it is freedom or food. When Brer Bear bumbles down the road with a bag of ready-to-eat turkeys, Brer Rabbit will do anything to get them, even if it means concocting a preposterous scheme and playing dead—not once but *twice*—in the middle of the road. Each of these interactions with Brer Bear and Brer Fox is a challenge, and once that challenge begins, he will do whatever it takes to win.

Your challenger may seem bigger and stronger than you, since it has been winning most of the battles in the past. You might already feel beaten down by Anxiety. But we are going to use completely different tactics than you've been relying on. You will no longer have to go toe-to-toe with your challenger. You don't have to be bigger or badder than your challenger. We're going for cunning, just like our model competitors Brer Rabbit and Mohammed Ali. To be cunning requires that you are daring. And brave, bold, audacious. You may even need to feel fool-hardy. I recommend that you emulate Brer Rabbit's tenacity. He knows what he wants, and through his clever and paradoxical manipulation, he sets about to get it.

As I've said from the beginning, we're here to change your attitude, your disposition, your mind-set, and your basic belief about how to get stronger. And then, with this specific tactic, we will manifest that change through messages you deliver to your challenger. You're going to ask for more of what you have been afraid of. Let's find out how your challenger handles *that*.

CHAPTER 18

Act as Though This Is Such a Clever Tactic

You've decided. You're going to the beach. Your calendar is strangely uncluttered and the sky remarkably clear, so there's nothing standing in your way. When worry predictably pops up and makes some lame excuse about elevated levels of ultraviolet radiation, you brush it aside and promptly tag it as noise.

"Chill out, Anxiety. It's the beach not the Arabian Desert. Just *try* to stop me. And P.S., it's called sunscreen."

And yet, as you load up the car with towels and blankets and swimsuits and sunblock and sandwiches, as you buckle your two-year-old into the car seat in advance of the thirty-minute drive to the ocean, it's only natural that Anxiety checks in to see how things are going, to infuse some discomfort, to make one last-ditch effort to royally stress you out. *Boy, you're bringing a lot of stuff to the beach. I think you're overdoing it. Maybe this is more trouble than it's worth. It could be too crowded when you get there, and then all of this preparation will be for nothing. How far are you going to be from home? What if something goes wrong while you're gone? This seems more and more like a bad idea. Wait! Aren't you terrified of the water?*

And then Anxiety suggests, oh so casually, *Perhaps it's better if you just stay home.*

This right here is the perfect occasion to "act as though." Anxiety knows that this is a make-or-break kind of moment. If it drums up enough apprehension over the threat of skin cancer and the tantrum-throwing toddler in the backseat and the various appliances that can spontaneously combust while you're away, then the whole trip will fall to pieces.

In this moment, any of us can respond in one of two ways. We can choose to tussle with Anxiety, which is what it wants—it wants to arm wrestle. It wants to struggle with us, because struggling means *stalling*. Struggling with Anxiety casts more doubt, causes us to second-guess our actions, and ultimately leaves us stagnant. Or we can simply keep moving forward. We can persevere in the face of doubt. We "act as though." We act as though we can protect ourselves from too much sun, and we will handle the crowd if it's there. We act as though, on the outside chance that something goes wrong, we'll manage it. And we act as though all this beach fun will be worth our effort.

When we "act as though," we move toward the feared situation as though it's all going to work out. We behave as though there's no major threat to fear. Full disclosure: this is not a radical new concept. We "act as though" all the time, without even knowing that we're doing it.

✧ We act as though we are going to live a long, fulfilling life.
✧ We purchase a gym membership and commit to an exercise program as though it will ensure an even longer, healthier, and more fulfilling life.

◇ We order an espresso as though the coffee is fresh and uncontaminated.

◇ We drive the car as though the drivers around us will honor the traffic signs and signals just as we do, as though the navigation system will not lead us astray (e.g., down a boat ramp into the lake).

◇ We ride the train to work as though the vast team of architects, engineers, and contractors who built this moving metal box were educated, experienced, and able.

◇ We go about our day as though the refrigerator will continue to run while we're at work, as though the day-care provider is attentive to our child's needs, as though the job we've held for the last decade will still be here tomorrow and the next day.

I'm only asking you to do something that you do every waking moment of every day. We *must* "act as though" in our daily lives. If we didn't, we could never accomplish anything. We couldn't assume that the water from the faucet was clean. We couldn't assume that gravity would continue to keep us grounded or that the earth would continue to spin. We make these assumptions without thinking about them. "Acting as though" *allows us to take action.* "Acting as though" permits us to drive to the beach on a day when there are no clouds and zero obligations.

As you program the GPS and pull out of the driveway, you act as though the trip will be effortless, the roads will be open, and your SUV will make it to your destination without incident. You'll assume that, while you're away, the oven won't turn itself on and burn the house down. When your daughter pines for some dried blueberries, you act as though she won't upend the bag and empty its contents onto her lap as you've asked her (on multiple occasions) not to do. You'll walk toward the water as though the car will be perfectly safe in the unattended lot. You'll run toward the shoreline as though your possessions will remain untouched and undisturbed on the blanket you've stretched out on the sand. You'll dive into those waves as if the sharks and sea creatures residing beneath the ocean's surface want little or nothing to do with you. And you'll wear sunblock because, well, that's just common sense.

You might find yourself saying, "Ugh, I'm not going to put myself through *that*. I don't want that terrible feeling of insecurity and discomfort. How do I *know* that the sharks want nothing to do with me?!" Catch yourself in that moment and shift your perspective to "Geez, I'm a little worried about this. But I'm going to *act* as though this is all right with me." Either support your excitement and pleasure about swimming in the ocean, or head back to the blanket. It's your choice.

By the way, this isn't some halfhearted "fake it till you make it" pretense. To "act as though" is a powerful intervention that can help you make a decision and then *take action*. It comes in two flavors.

⬧ **Act as though the content is irrelevant.** You may have previously decided that your worry about a particular topic is noise, but as you get closer to the threatening environment, you can expect Anxiety to come knocking and throw a little insecurity into the mix. In those moments, adopt this point of view (in your own words, of course): "I've already decided that these worries are noise. Even though I feel insecure about that decision right now, I'm going to act as though the content is irrelevant. I'm going to step toward this challenge and see what I learn." This will require your courage, because you are going to feel scared and step forward *despite* that fear.

⬧ **Act as though you have enough skills.** In many situations, Anxiety will stir up some doubt within you about whether you have what it takes to face the difficult task. This is not a true indication of your lack of skill; rather, this is Anxiety prohibiting you from trusting your skills. That shrewd challenger

Anxiety has generated a false *perception* that you don't have what it takes, that the challenge is too great for you. If your goal is to take on the challenge, you cannot wait until you are *certain* you have enough skills, because certainty is not available to you beforehand. If you delay, waiting for your confidence to show up, then you'll be waiting indefinitely. Therefore, it's best to *act as though* you have enough skills to face the challenge. This too will be a courageous act.

When we take a risk, we inevitably face some intimidation. No one is cool as a cucumber seconds before their first bungee jump off the bridge. On top of that insecurity, Anxiety has the ability to add another layer of uncertainty and a sense that you can't handle it. So you *need* the tactic of "act as though" to counter this stronger sense of doubt. When you decide to act as though you can handle whatever happens ("I'm going to assume the hotel housekeeping staff has cleaned the room and changed the sheets"), and when you hand that message off to your executive voice, then you're not going to let Anxiety question your decision. Instead, you'll say something to the tune of "Nope, I'm not going to analyze this decision again, Anxiety. I'm going to keep moving forward. Now beat it."

You need to recognize that *of course* some part of you is going to resist unpleasantness, difficulties, and threatening moments; *that's human nature.* (Sir Isaac Newton taught us in Chapter 8 with his Third Law of Motion.) So it's a given that your fearful side will voice its concerns. The goal is to not let that voice serve as the decision maker in the moment. Call up the side of you that is willing to push on through the doubts and difficulties rather than struggle against them.

"This 'act as though' thing is totally nuts," you say. "Why would I push forward without knowing that it is the right thing to do?" But wait a minute, you are already *backing away* from this challenge on the basis of uncertainty. That means you are acting as though certain beliefs are true without investigating. It's the old "better safe than sorry" stance that keeps you from taking action. Do these sound familiar?

- ✧ I *must* know the outcome of events before I participate in them.
- ✧ If I feel uncomfortable, there's *got* to be something wrong.
- ✧ Other people can apply skills and get stronger, but I don't have what it takes.
- ✧ I *have* to do it perfectly, or I shouldn't start.
- ✧ I can't tolerate people judging me.
- ✧ I can't feel awkward or clumsy while I'm learning a new skill.
- ✧ A panic attack could easily become a heart attack.
- ✧ I will suffocate and die if I get stuck in an elevator.
- ✧ Any spot of red could actually be a drop of blood containing HIV.

These aren't truisms. You are responding to an *interpretation* of the circumstance, not the circumstance itself. When we get scared, we make up these positions (positions like "all dogs can turn aggressive at any moment"), and we let them control our actions. We make decisions as though these momentary opinions are valid facts, but they are not. They are interpretations, and if they are needlessly limiting us, we need to challenge them. So I'm not proposing some crazy intervention (not this time, at least). Rather, I'm recommending that you call into question some preexisting points of view that are holding you back.

But here's the cunning part. It's difficult to go toe-to-toe with our firmly held beliefs. We aren't going to get rid of our belief first and *then* act. That's asking too much. And it's not necessary. "Act as though" is our secret weapon that allows us to sidestep those rigid beliefs. "Act as though" grants us the opportunity to discover something new. Instead of requiring yourself to dismantle that avoidant point of view, take the stance of "I can't really figure out if this is safe to do, but I'm going to act as though it's safe" or "I don't really know if I can handle this, but I'm going to act as though I can."

When "I can't tolerate people judging me" is preventing you from talking casually with your coworkers at your new job, that's a hard belief to completely extinguish. But it's not necessary to make a frontal attack on this mind-set. You don't have to say, "Yes, I can! I *can* handle it if people think I'm awkward. Be quiet!" Instead, you can take a different kind of firm stance: "Yes, I'm nervous about this, and I'm going to act as though I can handle their judgment."

Or let's say that you have long been afraid that your next panic attack might turn into a heart attack. Even if you've now collected enough evidence to reassure you of your heart's capacity, will you be able to hold on to that opinion as you approach a threatening scene? In that moment, it might be difficult to tell yourself, "I'm sure I'll be fine. Getting panicky is no fun, but I won't be putting my heart in danger." Doubt will slip in, and you have to accept that. But in the face of this insecurity, another option is to say, "Yes, I know I'm going to feel unsure, and I'm going to act as though I'll be fine."

Are you someone who compulsively checks the doors and windows and faucets and your car's interior light and emergency brake? Good luck being able to tell yourself not to worry because everything is fine. You can't reach your goals that way, because Anxiety won't let you. "I'm going to act as though everything is okay" is your ticket out of your suffering. And what would you do if you acted as though everything was okay? You'd step away from the front door, and those windows and faucets inside the house, and you'd head to your destination. You'd walk away from the car and into the mall. You'd still feel unsure and insecure about your decision to not check again. But you'd walk away *as though* you felt secure.

I worked with a woman who wanted to rein in her tendency to blush because it caused her neck and upper chest to blotch, which then triggered embarrassment and shame. She was getting married soon, and she *couldn't fathom* walking down the aisle with her neck and upper chest spotted red. That's not the kind of attention she wanted on her wedding day, and I could certainly sympathize with that concern. However, this was someone who wore a turtleneck or scarf to work every single day of the year as a means of shielding herself. Imagine her standing at the rear of the church, arm in arm with her dad, awaiting that momentous walk down the aisle, thinking to herself, *Oh God! This is it! This is the big test! If I blush now, my wedding day is ruined! Don't blush, don't blush!* Spoiler alert: This tactic would not work out favorably for our blushing bride. Can you see how her insistence on not turning red, and her abject fear that she might, would actually generate the very thing she fears the most? If that's true, then shifting her *attitude* about this possibility might be the best remedy.

So what did we do? First we addressed her daily activities. I gradually helped her shift her point of view from "I can't let my friends and coworkers see me blush" to "I can handle people seeing me blush. I can tolerate feeling embarrassed and even ashamed. I can cope with some people judging me as odd or weird." Those messages allowed her to experiment with wearing anything but a scarf or turtleneck.

But wait a minute. How could she be sure ahead of time? As she showed up at work in a blouse without a scarf, she didn't *know* she could handle people seeing her blush. If she started feeling ashamed that people might be judging her as weird, she didn't *know* that she could cope with that intense emotion. Yet if she required certainty, she would stay stuck. So to manage this conundrum, all these messages were within an even higher-level mind-set: "I'm going to act as though I can cope with blushing, with people judging me, and with feeling ashamed." Now she can step forward into her uncertainty.

Just so you don't make any false assumptions about my cunning brilliance as a psychologist, this revision of her attitude proved quite difficult. It took about twelve sessions over the course of four months to accomplish. But that is a profound change to shift from "I can't let myself feel ashamed" to "I'm going to act as though I can tolerate feeling ashamed."

Near the end of our work together, we developed the following approach. We personified her anxiety and completely turned the tables on it. Instead of only subvocalizing messages of fear, she invited Anxiety to give her precisely what intimidated her. When she stepped into public without covering her neck, she would say, "Gosh, Anxiety, please make me blush right now. I beg of you, *please* turn my neck bright red. Bring my cheeks up to about 101 degrees to the touch. If you will do that, I'll be so happy." (I haven't introduced that part to you yet. Call it a sneak peek into where we're headed in the next two chapters.) Once our bride mastered that tactic, she made great strides. By the time her wedding day arrived, she had adopted an entirely new point of view: "I can handle blushing during my wedding ceremony." Once she took on that attitude, Anxiety could no longer hold her hostage. I don't really remember whether she blushed on her wedding day. In the end, it doesn't really matter, because it no longer mattered to her.

PRACTICE TRUST

Here is my advice to you: Don't wait until you are certain that this approach will work for you. Take actions now, while you are feeling doubtful, scared, and insecure about my suggestions. Take actions because you understand the *principles* behind them. Take actions because you see the *logic* in them. Don't wait until you trust that this approach will work for you.

Why act before you have confidence? Because Anxiety won't *let* you feel confident about the outcome. If you wait for total assurance, you will be waiting a very long time. Anxiety's ploy is to convince you that you must be certain of the outcome *before* you step forward, and then it won't *allow* you to feel that level of confidence. So what happens? You step back rather than step forward. Anxiety gives you an intolerance of uncertainty and an urge to know that everything is going to turn out as planned. If you want to work your way free of Anxiety's dominance, you are going to have moments when you feel as though you are flying on a trapeze without a safety net. But you have to do it anyway. You have to take a courageous leap of faith so you can experiment with these new ideas.

Don't wait until you are certain that
this approach will work for you. Take actions now,
while you are feeling doubtful, scared, and
insecure about my suggestions.

Of course, you need to decide for yourself that the benefits of pushing through uncertainty and distress outweigh the risks. That's why in Chapter 21 we will clarify your goals for the future. Those objectives—whether it's a career change, more travel, more education, or simply getting your mind back so you can focus on the things you want out of life—need to be bigger than your fear of Anxiety.

Go have *experiences* to reinforce the belief that you can get stronger. You must face a challenge, feel insecure, choose to act as though you can handle it, and then step toward the challenge. You have to discover what happens as opposed to knowing ahead of time exactly what will happen. You will need to talk to yourself, and even though it may be a brief message, it should represent this decision: "I'm going to act as though this is the right action to take. I'm going to act as though I have enough skills to handle this. And I'll get through whatever happens." Then you need to act. You can adopt confidence only *after* you learn the lessons of repeated actions.

When you turn your car keys over to your seventeen-year-old daughter, who is taking her first weekend trip entirely on her own, you act as though she will keep herself safe. If you wait until you are *certain* she will act safely . . . well, you simply can't, or you will never let her grow up and have her own independent life. Trust is acting as though she has learned all the important lessons you have imparted to her, without knowing for certain she has. In this same way you must learn to trust yourself.

Of course some part of you is going to resist unpleasantness, difficulties, and threatening moments. Again, *it's human nature*. It's built into our subconscious to safeguard us. But you can choose not to let that part of you be the executive at the moment of action. Instead, summon the side of you that chooses to push into difficulties and not struggle against them. If you are willing to experiment with this new perspective and allow it to guide your actions, you make yourself available for that glorious "Aha!" moment. Whether it comes suddenly or builds over several weeks, here is the possible insight: "Hey! I actually *can* step forward into threat, and I *can* handle what happens."

CHAPTER 19

Talking to Anxiety

I love the Canadian Rockies, and a few years ago I had another opportunity to explore them. I was scheduled to teach in Vernon, British Columbia. With only a two-hour drive I could visit and hike trails throughout Mount Revelstoke National Park, which had several mountains topping 10,000 feet. In the months preceding my talk, I excitedly planned for this extra excursion. I booked a rental car, secured a bed-and-breakfast near the mountain, and planned my hike.

The day arrives as an exquisitely beautiful October morning. This park offers me a unique advantage. To access the trail head, I drive twenty-five minutes up the mountain and then have only a three-and-a-half-mile hike to reach one of the lower ridgelines. The trail will take me through a dense old-growth rainforest of giant cedars and pines, past a subalpine forest, and finally to high alpine meadows, within view of the ice-clad peaks of the Columbia Mountain Range.

I pull into the completely empty parking lot of Mount Revelstoke. I'm in a pristine environment, I can already see the snowcapped mountains, and I have it all to myself. Perfect. I head off, reminding myself to clap a few times as I get to each bend in the trail so as not to surprise any grizzly, since these 600-pound locals tend to amble down to the meadows in the fall to feed on the ripe berries.

It turns out I'm completely safe from the bears, but I am vulnerable to another predator: my obsessions. I begin to perseverate on a ridiculous topic that I am too embarrassed to reveal. Suffice it to say that I am exactly where I want to be right now, but I am totally not present. I am up in my head, and I am either obsessing or I am mad that I am obsessing. I see nothing of my surroundings because I can't focus on anything external. Oh, great.

This continues *ad nauseam*.

Then suddenly I have this thought: *What do you do for a living?!*

This is enough to shake me out of my nightmare, and, just as quickly, up pops a plan. From that moment forward, anytime I hear myself obsess, I will subvocalize the following instruction to my obsession, "Thank you! Would you give that to me again?" Then I will turn my attention back to this beautiful setting.

I implement the plan instantly. I step back and hear my obsession, I ask for more, and then I turn back to my surroundings. Within eight seconds, up pops the obsession again. I repeat, "Thank you! [With enthusiasm, too.] Would you give that to me again?" I allow not one moment's thought about whether the obsessions will disappear. I focus only on mentally stepping back to notice each obsession when it arrives, asking for more, and then turning my attention back to my hike. I don't check if it is gone, and I try to not even hope that it will be gone. I remain committed to the strategy. I decide to act as though this is how I will respond even if these obsessions keep sounding off for the rest of my life.

And then . . . it disappeared. Ten minutes after I committed to my paradoxical response, the obsession is gone as quickly as it showed up.

Do you think you can do something like this? Because your responsibility is to aggressively beat down the tall, brick walls that protect your old, firmly held beliefs about how to manage your worries. You start by making three moves: personify, externalize, and simplify. Personify: give your disordered thinking an identity, just like we've been doing throughout this book by calling it Anxiety. Externalize: perceive it outside of you, not part of you, but in a relationship with you. We've been doing that here, too. Simplify: reduce this relationship down to its bare bones. Anxiety gives you messages that you are weak in the face of threat, that you are not capable of stepping forward, that you need to listen very carefully to its instructions and back away from this threat. Now the task is to turn the tables on your challenger. In this case, I spoke directly to my obsessions with the simple, paradoxical message of "I want more of what you're dishing out." Whenever we can engage the symptom in any way other than fearing it or fighting it, we have our best chance of beating it.

FASTER, PLEASE

Now it's your turn. Imagine for a moment that roller coasters are not on the top of your thrill-rides-I-look-forward-to list. Now, however, you find yourself buckled in, listening to that haunting, rhythmic clicking as the train climbs the first big hill that inevitably leads to that steep, terrifying drop. So you start screaming at the top of your lungs, "I don't want to do this anymore! Make it stop! I can't take this! I can't stay on this ride! I can't handle it! Please make it stop!" But the roller-coaster operator, a sixteen-year-old suffering through summer employment, has no intention of pulling that emergency brake. The car is in motion, and you are not going anywhere else. You may agonize through the three-minute ordeal, hating every moment of it, but you are still going to experience it, whether you like it or not.

Now imagine holding a different attitude about the ride, one that is reflected in this subvocalized commentary: "Yes, we're heading up that first big hill. Okay. This is okay. I'm scared, but I can handle this. In fact, I'm a little terrified, well, really, really scared now—ahhhhhhhhhhhhh! Wow, that was a quick fall. But I made it . . . Uh, oh. *Still* terrified. But I don't want to stop. It's perfectly fine that I'm frightened out of my skin right now. I can handle this." Your executive voice is in First Responder mode, just like we discussed in Chapter 15. Anxiety isn't expecting you to take on this kind of attitude about the threat it throws at you. It counts on you to resist and block and avoid at the "I can't tolerate it," "I can't continue," and "Please make it stop!" level.

If you decide to ride the roller coaster a second time, you could consider yourself engaging in an exposure practice, facing the threatening situation in order to learn how to tolerate it. But that's not the game we're playing. No, for our challenge, you won't merely ride that roller coaster again. Instead, you step into your paradoxical "I want you to give me more of this" role. You purposely, voluntarily *seek* to up the ante by moving from the fourth row to the first row while you ask that teenaged ride operator to increase the speed a bit this time. You progress from agreeing to tolerate the ride to provoking the provocateur. "More, please!" So your messages become, "Make it faster! Make it more terrifying! I'm not uncomfortable enough! Not only can I handle this, I *want* this!" Rather than simply permitting and accepting that onslaught of discomfort and uncertainty, as well as all the physical symptoms that come with them, you *encourage* Anxiety to give you more. Keep in mind that your voice is quaking as you give the command. You are really scared! You aren't pretending to sound macho. But you're speaking courageously. You are frightened and you still push forward.

Let's try another scenario. Imagine you are sitting onstage, one of four people about to participate on a conference panel, and you become aware that your knees have begun to shake. Distracted, you put your attention on your relationship with Anxiety for a moment. You encourage Anxiety to intensify the shaking in your knees, to make it so intense that the stage floor rumbles beneath you, and then you return your focus back to the discussion about to take place on the stage.

Let me repeat this description, because it's an unorthodox move. Don't try to make your knees shake more, don't try to get the floor to shake. Ask *Anxiety* to serve in this capacity. "Please make the shaking worse. And give me some fearful thoughts while you're at it." Once you have delegated that responsibility, you are done with the transaction. Turn your attention back to whatever you'd like. You can look over your notes, scan the audience for friendly faces, or engage a panel member in small talk. If you get *distracted* again by your nervousness, you can compliment your challenger before you encourage it again: "Oh, that's excellent. But still not shaking enough. Try harder, please." Then return to your chosen activity.

It is possible that moments later you will have forgotten all about those shaking knees. Why? Maybe because they're not shaking anymore. Or maybe because you decided not to care anymore. Anxiety needed you to beg it to stop, or to try to shake off the worry, or press your hands against your kneecaps like you always do, forcing them to remain still. In fact, all your challenger wanted was for you to resist.

But no, you do the *exact opposite*.

Anxiety needed you to give in to the panic; to cross one knee over the other, over and over again; to make some excuse and flee the stage; to run and hide and seek out comfort.

But no, you talk directly to your challenger. Who is the challenger at this moment? It's Anxiety trying to scare you *about* your fear response. Once you've told it to keep provoking you, put your attention back on the present moment. You didn't remove your uncomfortable feelings. They're probably still there. But they don't require your attention, so you are redirecting your focus. Connect with your surroundings again until your worry or your physical discomfort grabs your attention once more.

That's how you apply this tactic as you take on a challenge.

This is not a permanent change. You won't forever have to beg for doubt or feign excitement at discomfort. However, it is a good starting place. Why? Because it shifts your consciousness away from resisting the present moment. When we fight against our current experience, Anxiety wins.

COULD YOU DRENCH MY SHIRT? PLEASE?

I imagine that when worry has relentlessly nagged you in the past, all you wanted was for worry and its distressing symptoms to subside. Perhaps it has pestered you so much that a big lump appeared to develop in your throat moments before your keynote address, or you ended up sweating through your shirt before you even arrived at the family gathering. "Stop worrying," you instructed yourself. "Relax. Enough with the sweating already! Calm down." And when the symptoms increased, your pleading increased. "Stop freaking out! Quit it! Get out of my throat, you stupid lump!"

But with all your attempts to quiet your worries and doubts, up they come again. "You can't do this. Trouble is coming, and you can't handle it. You're not ready, and you could make a fool of yourself. You must come across looking good. Don't let anyone see you struggle. No one!" All these demeaning, pessimistic, perfectionistic messages and all this anxious worrying and fear of humiliation is producing the lump in your throat or causing those pockets of sweat to accumulate on the armpits of your blouse or generating whatever other symptoms you're experiencing. Then when you react with "I can't stand all this anxiety," you produce even more symptoms.

So we have two problems in front of us: your doubts and insecurities, and your need to get rid of symptoms. To address both of these troubles, let's personify, externalize, and simplify. Bundle all these messages of threat and fear up into "the stuff Anxiety is saying to me." By doing that, you then have to address only this one identity, Anxiety, instead of having to counter every single new message that shows up in your mind. Now consider talking directly to Anxiety, making a completely different request. In fact, say just the opposite, one that is counter to the plea of "Please get rid of these anxious symptoms and these fear-inducing doubts."

In the same way that we can hit zero on the hotel room phone to speak to the reception desk, we have a direct line to our anxious pre-occupations. I suggest that whenever you get distracted or threatened by fearful thoughts, consider speaking to your challenger one-on-one. It need not be out loud (addressing Anxiety aloud at the post office or during Temple or in the middle of a moving eulogy could lead to negative consequences), but the notion of talking directly to your chal-lenger is significant. Give Anxiety a clear set of instructions, and make sure those instructions are the *opposite* of what Anxiety expects to hear. Then turn your attention back to the current activity, just like I was doing on my hike.

Have you ever had a hard time trying to fall asleep? You lie down, close your eyes, and attempt to put your mind into rest mode. After a few unsuccessful minutes, you tell yourself, "Look, I'm in bed, under the covers. Eyes are closed. It's nighttime. It's time to go to sleep." Then several more minutes pass . . . "I *have* to get to sleep! I can't believe I'm going to end up lying here for an hour. I can't *stand* this."

If in that very same situation you decide to lie in bed with the goal of *not* letting your eyes close, of making it your job to continue instructing your eyes to remain open, you'll have a better chance of falling asleep. Why? Because you are responding paradoxically to your frustration about not falling asleep. Your urge to "fall asleep *now*" is giving your amygdala a more than subtle message that something is wrong. There-fore, it responds by juicing you up a little, and you become more alert. When you commit yourself to the task of keeping your eyes open in your dark bedroom, that move requires you to let go of your struggle with falling asleep. Your negative talk may not disappear, but it quiets down, so your amygdala eventually quiets down, too. And this is the setting that is conducive to falling asleep.

We're employing this same paradoxical tactic with Anxiety in general, to tell it what it doesn't expect to hear. We're going to ask the challenger to give us more worries, more symptoms, more sweat, more discomfort . . . and we want it now. This catches the challenger off guard. "Anxiety, I want you to turn these pockets of sweat into pools of perspiration. I want you to drench my shirt in sweat. Soon, please!"

As with other parts of this book, I'm aware that this proposal sounds utterly ridiculous. You would never, ever want your armpits to sweat more than they have already. You're probably saying, "Hey, doc, I'm embarrassed enough here. You want me to get more embarrassed?! What is wrong with you? Can I get my money back?"

Well, yes and no. Yes, if we're talking about your fear of embarrassment, I want you to put yourself in situations where you may become embarrassed. You do have to go toward what you're afraid of in order to get stronger. That's a cardinal principle for most any tough endeavor. So I am asking that you *seek out* the opportunity for more embarrassment. But, no, I am not asking you to generate your embarrassment. The big twist is that you put yourself in the circumstance that has produced embarrassment in the past and you fear will produce it again now, but ask Anxiety to deliver the embarrassment to you. (Oh, and no, you can't get your money back.)

Imagine what you would sound like if you begged for even greater problems. "Anxiety, I urge you to make me more embarrassed. I want you to make my cheeks bright lobster red. I'm at a seven right now on the embarrassment scale. Make it a ten, please. No, make it eleven."

It's absurd, yes, but it's also formulaic. Whenever you feel threatened by your worried thoughts or your uncomfortable feelings in such a way that it interferes with your desired task, then request your challenger to increase whatever threatens you. If it's that lump in your throat, ask Anxiety to grow that lump larger. Even better, get more specific about what you want. Ask your challenger to upgrade that lump. "Anxiety, I'd really like you to make it a golf ball-sized lump. Please!" And then what do you do? Turn your attention back to your current activity. You'll talk to Anxiety again when it disturbs you again.

Of course, "make me more anxious" is not the same as, "I'd like to feel more anxious." Nobody likes to feel anxious. But if anxiousness comes with the territory of trying something new or difficult, then we can't let our fear of that distress distract us or cause us to back away. This intervention is about shifting the responsibility over to Anxiety in such a way that it no longer has the ability to dominate you. It's about shifting your attitude away from "This is going terribly wrong. I can't cope. It's got to stop!" Our goal is to get you as far away from resistance as possible. Once you understand the strategy, you will realize that this current tactic has four tasks. First, step toward what you're afraid of. Second, be cunning by pushing the responsibility of causing you more trouble over to Anxiety. This is a disruptive move in the relationship you have with the threat. Third, and just as important, let go of your need to remove your doubt and discomfort. For every one of us, these feelings come when we choose to expand our territory, to experiment with new behaviors, and to move toward difficult tasks. If you want to grow, you cannot run away from these feelings. Fourth, turn away from Anxiety and put your attention back on your current activity. You're done with this transaction. If you get distracted again, that's a whole new transaction.

If all this talking to Anxiety feels like a parody, you're on the right track. "Thank you, give that to me again. This is not enough. Can't you make it worse? *Please* make it worse." But anxiety disorders are maintained by the person's resistance. If you want to be a student of this therapeutic work, you need to realize that talking in this manner is not the central point; it is a means to accomplish our goal. The only reason to move to this theater of the absurd is to help you to stop resisting. The more you practice this extreme stance of asking for more, the less likely you will be thinking, *Oh, no, this is bad. I can't handle this.* Eventually when you hear those resisting thoughts, you'll notice them, decide they're not helpful, and drop them.

You will need to find your own messages to deliver to Anxiety whenever you feel threatened, and that's what we will address in Chapter 23. But in the meantime, keep in mind that we're looking for messages that resemble the disposition of "Really, Anxiety? Is that all you got? Come on. Bring it!" When that's your go-to attitude in the face of noisy worries and anxious symptoms, then you'll be the craftiest, most cunning challenger Anxiety has ever met.

CHAPTER 20

"Give Me Your Threats— Let Them Come"

The alarm clock glows pale green in an otherwise pitch-black room. It's minutes after 2 AM, and Bob is standing outside his bedroom door, racking his brain to come up with the opposite of *water*. This word, whatever it may be, is the only thing standing between him and slipping back into bed and under the covers. But at two o'clock in the morning, he's drawing a blank. Nothing's coming to mind.

He eventually settles on *sky*. Strike that. *Atmosphere,* he tells himself, "I'm sleeping in the atmosphere." And that thought, at this hour, is comfort enough so he can step back into his bedroom and settle into bed . . . that is, until the next fearful thought pops into his head moments later.

For Bob, every day is opposite day. It's the only way he's able to accomplish the most banal activities, things as fundamental to our existence as eating dinner or going to work or even falling asleep. Right now his theme is water. "So as I'm getting into bed I might think, *Well, I'm sleeping into the water.* I have to walk out of the room and correct that. First I have to decide what the opposite of water is."* Subvocalizing that new statement brings relief, and he can climb back into bed. It's a respite that often will last only a few seconds.

His behavior—"correcting" or "fixing" his negative thoughts by saying the opposite thought, or by replacing it with a positive thought—now has become a complex and taxing ritual, occurring five or ten or twenty times in any given night. Certain negative thoughts he's already "corrected" sometimes return, thus creating a vicious cycle with no promise of relief.

This routine, Bob's current compulsive behavior, is not restricted to bedtime. "It can happen when I'm eating," he says. "It can be when I'm getting into the car, thinking, *Oh, I'm breathing in the water.* I would have to get out of the car and mentally change that to *I'm breathing in the sky.*" The most rudimentary of tasks can turn into a series of repetitious actions.

Bob suddenly developed OCD at an early age. On a trip to New York City, walking through the streets of Manhattan, he was highly disturbed by the graphic propaganda on placards and bus stops, particularly a set of posters depicting babies and abortions. Within a day, ten-year-old Bob began obsessing, associating everyday objects like ketchup with blood and afflicted by thoughts and images of death. And when he returned home, these thoughts escalated into a genuine fear of dying: *Do I have cancer? Do I have a tumor? Is there blood in my lungs?* This young, confused boy couldn't figure out why these worries were plaguing him fifty or more times a day. He only knew that he had to find a way to get rid of them.

---

*Reid Wilson, *Treating the Severe OCD Client*, video, *psychotherapy.net*, http://www.psychotherapy .net/video/treatment-severe-OCD-Reid-Wilson, n.d. See Appendix B.

Sitting across from me now, Bob is noticeably well-built, confident, and charismatic. A passionate physical therapist, he immerses himself in his work and loves helping others reach their goals. He has goals for himself, too, and places he'd like to go in his career, but at this point in his life, he simply wants his mind back. "Whether other people notice it or not, I feel like I'm going crazy all the time. I want to be able to turn on the TV and watch it, not turn it on and off a million times, getting into some crazy, weird, complex ritual. Just to be able to put on my clothes without thinking about it, to be happy and excited about what I'm doing. That's all I want."

The last few months have been particularly hard, as Bob's compulsive behaviors are now impeding him from accomplishing daily tasks. Some nights he chooses to avoid going to sleep as a means to escape the incessant repetitions. That, of course, makes him exhausted and so he becomes weaker in his struggle against these intrusive thoughts. As he prepares for work, he can feel compelled to change his clothes a few dozen times. As he's finally ready to leave, he can get stuck repeating the process of walking out the front door. "By the time I get to work, I'm a wreck. Even if no one else sees it, I feel it." The threats of OCD are currently dominating his life, dictating his actions, and he's desperate to take back control.

TAKING THE POWER POSITION

Bob's problem represents what most people with anxiety go through, whether it's panic disorder, a specific phobia, social anxieties, or the broad worries of generalized anxiety disorder. You perceive a threat in front of you, and you automatically begin to look for protection or escape. If you can grab a protective mechanism or an escape hatch, you'll take it. If not, you'll face the threat with continued anxious worrying. This is the pattern you and I are going to interrupt.

Let me take you back to that first session with Bob. We're in the last fifteen minutes, and we're now discussing how he might experiment with some of these tactics over the next five days, specifically with his concerns about his bedtime rituals. Tonight, for instance, let's say Bob gets disturbed by one of his statements like, "I'm breathing water." And let's say he decides to experiment with tolerating doubt and distress by not getting out of bed and not replacing this statement with one that is more acceptable, such as, "I'm breathing air." Now he's faced with the fear of never being able to fall asleep. Here's how I introduce the new tactic:

> **Reid:** *Have you ever trained in any of the martial arts?*
> **Bob:** *Yeah. Karate and Okinawan.*
> **Reid:** *So that's what we're going to do. We're going to take advantage of OCD's energy. If OCD wins when I fight against uncertainty and distress, then I'm going to ask for more doubt and distress instead. You know this tactic, because you've been training in the martial arts.*

I remind Bob that OCD is focused on the distress of doubt. It doesn't care *at all* about the theme of breathing water or any other topic. It takes advantage of whatever it can in order to generate a sense of insecurity in his mind. I want Bob to take a power position over his disorder, and he can accomplish that by adopting a new point of view: "Wait a minute. OCD needs me to fight against uncertainty. If I want to break free from OCD, I need to do the opposite of that. So I ought to *ask* for more doubt. Ha!" Bob is a quick student. Read this brief exchange.

> **Reid:** *Our goal is to shift your relationship with OCD. The disorder lives in you only if you respond in a particular way. It needs you to take this stance: "I've got to get rid of my anxiety, and I've got to get rid of this preoccupation with this phrase in my head." Let's flip that. What's the opposite of "I've got to get rid of my anxiety"?*

Bob: *"I want it. I want my anxiety. I want it to stick around."*

Reid: *Okay, great. What's the opposite of "I've got to get rid of uncertainty"?*

Bob: *"I'm never going to be certain."*

Reid: *And . . .*

Bob: *"And, that's okay. I want it to be that way. I don't want to be sure about anything."*

Let's see if Bob can apply this strategy to one of his most difficult challenges, his sleep routine. If he wants to conduct an experiment by not getting out of bed to repeat a corrective statement, he must be ready for worry to show up. He's going to feel dread that withholding his ritual will cause him to stay up all night. Does he have the courage to purposely take an action that may cost him a whole night's sleep?

Reid: *This is when you might ask OCD to keep you awake all night. "Please, what I live for is for you to make me stay awake all night." It's a crazy way of talking. But the reason you want to talk that way is that you keep scaring yourself by saying, "Oh, God. I hope I don't stay awake all night. If I can't get rid of this thought, my night is going to be miserable." That fires off your amygdala in your midbrain, and that's your fight-or-flight response. So of course you're going to feel even more anxious when you talk like that. When you send a ridiculous message like "Come on, more, please," you are taking the game to OCD. You already know how to step forward. My job is to give you the move to step forward with, even though it might sound crazy to you.*

Bob: *Yeah, I need to talk to myself in a bring-it-on type of mentality, I think.*

Reid: *So you might say, "Hey, you can't give me enough doubt tonight. I am totally willing to stay up all night and dwell on this* *because you're forcing me to." I don't want you to* purposely *dwell on anything. I want you to go to sleep when you're able to go to sleep. Or watch a channel when you're able to watch a channel.*

Now I'm going to quiz him on this seemingly insane plan. And he will let me know whether he's catching on. I want him to realize that he's going to be on the receiving end of two mental events. First, his challenger, OCD, is going to give him the threatening message. Second, he will find himself immediately responding with an anxious urge to get rid of that message. There's no way he can interrupt those two events; they come as an automatic package. He needs to step back, notice that he's now getting played by OCD, and then deliver to his challenger a paradoxical response to the threat.

**Figure 8. Welcome doubt and distress
through the front door.**

You need to understand this, too. You are going to receive a threatening message, and then you will feel intimidated. That's why I am saying to you (perhaps more times than you want to hear) that you must expect and allow both doubt and discomfort to show up. They come bundled together and arrive at your doorstep in the blink of an eye. You cannot consciously stop something that is generated by your unconscious. So we're going to let these two in the front door instead of trying to lock them out. Now let's find out what happens when we invite Anxiety to help them stick around.

> **Reid:** *When you turn on the TV and you have that negative thought, your job would be to do what? Think what?*
>
> **Bob:** *"That's good that I got that thought."*
>
> **Reid:** *So the negative thought will show up, and you will automatically respond, "Oh, no. There it is. I've got to get rid of it!" That's going to happen automatically. But then you want to pair that with a something like, "Okay, great! Time to practice. I'm going to leave the TV on this channel and allow myself to feel freaked out. That's what that crazy psychologist today told me to do." You can say, "Thank you, OCD. I want this. But I am not preoccupied enough. Would you please make me even more freaked out right now?" Then turn your attention back to the TV or whatever you want to do. As soon as another negative thought comes in, you say, "Okay, good. That's what I want." You are looking to score points, and that's how you score a point. Not by enduring the fearful thought, but by pairing it with a response opposite of what OCD needs to fuel its fire. Okay?*

Learn to step back from the provocative messages of your anxious worries and obsessions. Push yourself away from those mental distractions just enough so that you can engage in the task of mastering this kind of provocative response. That's what I'm about to tell Bob. He must detach himself from the specific topic of his fear so that he can absorb himself in this experiment. He tells me he's ready to make this a competitive sport, and he's up for the challenge. That's what I want to hear.

> **Reid:** *Your job is to find opportunities to get this exchange going. So instead of dreading nighttime, when you are desperate to fall sleep, you say, "Okay. I'm looking for as many opportunities as I can to score points against OCD." How do you score a point? First, you notice that OCD is disturbing you. Then you say something to OCD, like, "Give me more, please." Or you say something to motivate yourself, like, "I want this."*

> **Bob:** *Right. Yeah. I have a competitive spirit. I need to get my fighting spirit going. I need to motivate myself to say, "I'm going to attack it." Make it a competitive sport.*

THIS IS NOT YOUR JOB

We are near the end of his first session, so I ask Bob if he has any further questions before I turn him loose for five days of experimentation. He has had to absorb a lot of information and a completely new way of thinking about how to handle his problems. So it's no surprise that I need to clarify one more point for him. (I'll assume you need to review this, too.)

> **Bob:** *Is part of my job to actually call up that negative thought in my mind, to say, "I want to think about this"?*

> **Reid:** *Wait, hold on. Your job is to ask OCD to make you think about it again. I don't want you to purposely think about it again. When it pops up spontaneously, ask OCD to "Give this to me again, please." Then you're done with the transaction. You're going to immediately return your attention to the task at hand, whether it is to close your eyes to go to sleep, or to continue to watch the current TV show. Don't go get the negative thought again. Make OCD go get it.*

Bob: *Yeah. So, it's more like my asking. It's not me saying, "Oh, I want to think of water now."*

Reid: *That's right. Your job is to create an activity, like turning on the TV, so that you might* provoke *the negative thought. That will give you a chance to score a point, because if the threatening thought pops up, you score a point by asking OCD to make that thought stay around and to make you feel worse. And then you go back to focusing on whatever your valued activity is at that moment, until OCD distracts you again. When it does, you say, "Thank you. That's great." Any message you deliver that is similar to "Great! Give me more!" will score you a point.*

Bob: *Okay, got it. I'm talking down to it, or talking back to it. That's how I score a point.*

Reid: *Yup.*

If he will actively engage in *that* project, he will further detach himself from the urge he feels to get rid of those thoughts and feelings.

Five days have now passed, and Bob is back for his second session. He's still the sturdy young man I met a week ago, but he's visibly more comfortable in his skin. He rubs his palms together and breathes deeply, trying to best articulate what he's discovered over the last days. Obviously, I'm curious whether Bob was able to apply the skills he learned here, and what effect they had, if any. Aren't you curious?

Reid: *Welcome back. Tell me what's been happening. What have you noticed?*

Bob: *Well, I've definitely been using a lot of the techniques. I've been challenging the OCD more. I'm seeing a lot of fast progress, I'll tell you that. It's nice to see. In the past, the problem has been that I never challenged it. Or at least I didn't challenge it enough. The phrases you gave me have helped. And I've come up with my own, to make it my own.*

> **Reid:** *What kind of messages have you been using?*
> **Bob:** *It changes a lot. But for me, a big one is "What's next?" It's like I mock it.*

This is going to be so helpful to Bob. He's not regurgitating some self-talk message I gave him. He's looking for messages that match his competitive spirit, and pretty quickly he adopts some excellent, aggressive phrases of his own. This is exactly what you need to do, too: find messages that fit you. Remember, using an aggressive tone with Anxiety is not your only option. You can even take on a more submissive stance by begging Anxiety to give you more distress, or pleading with it to make you more confused and intimidated.

It's clear that Bob's inner monologue has changed. He's as introspective and contemplative as he was a week ago, but now his thoughts are less fearful and more *strategic*. He's asking himself how he can get the most out of this experience, how he can adapt and personalize this experiment to get the best results in the shortest amount of time. It's wonderful to see this quality in Bob in his second session. It shows a resolve that surpasses simply committing to the work. He's learning to become the architect of his own treatment. "Doc, I did everything we talked about—and then I tried *this*, too!"

> **Bob:** *I tried to be mindful of when I'm starting an action that tends to be a trigger. One for me is when I'm going to the closet to change my clothes. That's an activity that triggers a lot of my obsessions.*

This "mindfulness" is something you can adopt as well. Be alert when you're approaching a scene where you tend to worry, and then mentally prepare yourself for how you want to respond. Because once you enter the scene, once you begin the activity, you will become more vulnerable to your worries, and it will be harder to break out of the pattern.

Let's say you're afraid of having a panic attack in public, and you decide to practice walking through the mall alone, this time without the crutch of your cell phone. Before you get out of your car in the parking lot, remind yourself of how you want to manage your fear. In the same way, if you are about to practice taking an elevator, before you step into the building, remind yourself of how you want to handle your anxiety. If you wait until you're standing in front of the elevator or the entrance to the mall, your anxious feelings and worries may get overwhelming. Plan your moves before you get there so that you're ready when they show up.

Like a quarterback discussing tactics and what he's learned from his experiences on the field, Bob explains what he does now when approaching that fearful activity.

> **Bob:** *For me, a big thing is vocalizing it to myself, actually saying it aloud. I will say, "Okay, I'm ready. I'm going to do this. I'm going to change my clothes now. I know I'm going to feel anxiety. I know things are going to come at me, things I don't like." And, I'll say, "I'm ready for the threats." And then I'll talk directly to OCD. "Let it go. Let them come. Give me your threats. I'm ready. I'm ready for whatever comes my way." I actually get pumped up about it. I try my best to feel that competitive spirit. Because I know it helps to talk to yourself. But you gotta feel it, you know? When I actually do it that way, I don't get a lot.*
>
> **Reid:** *What does that mean? "When I actually do it, I don't get a lot"?*
>
> **Bob:** *When I start the activity, after having that mentality, I don't get a lot of obsessions.*
>
> **Reid:** *Oh? What do you make of that? Let's make some sense of that.*
>
> **Bob:** *I can get a little scared, especially if it catches me off guard sometimes. But for the most part, if I can really take that mentality,*

then I tell myself beforehand, "I don't care what threats I get. I don't care what happens, or what obsessions come, or how much something bothers me, I'm not going to act on any threats I get." I say, "I'm not playing this game." I say, "You want to go? Let's go." I say, "Give it to me; give it to me. Let's go."

The best moments for me are when Bob relishes his tactical maneuvers—when he shares a clever approach or a devastating blow he delivered to Anxiety. It's natural for him to derive some enjoyment from this. In fact, I encourage it. Because that means that the man who was crippled by his obsessions, who couldn't get himself to sleep without a complex and exhausting ritual, is now taking the dominant stance. He's taking charge, and it's evident in his posture, in the assurance in his voice, and in the way he illustrates his encounters with Anxiety. Bob is eager to share more discoveries.

Bob: *A few of the days I started even getting to the point where I mocked it a little more. I'd say, "I can't hear you. I can't hear you anymore." Sometimes when an obsession slips through, it does shock me a little bit. But then I'll say, "That's a good one. That's a good one. Now give me more. Give me another one. What's next? What are you going to do? Let's go." And then I tell myself, "I'm going to keep doing what I'm doing, and I can handle this." Even before I start changing my clothes, I'm having that attitude of "Come and get me." You know what I mean? I feel I'm ready for it. And at least these last two days I have actually let a lot of those obsessions be there without redoing anything.*

Reid: *What tends to happen then?*

Bob: *The obsessions tend to dissipate, as long as I keep that mentality, and as long as I don't back away. Some of the obsessions do hang around longer. But if I continue that mentality as I go through the day into my next activities, they all dissipate.*

Are you listening to this? It's quite important. Bob doesn't say, "When I talk to OCD like this . . ." He doesn't say, "When I talk to myself like this . . ." No. He tells me, "When I take on this *mentality* . . ." That's the key. He is trying on a new *point of view*. He's taking on a fresh *orientation* toward his problem. He's shifting his *attitude* about how he is going to tackle this difficulty. And that's when I know he's getting a taste of what it's like to win. At that moment I say to him, "Now, if you'll keep that attitude the rest of your life, you've got it made."

Another crucial message is here. Bob is not just testing out a new frame of reference. He is committing himself to stay on course. Right now he is determined. No matter what he experiences, he's not going to fall for OCD's message. I encourage you to follow Bob's lead. If anxious worries have a grip on your life, make a strong-minded commitment to break that hold. Listen to Bob's expressions: I don't care what threats I get; I'm not going to act on any threats I get; I'm going to keep doing what I'm doing; it dissipates as long as I don't back away. Bob's sending you a message: Learn to become unyielding in the face of your fear.

Remember, Bob was deeply entrenched with his OCD, and he was able to accomplish all of this with only twenty minutes of instruction. One of the keys to his success is that he makes the protocol his own. He's not complying with a set of instructions handed to him by some psychologist. He listens to what I say, he chews on it, and then he metabolizes it. Who knows how long he can maintain this stance in the face of OCD, but for this first week he's got it.

The same goes for Mary. I gave her only about thirty minutes of instruction before she took it on as her own. As she was approaching that parking garage, she ran the logic through her mind as a reminder of what she needed to do. She deliberately entered that garage to face her fears. When the threat didn't become strong enough, she went right toward the most threatening location she could find. Far from withdrawing, she literally drove her car toward her doubt and discomfort!

You are receiving far more guidelines on how to challenge Anxiety than Bob or Mary did. If they can do it, then I'm certain that you can, too.

Anxiety is going to pitch you uncomfortable physical symptoms and insecurity about your future. It wins if it can get you to worry, to avoid threatening activities, and to fight the symptoms with the hope that they will go away. If you can switch that up and purposely encourage Anxiety to increase those symptoms, and if you can act as though you want them rather than dread them, you can begin to turn the tables. This is just one more way for you to discover that when you do anything other than resist symptoms, they begin to fade on their own.

PART THREE

Make Your Play

CHAPTER 21

You're Going Where?

Having an optimistic approach to life is not so much about believing that only good things will happen to you. One might call that a rather naïve outlook. Instead, true optimism is about belief in a successful outcome, or even the *possibility* of that outcome. It's why you don't stop watching your child's soccer match after the first half, even when their team is down four to zero. In those remaining forty-five minutes lives the possibility for resurgence, for the ultimate comeback, for the statistically impossible match-winning score of five unanswered points. Optimism is an inherent trait within all of us, and it materializes in moments big (e.g., feeling like you aced that job interview) and small (There will be a vacant seat on the subway!). Even those among us who might identify as pessimistic can learn to emphasize the positives and possibilities as we gaze into the future.

Obviously, I have no way of knowing your unique circumstances. Maybe you worry more than you would like, and you can't remember the last time you felt optimistic. Maybe your worries have become a nuisance, and you are looking for some fresh ideas on how to scale them back. Or perhaps you have a single fear that gets in your way, and you're ready to put it behind you with some new knowledge, a few tactics you learn here, and some courage. Mary's concern fit into this category. She wasn't overwhelmed by her anxiety, but it definitely got in her way. Here's what she said early in our first session:

> I get panic attacks and anxiety about feeling trapped in small places, especially like flying, which is really inconvenient because I love to travel. But it takes so much out of me just to get there. I'm afraid at some point that I'll stop flying, and I don't want to. I love to travel. I want to keep that option.

Mary's life was generally going quite well, but she felt motivated to take back this territory of closed-in spaces. If, like Mary, you have some specific arena that needs some work, this chapter can certainly be helpful to you, because we all have to see the advantages of pushing past our fears. But what if your struggles are more significant, affecting a broader range of your activities?

WHEN ANXIETY IS IN THE WAY, BIG TIME

How much trouble has Anxiety caused you? Can you see the opportunities you've missed out on: the invitations you've declined, the promotions and prospects you've passed up, or any other ways you have had to limit your activities? If Anxiety has run roughshod over your life and is limiting your freedom, then we need to take down this bully.

Bob belonged in this category. OCD was dramatically restricting his lifestyle, causing him to be late for work, limiting his social activities, preventing him from quality sleep, and injuring his self-esteem. Read what he wants:

I would love to have large goals, for my career and things like that. But, honestly, at this point I just want the simplest things. I want my mind back. I don't want to constantly feel like I'm going crazy. I want to be able to watch TV and not worry about some word coming up that will make me have to turn on and off the TV, or change the channel a million times, or get into some crazy, weird, complex ritual. I just want to be able to put on my clothes and go out and be happy and be excited about what I'm doing. My work is something I love. I'm so passionate about my work. I'd love to be more excited about that. But this problem cuts my excitement in half.

Bob made a commitment to his future. In essence, he said, "I have a powerful desire to get my mind back and my life back. That goal is so important that I am willing not to engage in my rituals and then risk being preoccupied with these terrible thoughts all day. If it makes my day miserable, that's the price I'm willing to pay." Only when he is willing to risk that feared consequence can he truly regain control of his life.

If Anxiety has intruded upon your life for a long time, imagine how life might have unfolded if you had never become tethered to your need for comfort and certainty and security. What would you have done differently? Would you have gone back to school or started your own business? Would you have conducted yourself differently in your relationships with others? Have your happiness, self-esteem, and general well-being suffered under the reign of worry?

Hey, why not take a moment to jot it all down. Ask yourself, "Which arenas of my life have suffered because of my anxiety?" Grab a piece of paper and write down your list of answers to the question "What have I missed out on?"

I'll help stimulate your thinking with a series of questions.

✧ Did you have trouble applying yourself in school? Did you end your education early?

◇ Did you miss out on any fun, recreation, pleasure, and happiness?

◇ Did you struggle with your faith or spirituality?

◇ Have you been limited in your community life or your ability to contribute to others?

◇ Has your work or career suffered? Do you wish you could have mastered certain skills?

◇ Has your financial security been jeopardized?

◇ How has Anxiety influenced your interaction with your family and friends? What kind of sibling have you been? What impact has it had on your role as a life partner or parent? Have you been able to hold up your end of these relationships?

◇ What about sleep, diet, exercise? Have your worries and anxieties influenced how you take care of yourself?

◇ How have your struggles affected your mental peace, confidence, and self-worth?

Now that you've read through the questions, I know what you're thinking: *Huh, that's an interesting idea. I'll come back to this later. I'll just read on and get the essence of what he's trying to say in this chapter. I didn't buy this as a workbook.*

My response: Come on. Since you've started reading, how many times have I asked you to stop and write something down? Right, this is the *very* first time. I promise it won't take that long. Plus, you and I are going to use what you write down as a jumping-off point in the next few paragraphs. So can you stop reading momentarily and do this for me, please? I'll wait.

[Musical interlude]

Hey, welcome back. How did you do? As you can probably see, Anxiety doesn't produce a private suffering without external consequences. When you limit your actions, you influence the world around you, your ability to show care for others, feel love, act productively, and make contributions, engage in a spiritual community, and so forth. Anxiety may be holding you back more than you ever realized.

Now, how about we create a transformation? Let's convert this list from "What I've Missed Out On" or "What I Would Have Done Differently" to a new list of intentions about *your future*. Let's call it "What I'd Like to Be Able to Do Differently in the Years to Come." (It's a long title, I know, so feel free to abbreviate.) Think of this as a list of experiences you want to move toward in your life. Perhaps, as you feel the freedom that comes with managing your anxiety, you will *want* to go back to school. You will *want* to repair a broken relationship. Or you will *want* to be happier, more social, more outgoing. You will *want* to regain your self-esteem. Make this the blueprint for the life that lies ahead. Make this a list of what you're fighting for. Because you're not fighting *against* Anxiety; you're fighting *for* the good life.

All of this can be summed up into what we'll call your "outcome picture." Outcome pictures reflect the values we want in our lives, the confidence to go out into the world and try new things, the social skills that may need some fine-tuning, etc. *The outcome picture reminds us of what we're fighting for.* "I want this future [outcome picture] strongly enough that I'm willing to face this [doubt, awkwardness, insecurity]."

Every time you take on a challenge and think, *I want this struggle right now*, it will be genuine, because you believe taking on the struggle can help lead you to any or all of the positive outcomes you desire in your future, whatever they might be:

Time	Relationships
Energy	Continuing education
Confidence	Productivity
Mental peace	Success
Family ties	Financial security
Happiness	Self-worth

If you decide to act courageously, what exactly will you fight for? Are you clear that this goal is *worth* fighting for? For any of us, our desired goals need to be bigger than our fears. That's how we gain our courage and determination.

To stand face-to-face with the threat is a difficult assignment. Stepping forward can seem too big and intimidating. But if you can simultaneously see past it, to the other side, where you have a chance to take back your life, you will gain strength. Ambrose Redmoon, a beatnik in the fifties and a radical hippie in the sixties, expressed the task well: "Courage is not the absence of fear, but rather the judgment that something else is more important than one's fear. . . . To take action when one is not afraid is easy. To refrain when afraid is also easy. To take action regardless of fear is brave."* As Redmoon conveys, you are not here to do the easy stuff. Nor are you here to back away whenever your fear becomes strong. This is a competition between two different mind-sets within you. And you are here to learn how to be brave and then apply a new mind-set.

If you really *want* that outcome, whether it's better relationships or more time for fun, education, or mental peace, we have a path to get you there. But, of course, you also have to want to do the work along the path. If it stands in the way of your desired future, then push into what you're afraid of. Invest your time and effort. The point of view to seek is "I truly want this outcome in my future. If pushing into this threat is what it takes to get there, hard as it may be, I'm going to do it. As I head toward my positive future, I'm going to take on whatever is in the way right now. And then I'll move to the step after this one. Until I arrive at my goal."

---

*Ambrose Redmoon, "No Peaceful Warriors!" in *Gnosis: A Journal of the Western Inner Traditions* (1991).

How do you motivate yourself? How about this equation: motivation = strong outcome picture + determination + courage. If you can create an outcome picture that has high value to you, and if you can feel determined to get there, and if you are willing to act courageously, then you will have greater strength to step toward the threat. You also have to trust that the strategy I am laying out in this book can help you get there. If you do, then it makes sense for you to *want* to do the hard work of this plan. That's what we're looking for. "This work is hard. And I welcome the hard work. Because it gives me the best chance to reach my prize."

Figure 9. Facing the threat can feel too frightening.

Figure 10. Your outcome picture will motivate you to push into threat.

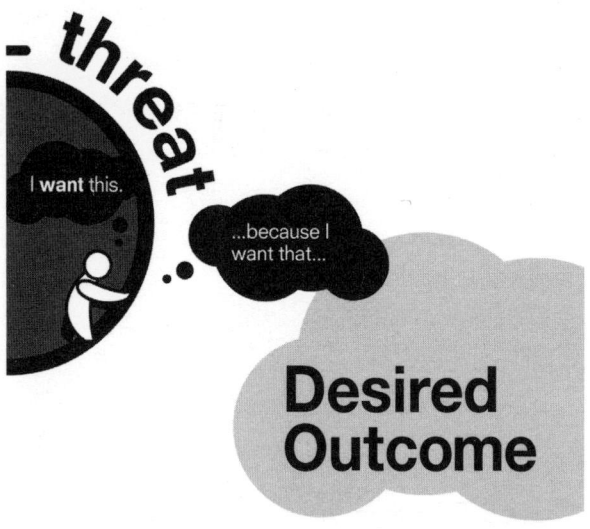

Nice work! You've got a hold on your desired outcomes, and throughout the book you've studied our plan to get you there. Now we'll narrow our focus to the specifics of how to make your play in this competition. In the next two chapters we'll tie down your personal strategy, including the important tactic of what you say moment-by-moment as you step toward the threat. Then Chapter 24 will put that strategy into the context of today's cutting-edge research on the process of change. And then . . . you play! Chapter 25 will tell you how.

CHAPTER 22

Plan Your Strategy

When it comes to preparing for competition, I want to take after the greats. I look to champion mixed martial artist Ronda Rousey. I summon the spirit of fierce tennis competitors like Roger Federer, Venus and Serena Williams, and Andre Agassi. Michael Jordan and Muhammad Ali. These powerhouse athletes dominated physically, but they also prepared relentlessly off the court and out of the ring. They walked into each match with a set strategy and a complex understanding of their challengers, equipped with a set of skills to help them succeed. And that's precisely what we should be doing for you. Throughout this book we have established the rationale for our strategy. Now let's touch on the highlights, because we must get you ready to play.

KNOW YOUR CHALLENGER

When we compete, we can increase our leverage by studying our challengers. If we know their typical moves, we can anticipate those moves and counter them, just as Annette Obrestad does at the poker table. Anxiety has been studying *us*. It's been watching the playback, learning how we behave, how we react. It's figured out how to hijack our weaknesses, our vulnerabilities, and our needs. Anxiety takes advantage of our instinct to protect ourselves from harm, especially after we have been traumatized in some manner. It becomes powerful by capturing our natural responses to threat, exaggerating them, and turning them against us. With all that information in hand, it constructs and delivers to us a set of beliefs that views our current difficulties as "threats" and reminds us that we don't have what it takes to face them. Those beliefs direct us to back away instead of step forward.

What are Anxiety's typical moves? One of its most formidable ploys is to keep us confused as to which worries are signals and which are noise. When our default position is "I gotta know for certain," then we are at its mercy. If you believe you should feel threatened because danger is likely/big/looming, then you are supposed to be preoccupied by your worries until you decide to back away. But you can't win your life back by backing away.

Our focus here is *not* the legitimate concerns that cause you to shift into emergency mode, or even to analyze a problem so you can generate solutions. Instead, we are addressing how you mistakenly label a noise as a signal, either because you are missing information, or because you have a psychological tendency toward that kind of worry, or both. Treating your noisy worries as though they are signals is the worst move you can make, one that *guarantees* you will lose. You need to do whatever work necessary to move your specific worries—whether it is fear of heights or panic attacks or contaminants—away from signals and over to noise so you can apply all the other tactics of this book.

Since Anxiety's biggest scheme is not to let you *know* if your worry is noise, and to convince you that you *must* know, then there will be times when you need to act as though an anxious worry is just irrelevant noise, even though you can't be certain. Anxiety isn't prepared for you to step forward with such courage. That's why it's a cunning move. It defies your challenger's expectations.

If you want to win this competition, then put the Laws of Motion on your side. Keep acting in ways that are opposite of what Anxiety expects; that will force it to change direction. Courageously step toward what scares you so you can do the important work of purposely choosing to feel insecure, uncertain, anxious, clumsy, and awkward. Embrace those feeling states. Make a significant and powerful shift in your point of view so that you can act in a counterintuitive way. Welcome what you fear.

YOUR FIRST MOVE AND YOUR LAST

Anxiety needs you to operate in the world while holding on to one or more of these points of view:

- ✧ be sure everything's okay
- ✧ get back to feeling comfortable
- ✧ treat all fearful thoughts seriously
- ✧ stay safe
- ✧ feel confident before acting

Anxiety will control your actions as long as it can keep you committed to these positions. Your work is to detach from them whenever they get in your way. That's no easy feat! But let's place them within the context of our pendulum. Check out Figure 11, and notice those five attitudes on the left side. Anytime you notice yourself backing away when you want to be stepping forward toward your positive future, look for how any of these viewpoints are restraining you, and work to detach yourself from them. Each time you hear your noisy worries start up, your first move is to detach from those worries and swing over to the new stance. When you let go of your commitment to protect and defend yourself, you will create a natural momentum that moves you toward the life you want.

Figure 11. Swinging over to a new stance.

Be sure everything is OK
Get comfortable
Treat fearful thoughts seriously
Stay safe
Feel confident before acting

Seek out doubt
Provoke your discomfort
Treat fearful thoughts absurdly
Aggress into new territory
Scare yourself

threat

Protect & Defend

Courageously Step Forward & Risk

DETACH

The simplest action you can take is to start that swing by labeling your fearful thought ("There's my worry again") and accepting that it has shown up ("It's fine I just had that thought") as a way to begin detaching from it ("I'm going to treat it as noise and let it go"). Figure 11 depicts using your energy to swing through detachment over to engagement. I'm not saying it will be easy. In fact, it will be hard, but it's also not complicated. Notice, detach, and then engage. Engage in what? In the principles that help you courageously step forward and take a risk:

✧ seek out doubt
✧ provoke your discomfort
✧ treat fearful thoughts absurdly
✧ aggress into new territory
✧ scare yourself

Step forward into whatever action you want to engage in. Yes, you may continue to feel anxious and doubtful as you swing into action. That's one of the reasons why you need courage, because you are stepping forward when a part of you still remains scared of the threat.

Imagine for a moment that you are literally swinging across on that pendulum, from the "protect and defend" stance over to the "courageously step forward and risk" stance. You will pass through a period in which you are letting go of—detaching from—all these tried-and-true positions you are well-acquainted with and have felt so protected by. Two points are important here, and they come in the form of good news, bad news.

First, the good news. It is vastly easier to grab on to a new stance when you have already let go of the old one. Your hands are free; you're not grasping on to the old ways; you're not arguing about the merits of each side. Letting go will free you up to make a change.

Now the bad news. After you've let go of your old point of view and before you've grabbed on to your new one, you are floating through the air without a point of view! Stepping toward the threat without your usual protections can be quite unnerving. You'll be scared. So grabbing a new point of view in so dramatic a fashion can require a great deal of courage during your first few attempts. Once you've tried it out a number of times, you begin to feel more confident in the benefits of the new strategy. But until then, you have no experience to lean on. You are operating only on the courage of faith and trust. On top of that, you are attempting a paradoxical move, one that on the surface seems illogical. So that makes it even tougher. Do it anyway.

When you are as strong as you need to be, your *last* move, the one you will repeat numerous times, will be to detach from the noise of those positions on the left side of the pendulum. They are going to pop up, and that's fine, because worries are a natural part of our life. You may still worry that everything won't go according to plan, and you may still have the urge to feel comfortable before you step forward. But your worries will no longer dominate your decisions about taking actions. You will hear them, accept them, and detach from them. "There's my worry again. It's fine I just had that thought. I'm letting it go and stepping forward."

But *don't wait* until you are strong to begin this process. *Anytime* you notice your noisy worries or your urge to avoid, starting now, experiment with simply letting them go and stepping forward. Sometimes it will work, and sometimes it won't. That doesn't matter. You still have all of our other tactics available. But I highly recommend that you spend time with Chapter 9 so you can develop the skills of being mindful of the moment and ultimately learning how to detach.

Got it? Great! But all of this is critically important to our work, so I'm going to explain it to you again.

SWING INTO DETACHMENT

Your first time flying can be a terrifying experience. Reading the overview on the TSNY (Trapeze School New York) website, you're told to expect a "truly unusual experience" involving an instructional, two swings, a knee hang, and something called a "catch." You're stuck on that word *catch*. Even more terrifying is the photograph of a woman gripping the wrists of an instructor in midair.

Of course, the folks at TSNY are accustomed to the fears of first-time flyers. So immediately after you sign their liability waiver, they go through the safety procedures and introduce you to the equipment. They place the harness snug around your waist, show you the cables, explain how the double-spotting system works, keep you clipped in on the platform, and direct your attention to the giant safety net that is beneath you at all times. And before you know it, you're twenty-three feet above ground, moments away from leaping to your death (okay, not really). You're prepared for the exercise: you've got chalk on your hands, harness around your waist, cables clipped on. You're warmed up and wearing the proper clothes. You're ready to follow the instructions: step up to the edge of the platform, grip the bar with one hand, grip it with both hands, bend your knees, breathe . . . and jump.

"There may be one moment of fear just as you commit your body to the task. Once you're off the platform it's all bliss."*

That's it. That's how you do it. I'm not agreeing to the "it's all bliss" thing. But if your goal is to get off the waiting platform, that's how you get off. Before you step into the action, you make a decision to act. You choose to act. Then you swing into action. You don't allow yourself to rethink the whole decision. (Although a part of you will actually do that, but you're not going to pay attention to that part, right?) You step out of your comfort zone and into the action. You will feel afraid, especially just before you step out. So expect that, accept that, and do the best you can to keep moving.

Anxiety needs you to feel intimidated and then respond by backing away. Anxiety needs you to step off the platform, climb back down the ladder, and opt not to participate. Therefore, your job is to feel intimidated and step forward into the action . . . and not just step forward, but step forward *while you feel intimidated*. As you step into the challenge, you can allow yourself to doubt that you have enough skills and yet *act as though* you have enough skills.

Let go of your comfort and swing out into that doubt, awkwardness, insecurity, and distress with as much determination as you can muster. By the second (proverbial) swing, step up to that platform more aggressively, accepting the idea and sensation of discomfort. Eventually you will work toward a "no lines" swing, i.e., one without safety cables. Way back in Chapter 3, I spoke about safety crutches, and those are the same crutches we're talking about now. The more you practice, the

---

*"Welcome First Time Flyers," TSNY, Trapeze School New York, n.d., *http://newyork.trapeze school.com/classes/Welcome1stTimeFlyers032504.pdf*

more prepared you'll be to peel off those safety crutches, to unclip those harnesses, and to just take flight.

Your most powerful first tactic is to detach from your fearful, protective stance. No arguing in your head! If you stay attached to your noisy worries, then you will find yourself arguing back and forth between two equally strong positions. Don't do that! Let go. Swinging over into this neutral position can be frightening because, well . . . you're in neutral. You aren't holding on to your old point of view, and you haven't yet grabbed your new viewpoint. In trapeze school, that's what's involved in a catch. Your job is to let go of the bar, experience the split-second floating in midair, then grab on to the instructor's wrists. You will have the urge to swing back to the comfort of certainty. You won't be alone in this urge, because we all know it. Who in the world wants to feel a sense of detachment, except those who want to grow stronger in their skills. So let me say again. Detaching from those six dysfunctional points of view will enable you to grab on to the mind-set of strength.

Learn to detach. Practice detaching again and again. Because then you can swing unencumbered to a higher level of abstraction, away from specific thoughts about your specific event, over to the paradoxical stance of wanting whatever you are afraid of. Anxiety uses your specific fearful content only to get you to resist by activating any of the positions on the left side of that pendulum. Your task is to swing over and *up* to the level of courageously stepping forward into risk. Grab on to that mind-set so you can compete on equal footing with Anxiety. Think of it as a three-step process, as illustrated in Figure 12. First, step back and notice your unhelpful point of view, expressed in self-talk and backing-away actions, and let go of it (which will definitely scare you). Second, maintaining your sense of detachment, grab on to a more courageous mind-set of "I want this." And, third, now that you have detached from your old stance and grabbed on to that "I want this" mind-set, step forward into your threat.

Figure 12. How to make your play.

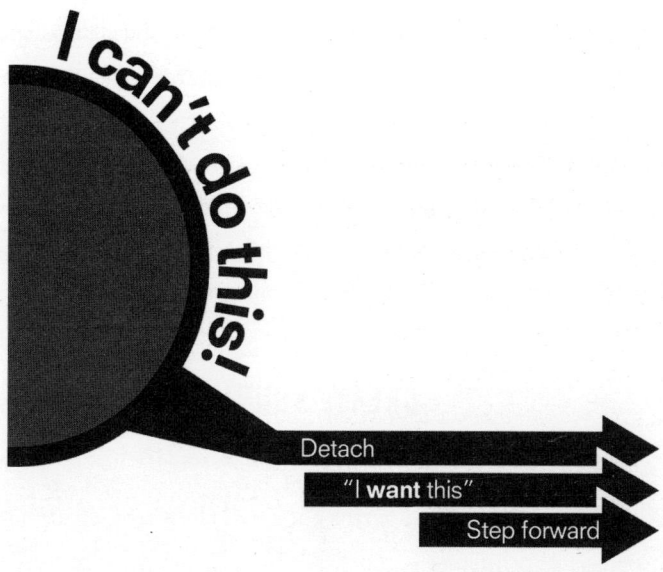

You remember that new want-it mind-set, right? We established it in Chapters 10, 11, and 12. Let's reminisce. Mary's issues with her heart and with suffocation, the profound toilet episode, the powers of your mind's working memory, embracing the wild roller-coaster ride, Cousin Don's "challenge accepted" stance during charades, Patrick's Tae Kwon Do competition, people who live on cobblestone streets, the purposeful instability of the Wright Flyer, and my former client with social anxiety who, tongue firmly embedded in cheek, said "What I really want is to *trip* on my way up to the podium, *stutter* the entire time, *blush* excessively, and have an extremely bad case of the *hiccups*." All of these stories reinforce this stance of *wanting* to feel the difficult feelings and *wanting* to do the hard stuff. This is the courageous "want it" mind-set.

In any of the activities related to your noisy worries, the work (if you choose to accept it) is to courageously step forward and take a risk. That might mean that you simply keep moving forward without responding to the noise in your head. But if you struggle with that forward motion, swing over to grab a mind-set on the right side of the pendulum. Purposely choose actions that will stimulate your doubt and provoke your discomfort. When those fearful thoughts pop up, treat them absurdly by ignoring them. Courageously decide to scare yourself by aggressing into new, unfamiliar territory. When you grab on to those commitments, you have a chance to win back the territory that Anxiety has been controlling.

CREATE YOUR OWN PRINCIPLES OF ACTION

With all you have learned in this book and elsewhere, create a simple and broad set of principles you believe should guide your actions as you step toward difficulties. What are the important components of getting stronger? Given what we know about the nature of anxiety and our relationship with it, what do you think you ought to do?

Our buddies Mary and Bob serve as good examples. Over the course of two sessions, Mary worked hard to experiment with new ideas, and she courageously immersed herself into the threat of her parking garage practice. At the close of our second meeting, I posed a question: "Imagine that ten people are coming in to see me tomorrow who face similar kinds of fears. What would you say are the most important principles they should apply if they want to get stronger?"

Mary had no trouble generating a list. Based on what we had discussed and, even more important, what she had experimented with in the sessions (like two pillowcases placed over her head and taped around her neck!) and in the parking garage the previous night, she promptly stated her five guidelines.

Mary's Principles

1) **Face your fears in small ways that you have control over**.

2) **Gradually do these things longer**.

3) **Then do the harder things**.

4) **Talk yourself through it in a really strong, commanding voice**.

5) **And talk to your primitive brain**. Let it overreact, and then say, "I like your expression, but you don't have to juice me up so much next time. I'm fine; save that for real situations."

Notice that she doesn't refer specifically to the fears of flying or claustrophobia, although she has been applying these guidelines to both of those problems. She has discovered *general* principles she believes will carry her forward. Anxiety is a master of disguises and can morph into a wide variety of threats. Her list of principles can be applied to lots of different forms that Anxiety may take in the future. And that's just what I wanted to hear.

I love her last item, and I recommend you include something like it on your list. She lets her body get aroused. That's how her amygdala will learn that it is overreacting. If she were to approach a cross-country flight or a dark tunnel on the highway with the self-message "I can't let myself get anxious here," she would stay stuck. And Mary is not interested in staying stuck.

What about Bob? When I asked him about the important components to getting stronger, he didn't regurgitate any of my messages. As you listen to our dialogue, perhaps you can pick up the sense that he has taken ownership in these principles. He's not just listing mantras to deliver to himself and to Anxiety; he's talking about taking on a new *mentality*. He wants to shift into a new *attitude*. Like Mary, his messages are a manifestation of that novel point of view.

Bob: *A big thing for people with OCD to remember is that you need to try something new. If they've been trying all these other ways their whole lives and there's no improvement, then why not try something else? It's like when I'm working with a patient. If we never try something, we will never know whether it can help them.*

Reid: *And what is it that they should try?*

Bob: *They need to take on the mentality of saying, "You know what? I'm going to be okay with experiencing uncertainty. I'm going to be okay with anxiety being in my life. I know things are going to bother me, and they're going to continue to bother me. It's okay for things to bother me."*

Reid: *So you're saying, "They're going to bother me, but they're not going to stop me."*

Bob: *Yeah. I think a big thing is to say, "No matter what I'm doing, I'm going to keep moving. I'm not going to let this OCD take up any more of my life." Because as I'm practicing, I'm saying, "Bring it on. Let's go. Game time. Come out and play." And as [OCD] backs down a little bit or actually surrenders, I've still got to tell myself, "Well, keep moving. Keep moving." As I'm grabbing my clothes or changing or grabbing my bag, I keep telling myself, "Keep moving."*

Reid: *So that sounds like another principle, which is, have things you say to yourself that represent . . .*

Bob: *I would say to take some of those phrases that you gave me and make them your own. For me, I'm seeing a result from it. You've got to motivate yourself. Even though getting your life back should be enough motivation, sometimes somebody with OCD is so depressed and down that they think, "Well, it's too hard to challenge it. It's too hard to fight it."*

Reid: *So then what should they do instead?*

Bob: *They have to make a decision. "Am I going to be depressed and lie here, or do I have something to live for?" They need to say, "Take on the challenge. Do it. Don't hold back." Do you know what I mean?*

Notice that he starts with the principle of acceptance. Instead of fighting to get rid of his obsessions, he makes it acceptable for them to exist. Then he's chosen to talk in a more cunning way to Anxiety. Most important, he tells himself to keep moving, to be in action.

Bob's Principles

1) **Make a decision.** Ask yourself, "Am I going to be depressed and think about how much of my life has been wasted by Anxiety, or do I have something to live for?"
2) **Try something new.** Take on the challenge. Do it. Don't hold back. If you never try it, you will never know whether it can help you.
3) **Take some of those self-talk phrases and make them your own.**
4) **Remind yourself:** "I know things are going to bother me, and they're going to continue to bother me. I'm okay with anxiety and uncertainty in my life. In fact, I invite them."
5) **Keep moving.** Don't let this problem take up any more of your life. Tell yourself, again and again, "Keep moving."
6) **Talk to Anxiety:** "Bring it on! Let's go. Game time. Come out and play."

Take whatever time you need to think about and then write out your personal principles. Because it's just about time to get specific about how to play this game.

THE GAME STRATEGY

You and I have studied a great deal together, and now we have all the pieces of a strategy. I'm going to describe a specific game for you to play. The *only* function of this game is to train you in the tactics of our strategy.

On the surface it appears as though you are playing against Anxiety, and I am going to continue to portray it that way. More accurate, though, the competitors are two different points of view. Yes, they can both reside within you, but they are *not* you. They are points of view you can hold onto or let go of. The first one makes you vulnerable to Anxiety. The second one initiates your independence.

> **The first:** "I need to protect myself and others from getting hurt." Then, "So I *should* worry about this. It just seems too risky," or, "So I shouldn't *do* this. It just seems wrong and unsafe."
>
> **The second:** "I will purposely and voluntarily choose to let go of these worries," or, "I'm going to push into these difficult tasks, because then I will get closer to the goals that are important to me."

In this competition, our mission is to put this second point of view in control, to make it take precedence over the first. We're not going to get rid of that first point of view ("I don't want this"). Part of our strategy is to permit it to live on inside you, but it no longer gets to dominate your actions (or lack thereof).

Let's assume that up until now you've been acting according to Anxiety's rules. Now we're going to play our own little game. Here are the primary components of our strategy.

Continuing to *think* about this stuff is not going to cut it. Your competitor *loves* it when you start worrying, because it knows how to dominate your judgments, opinions, and beliefs. You cannot win this game through thinking. The thinking game is over. This is a competition of action. The only way you will win is by shifting your point of view so that you can *step forward*. It's true that you need to change some of your thinking, but those new thoughts will always be *in service of* your actions. Your objective is to change up your thoughts and then change up your actions.

If you find yourself continually mulling over what you should do and waiting for the right time to do it, that should be a red flag warning you that Anxiety is dominating yet again. Figure out how to get all that thinking out of the way so you can act on your best interests. If you don't feel *ready* to take action, find someone to coach you. (More on how to find a helpful coach is in Appendix A: Need Coaching? Get Treatment.) You must be in action if you want to get stronger.

Your actions are to be paradoxical. You need to move in the direction of what you fear so you can move through it and on toward what you want in life. Simultaneously, your job is to want whatever is happening *right now*. It's certainly paradoxical to move toward something else that you want and at the same time accept what you are experiencing in the present moment, which is often something you don't like. Yikes! And yet, that's precisely how you win.

The Game Strategy

- *Thinking* about this stuff is not going to cut it.
- Your actions are to be paradoxical.
- It's not how big or small a step you take. It's that you take a step toward the threat.
- Only do what you want to do.
- To get stronger, you *have* to want to do the hard stuff.
- There will be times when you must "act as though."
- When you don't know what you want, want *that*.
- Hold fast to your strategy as you step forward.

It's not how big or small a step you take. It's that you take a step toward threat. Keep moving forward. You can't win unless you move forward. You can take the slightest action in a forward direction as long as you expect that small step to generate some unpleasant doubt and discomfort. You lose by standing still or backing up while you think, think, think.

Only do what you want to do. This stance is one of the cornerstones of our strategy, and I first talked about it in Chapter 12. Don't work on this stuff because you have to, or because you need to, or because someone has told you that you should, or because you think it's the right thing to do, or because you've read these directions. All of these may be good reasons to take action: you have important goals, this difficulty is in your way, you know you should work on it, you know it's the right thing to do, and everybody says you should do it. Nonetheless, when you do step forward into the difficulty, step forward only because you want to *in that exact moment.* Even if you're about to try something quite difficult, and even if a part of you is saying, "Don't do this," find that executive voice that says, "I want to do this." Then begin the action. And throughout the entire task, keep stepping up to the stance of "I want this."

If you don't want to practice, then don't practice. If you don't want to do something difficult, then don't do it. If you want to avoid, then avoid. Obviously, those decisions have consequences. Nonetheless, only do what you want to do.

To get stronger, you *have* to want to do the hard stuff. Let me say again, "I want this" is a cornerstone of our strategy. It's also another paradoxical tactic. Who in their right mind would want to do actions that cause them to feel awkward, clumsy, unsure, and insecure? Hmmm. Well, I can name a few we've already talked about: rock climber Chris Sharma, gymnasts Paul Hamm and Kerri Strug, boxers Muhammad Ali and George Foreman, children who want to learn to dive, and students of

Tae Kwon Do. Of course, Mary and Bob belong on the list. So does cousin Don. And so does champion swimmer Michael Phelps (whom we'll discuss in Chapter 25).

Figure out how to willingly and voluntarily choose the difficult tasks. The message-to-self that will give you the biggest leverage is "This is hard, and I want to do it."

There will be times when you must "act as though." Let me state the obvious. In the future, you are going to approach lots of difficult situations with reluctance, because you're just like the rest of us. I encourage you to act as though you want to step toward them. What does that mean? It sounds like I'm asking you to pretend that you want to do the hard stuff. That's not quite it.

Consider for a moment how you behave when you actually *do* want to take an action. Let's say you want to take a friend out to the movies tomorrow night, and you expect that you both will have fun together. Imagine how you will now behave. Will you procrastinate on calling her, running the risk that she will have already made other plans? Or will you call her in a timely fashion? How will your tone of voice sound when you invite her? Will you sound hesitant? Or will your voice convey eagerness? Will you pick her up on time? Or will you drag your feet? What will your basic attitude be as you think about going? Given a choice between "ugh" and "I'm really looking forward to this," which one expresses your feelings about this outing?

That's what I mean by "acting as though." When any of us believes an action is absolutely the right step to take, and when we want to take it, then we move forward with positive expectations, timely stepwise decisions, and an upbeat tone. We willingly choose to step forward. That's how I suggest you approach your difficult task. You *don't* have to like it, and it may very well be unpleasant, but freely choose it—want it—because you decide that it is an important step toward what you want in your future. That's why Chapter 21 precedes this one, because you need a positive goal that is bigger than your fear. Then you should use that desired goal to pull you *into and through* your fear.

Choosing to "act as though" is another exceedingly important cornerstone of our strategy. If you need a refresher about its value, please review Chapter 18, "Act as Though This Is Such a Clever Tactic."

When you don't know what you want, want *that*. You might be one of those people who gets stuck obsessing on this: "Do I *really* want this goal? What if I start moving down this path but it's not the right one? I'm just not sure." Here's my advice about this stall tactic. If you are confused as to what you really want to do, then *want* your present experience. *Want* that confusion, then take action anyway. *Choose* to feel muddled, and step forward into your day. Welcome your uncertainty. "I'm going to move into action even while I feel unclear if this is what I want." That is an example of paradoxically accepting the current moment as you move toward the future. Whatever experience you are being subjected to, purposely and voluntarily choose to be subjected to it. Don't bother wasting time fighting it. Act as though that's exactly what you want to do or feel. Then take your next action.

I guarantee you that Anxiety won't know how to respond if you approach an activity while engaged in this kind of attitude. And that's what we want: to put Anxiety back on its heels for a change.

Hold fast to your strategy as you step forward. Once you decide how you want to apply your principles to any given difficulty, hold fast, because Anxiety will challenge your resolve. Expect that the closer you get to the difficult situation, the more doubts you will have about sticking to that plan and the louder that voice inside you will yell, "This seems like a *VERY* BAD IDEA!" In fact, that voice is typically a cue that you are on the right track.

As any of us becomes more frightened, our minds tend to regress to a defensive mode. *Of course* a part of you is going to want to back away! (This can't be news to you at this point in the book.) As you become scared, do your best not to question the tactics you've chosen. Act as though you are simply the player in this momentary drama. Since you are also the writer, producer, and director, you have given yourself, the actor, a script you wrote during the planning phase. You will hear that loud voice inside you saying, "Don't do this! Keep doing what you've always done." Stick with your script anyway. The writing's good! Don't argue in your head about whether or not to go forward. Don't allow your executive voice to be on equal footing with your frightened part. As I described earlier in the chapter (see Figure 12 on page 295), detach from the voice that tells you to escape, regardless of how loud it might get. Feel free to be mindful of that defensive voice. There's no need to block it out. You can acknowledge it, but just don't allow it to control your behavior. Swing over to your courageous side and keep stepping forward.

As you will learn in Chapter 25, the only way to win this competition is to become *bothered* by worried thoughts and anxious feelings. But it's poor strategy to allow that moment of threat to alter your plan. Generate firm rules for what you're going to pay attention to and how you are going to act, and then follow those rules resolutely during those threatening moments.

CHAPTER 23

Change Your Voice

To override your habitual, built-in fear response, you must make a firm and conscious decision to adopt a new point of view. What would that attitude be? Consider this one: "I want to practice going toward what I'm afraid of." Once you've established your orientation to this work, you will then need to remind yourself of your intention as you meet up with your resistance. In this chapter we are going to develop what you can say to yourself *based on this shift in your attitude*.

If you are afraid of heights and your fear includes standing next to an open railing a few stories up, do you believe you can't withstand this anxiety? Do you want to overcome your anxiety so you don't let your intimidation stop you when you're near open railings? Then that defines your strategy: to work on tolerating your anxiety of upper-floor railings. Once you've made that decision, start creating some messages that will manifest that strategy. As you decide to practice standing near a railing in order to provoke your distress, you can offer yourself supportive and instructional messages such as, "Go ahead and step forward. Grab hold of the railing. You can do this," or, "You can handle feeling this anxious. Just linger here a while longer."

If you want to work on overcoming your fear of driving on highways, you might spend thirty minutes driving between two exits, turning around, and driving back, again and again. You might offer yourself a number of messages during this time:

"It's okay to merge now. Go ahead and gather up speed."

"I can handle this anxiety."

"Put on the turning signal now."

"I can take a break at the exit if I want."

"I'm doing great."

"Ten more minutes and then I'll have done it!"

Let's say you're worried about work or school performance and you had one of these thoughts:

✧ I have to be sure that I succeed. What if I fail? What if I'm demoted?

✧ I can't make a mistake, but I think I just did. This could be a *big* mistake. Oh, no!

✧ I'm not smart enough. I don't think I'm going to figure this out. But I *have* to figure it out.

✧ I didn't study enough. I'm worried that I won't get an A on this test.

✧ I can't do poorly in that presentation, because if I do, I'm sure I'll be fired.

✧ What if I don't have enough money?

If you believe that any of those thoughts is a signal, then your job is to problem solve, just like we talked about in Chapters 5, 6, and 7. But if you decide that these thoughts are noise, or that you are going to act as though they are noise even though you aren't sure, then your next move is to welcome them. You can say anything to yourself that reflects the stance of "It's fine I just had that thought. I expected it, since I'm moving toward something difficult."

Next, subvocalize a message that helps you return your focus to your chosen activity. You can offer yourself any or all of these three types of responses: encourage yourself, instruct yourself, or talk in a cunning way to Anxiety.

Giving yourself encouragement will typically involve reminding yourself that you can tolerate doubt or distress and to do so moves you toward your desired goals. So you might say, "I'm willing not to know whether I'll succeed," or "I can handle being scared about making a mistake." You could tell yourself, "I can keep going even though I feel insecure," or "I *want* not to know if I'll make an A. Now I'm practicing my skills." Or maybe you say something like, "It's good that question just popped up. And now I'm not going to answer it. I'm looking to tolerate doubts about money."

TAKING A STAND

All messages-to-self should come from what you've decided is your best strategy. Don't just pick from my list of self-talk suggestions in this chapter. You can certainly look through the list for those that resonate with you. But shape them over time into messages that help you to step *toward* the struggle as opposed to avoiding or resisting. The wording is entirely up to you. Our goal is to support and guide each of your actions through a clear and simple instruction ("Speak up now") or motivating message that supports your actions (e.g., "This is hard, and I can do it"). You may say it reluctantly ("Ugh, I need to keep exercising if I want to stay healthy, so I'm heading to the gym now"). You can even try saying it sarcastically ("Oh, I am *so* excited right now to have my heart pounding through my chest"). But that message still needs to serve as a reminder. And if you are delivering a message as an instruction, it should be firm enough to empower you to move forward, just as my brother did while he learned to run those hills ("Pick up the tempo!").

You might learn new information about the challenge you face, and that will influence these self-statements. As I talked about in the earlier chapters, make sure you correct any misunderstandings. Then you can remind yourself that what you thought was a signal is really noise. As you read in Chapter 16, Mary decided that suffocation was not an issue she needed to pay attention to. So as she entered that garage and faced one of her biggest threats, she told herself with a commanding voice, "It's not going to be pleasant, but there *is* enough air, and I'm *not* going to suffocate." She delivered that statement as an expression of a newfound belief stemming from what she learned in her treatment session earlier that day.

We're going to create these new messages for you because—yes, you guessed it—you're already operating from Anxiety's set of old messages that in the past might have been helpful: "Get out!" "Don't do anything unless you are sure you figure this out." "Tense up!" "Avoid!" "Run!" As soon as you encounter the threat, that powerful belief system of "avoid doubt and discomfort" will arise automatically from your unconscious and generate those avoidant messages. You need a competing response at the ready. Your conscious intention must counter your unconscious urge by encouraging you to step *toward* the problem, like, "Stick with it. Power through. Stay the course." Think of them, if you will, as bite-sized mantras you can put in your pocket and pull out whenever you approach a feared situation.

MOMENT-BY-MOMENT

Let me again make one point perfectly clear. Your new and improved messages won't *replace* the outdated ones that are telling you to run in the opposite direction. That's too high of an expectation. You can't simply give yourself an instruction to step forward into the threat and then assume all your worries and resistance will fall away. As you will see when you try it out, you have to talk to yourself frequently. Assume that while you're feeling afraid, all those pleas to "get out" will spontaneously and repeatedly sound off in your mind, and they will be joined by an urge to stop the action, just like what happened to me when I got panicky in the boat. Again and again and again, as you keep stepping forward, you'll hear a voice that says, "Step back!" Our new messages are designed to come immediately *after* any instruction to run. At that moment, mentally detach from that instruction and give yourself the "step forward" message.

Let's return to the scene of my panicking while rowing. Do you remember the mental exchange? I had to *continually* encourage myself to "keep going," because even as I followed that instruction, I remained scared. My fear immediately generated another demand, "Stop this madness!" And I had to quickly counter it so I could continue to move forward. (Actually, you row backward, but that's beside the point.) This is just what it's like, a moment-by-moment challenge between the urge to escape our distress and our intention to push forward. That's how it's going to go for you, for me, and for everybody else who wants to take what seems like a significant risk.

We are *not* removing your obsessive voice. We're not trying to extinguish it. We are bringing up a parallel voice and then elevating it so that it becomes the executive voice, the one in charge. You need to separate yourself enough from your worries to recognize them as irrelevant, even harmful, noise. Then detach yourself from them and absorb yourself in the messages of your executive. This is the principle of absorption and detachment we talked about in Chapter 15. To pull your attention away from one stimulus, it is best to redirect your attention to your new frame of mind. To move forward, you need to detach from the instruction to escape. Yes, notice your fearful thoughts. Yes, hear them, but then step back from them. Instead, absorb your mind in self-talk that manifests the principles of change, the ones that will make you stronger.

SHIFTING YOUR ATTITUDE UP

When you are ready to experiment with all this self-talk stuff, consider trying out one of these three messages. They all reflect a change in attitude. They come from above the fray of the moment and above the specific content of your fear.

✧ *"This is a good opportunity to practice."* When you're feeling clumsy or awkward and you start thinking that you want to pull back from an activity, rise up above the urge so you can give yourself a message from one level above the fray. Even while you're feeling quite uncomfortable and you want to escape, remind yourself that this is a chance to push through your urge to avoid so you can generate an opportunity to learn a new skill.

✧ *"I want to be uncomfortable here."* Feeling uncomfortable is a sign that you are stretching your boundaries out of your safe zone. As you notice yourself struggling, rise up to a level of perspective that allows you to welcome this insecurity, because you have to tolerate such discomfort in order to grow. The message "I want this" is the opposite of what Anxiety needs you to say: "I don't want this."

✧ *"I'm going to handle this."* To expand our territory, all of us need to tolerate clumsiness, embarrassment, and big and little mistakes. The reason you stay the course in the face of doubt is because of your positive intentions. To reach your goals you have to pass *through* difficulties instead of always backing up in the face of them. When you give yourself this message, it doesn't imply that you *know* how you're going to handle the struggle; it says you are going to *act as though* you'll be able to handle it. This simple message reflects the central theme of the work: "This is hard, and I want to go through it anyway, and I'll find a way to handle it."

So play with the expression "This is a good opportunity to practice." As soon as you're in a situation where your heart starts racing and your knees begin shaking, remind yourself that this is the perfect opportunity to practice responding to these threatening circumstances in a new and helpful way.

Try out the intention behind "I want to be uncomfortable." For that stance, look for opportunities every day to leave your safe zone and welcome insecurity.

See if you can live into the message "I can handle this. *This is hard*, and I can handle it." Be willing to withstand the disturbance that worry will generate from time to time.

Remember that your work is first to mentally step back in those threatening moments, then step *up* one level of abstraction, where you will find the principles of getting stronger. Following are some of the biggest principles we've covered:

- ✧ Anxiety needs you to back away from challenges. You *have* to take risks to get stronger. Permit yourself to risk failing.
- ✧ Expect that you will feel uncertain and uncomfortable as you step forward. It comes with the territory, and it's a sign that you are working on the right stuff. Anxiety needs you to feel intimidated by doubt and discomfort when they show up.
- ✧ The closer you get to the challenge, the more those scary but unhelpful worries will show up. They will *feel* as though they are signals, and they will instruct you to step away and to protect yourself from danger. You must learn to detach

from those messages. You are going to hear them, but don't believe them.

✧ *Want* whatever insecurity or discomfort shows up. *Want* to take on challenges. *Seek out* the tough encounters. These are the attitudes that give you power.

✧ You'll be dominated by Anxiety if you keep seeking perfection. Willingly choose to feel awkward and clumsy and to make mistakes as you engage in any challenging new activity.

What might you say to yourself to manifest these principles as you are stepping toward your challenge? The chart "Examples of Self-Talk" will give you an idea of how your self-talk might sound.

Examples of Self-Talk	
PRINCIPLE	**SELF-TALK**
Anxiety needs you to avoid. To get stronger, take risks, including the risk of failing.	"I want to do this, even though it feels risky. I want to get stronger."
To step forward, you need to feel uncertain and uncomfortable. Anxiety needs you to avoid those feelings by *not* stepping forward.	"It's okay that I'm anxious right now. I can handle not knowing how this will turn out. I need to do this. I'm glad I'm doing this, even though it's hard."
The closer you get to the challenge, the more your noisy worries will show up. They will *feel* as though they are signals of danger. You must learn to detach from those messages. Don't fall for them.	"I expected these worries would show up. I don't need to pay attention to them. But I do need to tolerate this anxiety that they're generating."
Want whatever doubt or discomfort shows up.	"Good. I want these feelings, even though they make me really uncomfortable."

Want to take on challenges. *Seek out* the tough encounters. That attitude gives you power.	"This is really scaring me right now, but I want to keep going. I can handle this."
You'll be dominated by Anxiety if you seek perfection. Willingly choose to feel awkward and clumsy as you engage in any challenging activity.	"I've *got* to feel awkward before I can feel competent. And I want to master this."

SCORING WITH SELF-TALK

Anxiety will deliver some strong messages about how you should keep worrying about this topic or how you should back away from anything that seems the least bit risky. Once you hear those messages or feel the pull to back up and avoid, that's when to kick into gear. There will be plenty of times when the most important response is to tell yourself how to step forward. You may need to say something like, "Ignore that and get back to work." At other times, a few words of encouragement can keep you going: "I'm going to get through this." The chart "Examples: Self-Talk to Encourage or Instruct" gives you some samples of how to offer yourself supportive messages or instructions. Notice that one even expresses excitement about getting to "score a point." That's foreshadowing of our next chapter, when we convert all of this into an action game.

Examples: Self-Talk to Encourage or Instruct		
NOTICE the Noisy Worry	**THEN** Encourage Yourself	**OR** Instruct Yourself
I didn't study enough. And if I don't get an A on this test, I'm screwed.	I can handle not knowing. It's okay to be anxious right now.	I'm letting that thought go now. I'm going to pay attention to question three.

If my heart starts beating too fast, I'll panic.	I was looking for an opportunity to get scared like this.	There I go again, scaring myself. I'm going to focus on finishing this run.
Am I certain my hands are clean?	I *want* not to know right now. Plus, I get to be uncomfortable! That's what I'm looking for!	Don't answer that. Step away from the sink and walk out of the bathroom now!
What if there's a spider out there and I don't see it? That's freaking me out!	This is exactly what I want, another chance to feel scared about spiders.	I expected those worries because I'm practicing now. Now let's see if I can find another web.
What are they thinking of me? I'm probably disappointing them.	This lets me practice feeling unsure. Plus, I get to score a point!	I'm not answering that question. I'm going to focus back on the presentation.

Consider experimenting with some of the self-talk given in the chart "Motivating Messages." Keep in mind that the only way they are beneficial is if you embrace the point of view from which the message is created. For instance, saying, "Let go and let God" implies that you actually want to stop trying to control everything and you want to practice trusting that all will work out in the end. So telling yourself to "Let go and let God" will assist you only if you believe the message.

Motivating Messages			
I'm willing to feel unsure *right now.*	I *want* this to feel intense.	I can handle this.	I *want* this to stick around.

I'm willing to feel anxious *right now.*	Gimme your best shot!	I can take the heat.	I want my life back!
Be scared and do it anyway.	This is a good opportunity to practice.	Seek out discomfort.	My job is to move forward.
Go *toward* what scares you.	Love the mat.	I want this.	Choose active over passive.
Do the *opposite* of what Anxiety expects.	Seek out uncertainty.	I must risk.	I'm *willing* to feel awkward and clumsy.

TALKING TO ANXIETY

We are personifying Anxiety as your challenger who gives you that uncertainty and distress. If you want to make a really cunning move, talk directly to Anxiety.

Focus on asking Anxiety to produce even more insecurity and more discomfort, more fearful thoughts, more questions that threaten you. In other words, request the absolute opposite of what you would typically request. When you hear yourself say that message of resistance, "Oh, no . . . ," shift your attitude and deliver the message, "Oh, great! That's a wonderfully scary thought. Could you suggest a few more ways I might fail?" or, "Please make me more [uncomfortable, scared, confused, intimidated, embarrassed], and could you get it to stick around longer, too?"

This tactic starts the same as any of the others. You notice that you are now bothered, then you shift your attitude to want this experience instead of resisting it. Now the new part: you respond by sending

Anxiety a message that's opposite of what it expects, like thanking it for stirring you up and asking it to give you more. Then put your attention back on your desired activity.

If you've been in cognitive-behavioral treatment (CBT), you may have learned the instructions of traditional exposure practice, where it is *your* job to keep yourself anxious and worried. Not here! It's true that you have to *initiate* contact with the circumstance that generates your anxious worrying. Everybody has to do that to get stronger. But once your doubt or distress shows up, turn over to Anxiety the task of maintaining or increasing those unhelpful thoughts and feelings. Bob, for instance, sets up the possibility of hearing an obsessive thought by standing in front of his closet as he prepared to change his clothes, or by turning on his TV. OCD then gives him an upsetting thought and provokes his urge to fix the thought so it doesn't plague him the rest of the day. That's what he is looking for, the urge from OCD. Now he can say, "That's a good one. Now give me another one. Let's go."

Here's the caveat: There is only one exchange in this transaction. Anxiety signals that you should feel threatened, and you respond by saying you aren't threatened enough and to please give you more. Once you make this request, you are done with the transaction. No matter what happens next, this exchange is over. You are finished with it. You got that? You are not having a *conversation* with Anxiety. You instruct it or make a request of it or give it a demand. Essentially you are saying, "I will tell you what I want, and it is not open for discussion." But do it through your courage. And once you send your message, that transaction is over. To the best of your ability, bring your attention back to whatever you *want* to be doing in the moment. Get back to studying, or crossing the soccer field, or opening the can of soup.

Once you have put your attention back on the current activity, be prepared for those moments when Anxiety grabs your attention yet again. This will often occur within a matter of seconds. What do you do then?

Just repeat the same steps: notice it, want it, make a cunning request of Anxiety (you can thank it for stirring you up and ask it to give you more), then turn your attention back to your desired activity. (Oh, by the way, CBT and exposure practice are the gold standards of treatment for anxiety and OCD. If you hate my suggestions, just throw them out.)

Your job is *not* to get rid of your dread and insecurity. It is to change your response. You get stronger by allowing yourself to experience these reactions without resisting them. One of the best ways to do that is to disrupt the pattern that's been established by Anxiety. The chart "Examples of Talking to Anxiety" provides different ways to address a message directly to Anxiety. Notice that some of these are simply declarations that you are enthusiastically embracing your struggle. If you become uncomfortable, feel *pleased* that you are now distressed. "Yes! I scored a point!" Don't worry, Anxiety is listening.

Examples of Talking to Anxiety	
Notice the Noisy Worry	**Then Respond in a Cunning Way**
I'm afraid I won't have enough money.	Yes! I scored a point!
If my face turns red, I'll be humiliated.	Oh, thanks for that! Would you give me that thought again?
If I don't know how crowded it's going to be, I'm afraid to go.	Excellent! Could you scare me more, please?
I think I felt a bump. Did I just hit someone? I've got to find out!	All right, OCD! Thanks for showing up. I was looking for another point. Keep them coming!
What if he's not the right one? Maybe my soul mate is still out there. But then what if I break up with him, never meet anybody else, and lead a sad, lonely life?	Is that the best you can do? Can't you throw a little more fear of God into me? Come on . . . bring it!

You can create your own messages to Anxiety using a simple formula. Use Figure 13 like a menu. Think of requests as appetizers, the increases as entrées, and the threats as dessert. You can mix and match courses. "Plead" for "scarier" fearful thoughts or "invite" Anxiety to give you "more frequent" heart palpitations. The manner, style, or volume of your provocation need have no limit. The choice is entirely yours. You can demand Anxiety to make you feel worse; you can beg it; you can sweet-talk, rough-talk, condescend, command, cajole, goad, joke, or bray. You can execute the order like a drill sergeant or like a mother instructing her child to go to his room. Your goal is to pass the job over to Anxiety to make your symptoms worse, by whatever means and tone of voice you prefer. If you get stuck, remember that you can always ask for more: more self-doubt, more mistakes, more physical manifestations of the fear, etc.

Figure 13. How to talk to anxiety—the formula.

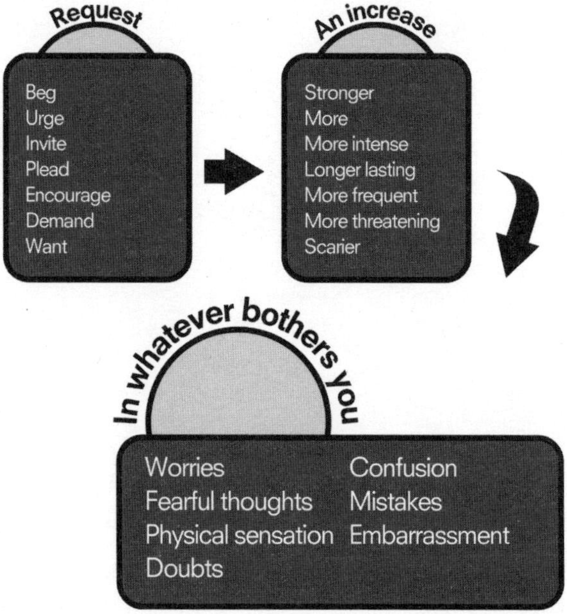

Request

Beg
Urge
Invite
Plead
Encourage
Demand
Want

An increase

Stronger
More
More intense
Longer lasting
More frequent
More threatening
Scarier

In whatever bothers you

Worries   Confusion
Fearful thoughts   Mistakes
Physical sensation Embarrassment
Doubts

The best part of all of this is not the nature of the paradox (instructing Anxiety to give you more of what you fear) but what results from diving into this extreme experiment. When you deliver a clear, paradoxical instruction, you give yourself an opportunity to discover the possibility that Anxiety can't live up to the challenge. Moreover, you'll learn that in some instances—SPOILER ALERT—the threatening symptoms begin to fade. So get ready for a surprise gift in the form of a powerful, sudden flash of insight: "I don't have to resist Anxiety!"

Figure 14. The paradoxical moment—"Please give me more."

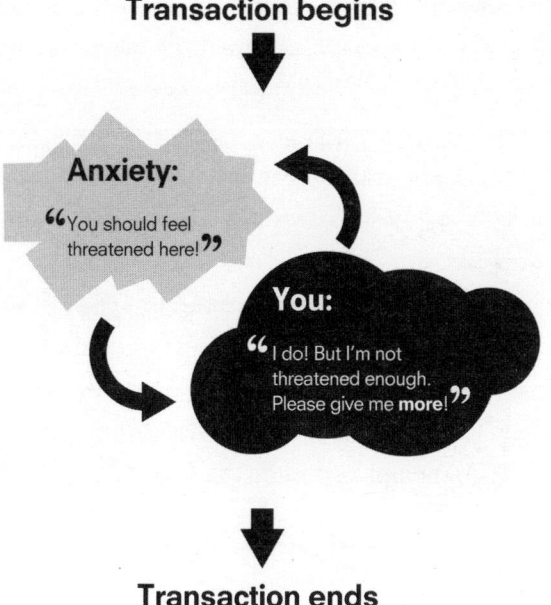

Your sole responsibility is to change your responses to the stimulus of doubt or distress, and that's what we're doing here. Now swing your attention back to your chosen activity. Absolutely *do not* check to see whether it's "working," because your definition of "working" tends to be that your symptoms are reducing or your worries are quieting down. Here's the proper definition of whether it's working: you are following the instructions about what to say, and then you are turning your attention back to your valued task. Don't wait to find out how Anxiety responds. Don't even *care* if Anxiety responds. And how your body and mind respond to your instructions is none of your business, either. This is a critical component of the intervention, and it is where most people stumble. (So I'm going to say it all over again in the next chapter.)

Once you place your mind back onto your chosen activity, if your fearful thoughts or sensations grab your attention again, consider that as a brand-new transaction. Your focus has just been disrupted by your challenger's message: "You must pay attention to this scary possibility!" Thankfully, your job is simply to repeat the same steps: notice what's happening; welcome the opportunity; speak directly to yourself or Anxiety; and then swing your attention back over to your current activity.

When you are practicing any of these tactics, I suggest you take this stance: "I don't care how many times that symptom, that insecurity, that doubt shows up right now. I'm going to continue to respond in this way." When you deliver these messages to yourself or to Anxiety, it represents the attitude shift, "I'm now going to treat these thoughts and feelings *as though* I don't care if they keep interrupting me. Each time it recurs I'm going to consider it another opportunity to run my protocol. The doubt and distress do not have to go away. I can handle them if they stay."

PLAY AGGRESSIVELY AND SCORE POINTS

In the last chapter I asked you to develop your personal principles of action, based on all you have learned so far, and I then outlined the best strategy for this competition. In this chapter we conducted the important work of translating these principles into messages of encouragement as you move into action. We also talked about the value of creating instructions you can deliver to yourself as you get scared so you can override the messages of escape. You have the option to turn them into commands if you need a stronger message. And when you want to be even more cunning, you can make direct requests of Anxiety.

All of this surely must seem radical. But when any of us gets stuck in a pattern we haven't been able to break, we *must* act more aggressively. Timid play is a losing strategy.

Where are you heading with all this action? Your intention should be to move *through* Anxiety, not around it, toward your positive goals. That's why Mary drove into the parking garage, and that's why she took that flight, to provoke her fears so that she could get stronger and fly with more ease. If those goals you created in Chapter 21 have high value to you, then they will be worth all of this effort.

CHAPTER 24

Shift Your Attitude

W ell, it's nearly time for you to start acting on all we've designed together. After all these pages of information, ideas, and suggestions, I will ask you to shift your attention to a radically simple game in which you score points by becoming bothered and then changing what you say inside your mind at that moment. I firmly believe that if you join me in this competition, you have a chance to win. What I'm suggesting is such a fundamental shift in your thinking that I want to place these instructions in their proper context. I promise you, I am not pulling this strategy out of thin air. Rather, it is backed by over fifty years of research science and aligned with the trailblazing concepts and practices of some of the top theorists in our field. After thirty-five years of my own work with those struggling with anxiety, I believe the most important change you can make is to shift your attitude and to express that shift through your emotions moment-by-moment.

We have made giant leaps in our understanding of how to produce change in people who are anxious and worried. In 1958, a South African psychiatrist named Joseph Wolpe created a procedure called systematic desensitization, within the fledgling field of behavior therapy. Dr. Wolpe discovered that if he could teach people a psychophysiological state that was opposite of fear, he could help them recover from their phobias. What procedure did he create that was counter to feeling afraid? He taught his patients to overcome fear by becoming relaxed.

Imagine for a moment that Dr. Wolpe was working with people who are terrified of spiders. He would teach them how to relax, and once they were calm, he would present them with a minor representation of the phobic object—in this case, perhaps a black-and-white drawing of a spider. When they then became anxious, he would remove the drawing and help them relax again. After several repetitions, seeing that drawing became tolerable, and he would introduce something slightly more threatening, like a larger color photo of a spider. Eventually the patients would become capable of tolerating the presence of spiders in real life.

In the 1960s, Dr. Victor Meyer experimented with a different approach while working with patients who were diagnosed with OCD. Aware that their tendency was to perform rituals to allay their fears, he took the opposite tact. He prevented them from engaging in their rituals, forcing them to remain in contact with their fears for a prolonged time. His successful experiments produced our first breakthrough in the behavioral treatment of OCD.

Do you see the similarity in these two groundbreaking approaches? Wolpe focused on relaxation as the opposite of fear. Meyer focused on remaining in a distressed state despite the strong urge to avoid that distress. Both of these scientists studied the pattern in our responses to fear and then encouraged actions that were opposite of the pattern.

Now, after half a century of research and innovations, we know without question that all of us have the ability to access emotional states that are opposite of fear. If we can summon one of those new emotions as we approach a relatively safe event that threatens us, we can transform our experience. Today, at the cutting edge of our current innovations, we know the following about our psychophysiological response to feared situations:

✧ How you react in any moment is triggered by whatever personal meaning you express about the event: it seems safe; it sounds exciting; it's going to be boring; it looks dangerous.

✧ You may not even be conscious of that meaningful message. It can simply rise up in your unconscious without your awareness.

✧ Once you've engaged in that meaning, consciously or unconsciously, it triggers a cascade of responses that can show up in your thoughts, your emotions, your facial expressions, and other changes in your body.

✧ At that very moment, you begin to sense your emotion, whether that emotion is joy, interest and curiosity, excitement, disgust, or fear. You may suddenly notice that you feel excited, or you may register how scared you are.

✧ And if it is a distinct emotion, it will direct your actions. Anger kindles your urge to attack. Desire gives you an urge to approach. Fear stimulates your urge to escape.

Oh, hey, did you get that? Fear automatically stimulates your urge to escape. Desire automatically stimulates your urge to approach. Our job is to help you *approach* situations you perceive as threatening. Therefore, we need to help you access the *emotion* that encourages approach. When you feel threatened, your automatic response is to want to avoid. We don't need to stop that from happening, but we do need to undo the pattern that generates from your automatic response. How on earth can we do that?

TRANSFORMING YOUR RESPONSE

Your job here is *not* to get yourself to approach an unnecessarily threatening situation you have been avoiding. Of course, that is *part* of our project. But we have a more important task. To produce a more stable, long-term change, your task is to allow all the systems of your body and mind to make a shift as you approach that threatening situation. What if we help you cultivate interest, curiosity, and desire in the face of fear? To feel curious in the face of threat seems like an unreasonable suggestion. But it is also a simple action that can accomplish some complex tasks, such as to reset your belief system and to reset your body and mind's automatic responses. Is it a big and crazy task? Of course. Can you do it? Absolutely. How can you do it? By focusing on your moment-by-moment experience. That's going to be your play.

The best work you can possibly do is to generate meaningful self-talk as you approach your difficult circumstances, just as we discussed in the previous chapter. Self-talk is meaningful when it manifests an attitude you want to hold on to. Remember the four big tasks in our strategy? Step back, want it, step forward, and be cunning. Your job is to turn those four tasks into an attitude of commitment. "I'm going to step back and see this pattern of threat unfolding. Then I'm going to *want* whatever is happening in the moment. Then I'm going to step forward with a purpose in mind. And I'll be as cunning as I need to be in response to Anxiety's antics."

As you call up that attitude in the moment, your self-talk can support it as well as express it. Now you are doing the good work. You are manifesting an intention to approach instead of escape. To willingly approach in the face of an urge to escape is exactly what we're looking for. We have a growing scientific foundation that justifies this strategy. We are not looking for short-term change. We want to help you develop a lasting ability to face challenges with resilience.

What does overcoming this problem *mean* to you? Why is it *important* to bother with facing your difficulties? Once you have your answers to those questions, call up those desires as part of your intention when you step forward. As you choose to move toward your difficulty, if you can shift your focus to your *interest* in approaching and your *desire* to push on toward the unknown and the uncomfortable, and if you can repeat that pattern over time, you will develop an internal signal to approach. I promise that if you can develop this internal signal to approach, it will take you places you never expected you could go. And you will be stronger because of it.

How might your intention sound? "*I want this* outcome [a return to school, emotional connection with my family, greater independence, etc.]. I believe that purposely choosing to approach this difficulty will help me move forward toward that outcome. So *I want this* doubt and discomfort I am generating by stepping forward." You can literally call up the image of your desired outcome at the same time you are facing your difficulty.

Or you could frame your intention a little differently: "*I want to* explore the possibility that when I willingly step forward, I also compete with Anxiety's goal of getting me to step back. So I'm going to practice choosing to step forward, purposely and voluntarily, into this uncertainty and discomfort."

Both of these stances can be represented through self-talk as you approach the difficulty, as well as during and after it. Of course, there's no way you can go into a monologue about your intentions when you're in the midst of a threatening moment. Any reasonable facsimile of the message "I want this" can serve as a simple representation of your commitment.

But here is an important caveat. As we've discussed, when you choose to step forward into difficulty, it's highly likely that a voice inside you will say, "I don't want this." That message will instantly activate physiological changes. Your body will automatically respond to your resistance by producing fear, arousal, and the urge to run. Don't worry about that response. We *don't* have to get rid of that. In fact, when you feel your resistance, it can be a signal that you're working on the right stuff.

Let me take that a step further. Based on our most current scientific knowledge (which I'll share with you momentarily), our work *requires* your resistance. So when it shows up, that's good news! We want to activate the circuitry in the brain associated with your fear of the situation. That's the only way we can get access to that circuitry so we can change it. And we are going to change it by helping you to shift your attention once you recognize those moments. Again let me say, when you notice yourself resisting your intention to step forward, your response can be, "Good! I was looking for that feeling!" If you can swing your stance over to, "It's fine that I'm afraid. I want this," then you will begin to activate the physiology of approach. If you can master that, it is a profound change. Even by *struggling* to master it, you will change, because you will no longer be mobilizing support for that urge to run.

Dr. Barbara Frederickson, a brilliant, innovative, and award-winning positive psychology scientist, is also a colleague-friend of mine at UNC. Based on the conclusions she has drawn from years of research findings on the process of change, she might summarize it all by saying, "If you will pull up a positive emotion on the heels of these negative feelings, you can literally dismantle all that mental and physical preparation to run." That matches up with the work we've been doing about your self-talk. Your job is to learn how to tell yourself, when you're feeling threatened, such messages as "I want my life back," "I'm doing this for my family," "I want to get stronger," and, "This is going to help me."

Based on the significant results of her insightful research, Dr. Frederickson might also say to you, "If you will continue to call to mind your commitment to step forward and explore, and if you will keep acting on that commitment to absorb new information and experiences, you will build enduring personal resources in all your domains: physical, intellectual, social, and psychological." What does she want you to do? She encourages you to actively generate a positive meaning for why you are letting yourself generate feelings of threat. Once you become aware of that feeling, if you will step forward voluntarily (because you see it in the broader context of your life's goals and that reason has *meaning* to you), your intentions can transform your experience.

In case Anxiety has had you in knots for so long that you feel a little lost about where you want to go in your future and just want some relief in your daily life, here's the added twist to our work. Dr. Frederickson would say that simply changing your attitude during these moments of practice should increase the likelihood that you will be able to find positive meaning in your future. Why? Because negative emotions narrow your thinking ("I can't do this. Tomorrow's going to be just like yesterday. What's the point?"), and positive emotions broaden your thinking. So as you develop the ability to step forward toward each threat while holding on to a positive intent, you create a more powerful ability to entertain the possibility of a positive future.

GRABBING ON TO A NEW EMOTION

Dr. Leslie Greenberg is one of the most highly respected researchers in the psychology of emotion. He has spent the entirety of his thirty-five-year career studying how we can *change* our unhelpful emotions, so he definitely has something to teach us. Like Dr. Fredrickson, he uses powerful language to describe what's possible. With decades of research supporting his statements, he believes that once you access negative or maladaptive emotions, you can *transform* them by activating more adaptable emotions. Think about what he's saying. He has figured out that you need to first *access* your negative feelings if you want to produce change in them. And you're not just switching them out for a new feeling or sitting with them until they change. You're "undoing" them. That's a radical stance. But Dr. Greenberg is no maverick. In 2012, he won the American Psychological Association's Award for Distinguished Professional Contributions to Applied Research. In reviewing his findings, I consider this as the most important to us: When you let yourself become afraid, and then you call up a competing emotion, you can *transform* your fear reaction. That sounds a whole lot like what Dr. Frederickson is trying to convey, doesn't it? You can actually *replace* the emotions of withdrawal with the emotions of approach if you are willing to work at it.

You're not changing your emotions by *thinking* or *reasoning*. And you are not simply allowing the feeling, letting go of the feeling, or facing the feeling. This is not mere exposure or extinction or habituation, to use terms of our trade. You're changing your emotions by activating a competing *emotion* that expresses a competing *point of view*. Accessing a strong and meaningful desire to step forward will, over time, undo the neurochemistry, the physiology, and the experience of your fear. You will not be replacing your fear; you will be *undoing* its effect on your mind and body. How do you do it? Your job is to elevate your sense of willingness to embrace doubt and discomfort *while* you're feeling afraid. That will spontaneously begin to lower the primacy of your fear.

That's why when I ask you to express some reasonable facsimile of "I'm willing to feel these feelings," I am also asking you to mean it, to attach the emotion of wanting something onto that statement. *Want* to get stronger. *Want* to experiment with these new ideas. *Want* to go through this to get to the other side. *Want* that outcome picture you developed in Chapter 21. Even accessing feelings of self-compassion ("I know this is hard, but if I hang in there, I'll get through it.") can undo the desire to escape.

As Bob has described, when he is standing in front of his closet, putting on his clothes for the day, OCD hits him with a vengeance, giving him fears that he might stay preoccupied with this moment throughout his whole day if he doesn't take his clothes off and put them back on again. As he's practicing his new skills, Bob *thrusts forward* toward OCD. That is absolutely opposite of his usual recoiling behavior. He is violating OCD's rules while he simultaneously provokes his challenger: "Is that all you got? Give me your threats. Let them come." That aggressive stance is the start of transforming his fear and forging a new state.

IS IT COMPLEX? OR SIMPLE?

Boy, we PhDs can write some complex stuff. Have you ever tried to read one of our research publications? It's enough to make you want to chuck the journal articles we've toiled over into the nearest body of water. *But* our task here need not be so complex. Let me give you an example of what I mean about the possibility of *simple* change.

Dr. Alison Brooks of Harvard Business School conducted four intriguing experiments, reported recently in the *Journal of Experimental Psychology*, that support just what we've been talking about.* She asked the question: if people change their interpretation of an anxiety-provoking performance, what influence will that have on their performance? What if, instead of simply feeling anxious before the performance, a person attempts to conjure up a feeling of excitement? Physiologically, anxiety and excitement are quite similar in that they both tend to be felt before an event, and they both tend to generate high arousal. This could be good news, because if feeling excited produces a similar arousal as feeling afraid, and if feeling excited helps people perform, then they don't have to calm down in order to perform better. That makes the work of transforming their anxiety a *lot* easier. Imagine that you're approaching an important performance—let's say a big talk in front of a throng of people—and you're feeling anxious as you anticipate the event (as most of us would). If you now must *relax* in order to perform better, you will have to change your whole psychology and physiology to a non-aroused state. Imagine how much work that takes to shift from

---

*A. W. Brooks, "Get Excited: Reappraising Pre-Performance Anxiety as Excitement," *Journal of Experimental Psychology: General*, December 23, 2013.

a state of high arousal to one of tranquility. Wouldn't it be easier if you had to change only your *attitude* about being aroused?

In her first experiment, Dr. Brooks studied 113 subjects who were required to sing a karaoke song in front of an experimenter, and they were told that they would be paid on the basis of their singing accuracy score. She then divided the subjects into three groups. Just prior to singing, the experimenter asked each subject, "How are you feeling?" In the first group, each person was to answer, "I am anxious." In the second group, each person was to say, "I am excited." The experimenter did not ask the question of the third group. Analyzing the data, Dr. Brooks found that simply by stating out loud "I am excited," individuals actually reappraised their anxiety more as excitement and then improved their subsequent singing performance. The group with the weakest performances? Those who said "I am anxious" before they performed.

So maybe saying "I am excited" represents an emotion that is opposite of being anxious. What if they told themselves they were calm? Isn't that the opposite of being anxious? So in her second experiment, she tested that possibility by studying public speaking anxiety with 140 subjects. Each participant was given two minutes to prepare a persuasive speech. They were told that they would deliver a two- to three-minute speech in front of an experimenter and that it would be videotaped and judged later by a committee of their peers. Participants were divided into two groups. The first group was asked to begin by telling the experimenter, "I am excited," and the second group was to say, "I am calm." She found that those who reappraised their anxiety as excitement before the speech then a) gave a longer speech, b) felt more excited, and c) were perceived by evaluators as more persuasive, competent, confident, and persistent. Geez, that's a lot of benefit from one simple statement!

In a third experiment, Dr. Brooks moved closer to the sort of task I am assigning you in our competition with Anxiety. She recruited 188 subjects who were asked to complete a difficult math task under the pressure of time and were told that they would be paid based on accuracy. Three groups were created, and this time none of the groups were asked to verbalize anything before they began. Just prior to the performance, the first group was instructed to "try to get excited," the second group was told to "try to stay calm," and the third group was given no instruction. The results? The average heart rate of the participants remained high across all three groups leading up to and throughout the task. When the second group tried to stay calm, it had no effect on that group's ability to calm down. However, the group who tried to get excited increased their subjective feelings of excitement and performed better on the math assessment. Again, notice how little was asked of the participants, and yet they produced a significant change.

Her fourth experiment was set up in a similar way, but she took different measurements. Brooks found that when participants in an anxiety-inducing math performance were asked to "try to get excited," they changed how they perceived the event. They viewed it more as a challenge, as an opportunity, instead of as a threat. And that group improved their performance.

What can we take from Professor Brooks's studies? You might have thought that learning how to calm yourself is the best tactic to combat Anxiety. But calming yourself when you are about to perform is a major undertaking. You might want to call that tactic into question. And what if it's not necessary? What if you can perform just as well without calming down? Maybe, instead of working so hard to calm down, you will benefit more from changing what you tell yourself. If you experiment with the messages we've discussed, like, "This is hard, and I *want* to do it," you may be surprised at the results.

All of Dr. Brooks's subjects were college students, and none of them were diagnosed with anxiety. Her results are therefore interesting but not necessarily conclusive. Therefore, let me bring in the big guns in our field. Dr. David Barlow, founder of the Center for Anxiety and Related

Disorders at Boston University, is a colleague-friend whom I respect and have learned from my entire career. In my mind, Dr. Barlow stands beside Dr. Aaron Beck, the father of cognitive therapy, as one of the two greatest innovators our field has ever seen.

At the pinnacle of his career, what is Dr. Barlow studying now? He believes that we clinicians should not be paying much attention to the nuances of each anxiety disorder, nor should we be addressing each discrete problem faced by our anxious clients. We should be working on the Big Picture issues and, among other tasks, helping our clients learn to push forward and feel all the negative emotions that are triggered by their feared situations. He thinks one of our most important tasks is to teach clients how to step forward into their feared events in order to tolerate distress *in general* and not simply tolerate the specific distress of heights, public speaking, claustrophobia, or other specific arenas. Hundreds of researchers are now working to sort out which features of this universal protocol are the most essential. But I can assure you that they have already concluded that we need to be going toward, instead of backing away from, the unnecessary threats that stand in our way.

Who else is doing the most creative exploration in our field today? A longtime research collaborator with Dr. Barlow, Dr. Michelle Craske is Director of the Anxiety and Depression Research Center at UCLA and is committed to studying exactly how we can help those with anxiety achieve stable and long-lasting change. What is she discovering is the most effective avenue? To mess with the pattern!

Okay, that's my expression, not hers. But still, that's what she's doing. She is calling into question all of our existing assumptions about how to produce change. Her center is testing out such variables as the effect of labeling feelings at the same moment that you are experiencing them, of changing the order in which we introduce fears (instead of starting with lower fears and gradually stepping up to higher fears), and of frequently changing the length of each client's exposure practice. Craske's group is measuring what happens if they introduce more than one source of threat at a time, like two tarantulas instead of just one. Yikes!

And, within all that, they are exploring what happens when they encourage an emotion that is diametrically opposed to fear while the subject is facing a fear. For instance, in the midst of an exposure practice with someone who has a spider phobia, they stop long enough for the subject to watch a brief clip from *Charlotte's Web*. Why? Because in that movie, the spider is the hero, saving . . . well, I won't spoil it for you in case you haven't seen it. The intention of viewing that clip is to help the person access a feeling that is distinctly different from fear while facing the feared object. I assume you've already guessed that such a move enhances the subject's ability to tolerate the distress of sitting a few inches from a tarantula in its cage. In fact, her studies show that all these changes I just mentioned will strengthen a person's abilities.

This may sound like Dr. Craske is espousing a complex protocol for overcoming your irrational fears. But she's not. She's looking for the fewest, simplest moves we can make to help someone get stronger. And all the newest additions to her protocol involve messing with the pattern that maintains Anxiety's control. You and I have that same task in front of us now.

I'm about to teach you how to play a specific game to master these skills. In this competition, every time you score a single point against Anxiety, you will be winning. And you score a point by doing what it doesn't expect: by pushing toward doubt and thrusting yourself into the fray, especially while feeling intimidated. Don't wait until you *believe* you can handle whatever Anxiety might throw at you. You need to act as though you believe. Act as though you can *survive* the symptom, the mistake, the embarrassment, the failure, or whatever it may be. That's how you build strength. And in time you will believe in yourself.

CHAPTER 25

Make Your Play

Truth be told, I'm not all that great at the coach's pep talk before play begins. But in the spirit of competition, listen up.

As you take everything you've learned here, make it your own, and put it into practice, I want you to know that you can't expect to be perfect. You won't be perfect. You will stumble. The most you can ask of yourself is that you bring your all to this competition and that you commit yourself fully to the rules of the game. Only then can you determine if this strategy will truly benefit you. I'm excited to see what you'll discover.

Whenever you are ready to take back the territory that Anxiety now controls, you can apply the strategy laid out in Chapter 22. Your job is to turn those guidelines into an attitude that you take with you, right into any difficulties. But if you want help calling up this new attitude—if you find yourself pulling back from challenges or approaching them with clenched teeth and noisy worries—then I've got just the game for you. It will train you in tactics that apply our strategy moment-by-moment until these moves come more naturally to you. It has a highly specific set of rules to help you take back control. Every aspect of this game reflects the principles I've laid out in this book.

Ready? Here's how you play:

There's only one play in this competition, and only one point can be scored in that play. The play begins and ends in a brief few moments.

Yes, you are engaging in tasks with the intention of completing them, whether it's dinner with friends, driving to an appointment, or locking up the house before a weeklong vacation. But in this competition you are to use challenging activities primarily as a stimulus to generate doubt and distress. Your objective is to practice often and to pair up your awareness of any moment-by-moment doubt and distress with new messages and actions that reflect our strategy.

You complete each play by turning your attention back to your chosen task. That's when you score the point. As you are moving about your activities, you notice that you are bothered by Anxiety's intrusion. You will then respond (as described below). Once you respond, your job is to turn your attention back to your chosen task. That's the play, and that's one point. Once you've completed a play, you're ready for Anxiety's next disturbance, so you have a chance to score again.

You can score a point in three ways. Your job is to score *as many points as possible*. Keep moving toward tasks you predict will generate at least some degree of uncertainty and distress regarding your worried theme. (For example, if you tend to worry unnecessarily about finances, then whenever you look over your online bank statement or review your monthly budget, you can seek out opportunities for noisy worries to show up.)

Whatever you choose to do, you will have chances to score points before, during, and after the task. When you *notice* yourself feeling *bothered* by your worries or anxiety, you've taken the first step, which is to mentally step back and identify the opportunity to score a point. At that moment you have three ways to respond, and these reflect the self-talk we developed in Chapter 23:

1) Subvocalize a meaningful message that supports your intention.
2) Instruct yourself to take an action.
3) Talk to Anxiety in a cunning way.

Then turn your attention back to your chosen task, even while you still feel uncertain and uncomfortable. Great! You've scored a point!

In our example . . .

1) Tell yourself something like, "I can handle this anxiety." (encouraging message)
2) Say, "Fine, my worry just showed up. Now I'm going to put my attention back on balancing the numbers." (instruction to act)
3) Or say, "Hey, Anxiety, thanks for disturbing me! Stay with it!" (cunning and paradoxical retort)

Whatever you might say, your next move is to turn your attention back to your chosen task, whether it's balancing the budget or accounting for all the checks in the bank statement. You just scored a point! If you get bothered again, even if it is only a few moments later, that's a brand-new chance to score a point.

Do you remember my anecdote about hiking in the Canadian Rockies? I was bothered by a specific worry, and I decided to make a request of Anxiety: "Thank you! Could you give that to me again?" And then I directed my attention back to the beauty surrounding me. That's how you score a point. And I scored numerous points by repeating that process over the next half hour.

THE RULES OF THE GAME
How to Play with Anxiety

- There's only one play in this competition, and only one point can be scored in that play.
- You complete each play by turning your attention back to your chosen task.
- You can score a point in three ways: subvocalize encouragement, instruct yourself to take action, or deliver a cunning message to Anxiety.
- You score a point only when you're being *bothered* by Anxiety.
- You score points even when you are *anticipating* a difficult task.
- You can score points back-to-back.
- Scoring a point may scare you, and that's okay.
- Don't look for the benefits of scoring a point.
- It's an attitude shift, really.
- In this competition, you win every time you score a point. Focus on scoring *as many points as possible*.

You score a point only when you're being *bothered* by Anxiety. Worries, apprehensions, and anxiety are likely to pop up when we engage in a challenging activity. So expect them to appear, and when they are noise and not a signal, you can simply keep moving along with your activity, right through that momentary interruption. Nothing needs to be fixed, so you don't score points in those moments.

The only opportunity you have to score a point is when some distress or a noisy worry is *bothering* you. It will show up as a two-step process. First will be the event: you'll notice a feeling in your body, or you'll remind yourself you're about to take a risk, or an uncomfortable image will pop up in your mind, or you'll feel apprehension as you begin to

step forward. Second, you'll feel bothered. You'll hear yourself spontaneously responding along the lines of "Ugh, this is too much for me.
I'm not going to be able to concentrate. I need to back away." Now you
begin your work of *responding to your response*. Notice it, subvocalize one
of our new messages to yourself or to Anxiety, and then turn away and
refocus your attention on your task. Great! Point scored!

You score points even when you are *anticipating* a difficult task.
Remember, you have a chance to score a point *anytime* you feel bothered
by your distress or noisy worry. So, of course, as you consider facing a
difficult task you aren't sure you can handle, there's a good chance you
will get distracted and become bothered by your anxious doubts. Don't
forget to take advantage of those moments to score on Anxiety. In fact,
you may score the most points before you take any action. So be alert!
Look for those opportunities to score!

You can score points back-to-back. Scoring a point takes only a few
moments. You notice that you are bothered, you deliver your meaningful or cunning message, and you return your attention to your task.
That's a point. If you become bothered again moments later, that's
another chance to score a point.

Do you recall my story about getting panicky as we were racing
on the water? I was trying to manage an intense situation that was
unfolding quite rapidly. I really wanted our boat to stay in the race,
yet I was experiencing anaerobic symptoms that scared me, and a part
of me was insisting that I stop the boat so I could recover. I heard that
frightened voice saying, "I gotta stop!" I made a quick assessment and
decided to push forward. I responded by mentally yelling, "Keep going,"
and I returned my attention to the task of rowing in unison with my
other three crewmates. But that focus was immediately interrupted with
another threatening message. I can assure you that I wasn't thinking
of points in those moments. I was just trying to get to the end of the
race. But if I had been playing this game, each time I heard "stop" and

I responded with "keep going" and then returned to my task, I would have scored a point.

How to Score a Point

1) Move toward any task you predict will generate at least some uncertainty or distress regarding your worried theme.
2) When you notice feeling *bothered* by doubt or distress (whether before, during, or *after* that task):
   A. Step back and acknowledge that it's happening ("Ugh. This is hard");
   B. Welcome exactly what's happening ("Yes, and this is what I'm looking for"); and
   C. Subvocalize a message that helps you stay engaged in your chosen activity:
      1) Encourage yourself ("I can do this");
      2) Instruct yourself ("Keep moving!"); or
      3) Talk in a cunning way to Anxiety ("Give me more, please").
3) Then turn your attention back to your chosen task, even while you still feel uncertain and uncomfortable.

SCORE!

Scoring a point may scare you, and that's okay. To score a point, you are going to choose to turn away from your noisy worries without solving the fearful questions they generate. Therefore, at least in the beginning, you will feel scared. And why shouldn't you? You've just ignored what some part of you believes to be a protective defense mechanism, and now you're feeling more exposed and vulnerable. Remember, you have been using avoidance to guard against harm, so this will feel different. Those worries are going to make a lot of noise, and they will demand that you pay attention to their warnings. Now you're stepping forward despite the warnings, and that's why you are likely to feel more scared. Your job is to expect all of those reactions and be okay with them. ("Of course I'm scared. This feels risky.")

Don't look for the benefits of scoring a point. *Do not* check in to see if your intervention is "working" by evaluating whether your symptoms are quieting down. Your comfort is totally irrelevant. (Sorry.) Don't start monitoring your body or your thoughts to see if the tactic was successful. You might have the urge to do so, but that's none of your business. The definition of "it's working" should be whether you are saying what you've decided to say in these moments, not whether the symptoms are fading in response. *Do not* check to see if Anxiety has backed off. That's also none of your business. You are not making these changes to make Anxiety go away. You are shifting your attitude and your actions so that you no longer are an unintended participant in Anxiety's dominance.

The only way you score a point is if you turn your attention back to your original task after your intervention. To immediately seek out some outcome from the tactic is a bad move and prevents you from scoring a point. Simply play the game through this method of scoring points. Keep stepping forward. Then look for any new opportunities to score another point.

It's an attitude shift, really. That's the underlying message here: take on a new attitude, then take actions from out of that attitude. *Look for opportunities* to practice your tactics. *Seek out chances* to score points. Consider that facing your difficulties is a *challenge*, not a threat. These positions represent a shift in point of view, and that's what we're looking for. Your best tactic is to voluntarily and purposely *want* to feel unsure, distressed, awkward, insecure, embarrassed, or any other state you tend to fear. Why? Because those feelings come with engaging in something that's new and hard for you, and because Anxiety lives off of your trying to get rid of those feelings. You must courageously enter arenas that typically provoke your fear. You will know you are doing the good work of aggressing into new, unfamiliar territory when you *purposely scare yourself.* The attitude to strive for is "What can I do right now to score a point? I really want another point."

In this competition, you win every time you score a point. How many points you score is not important. Focus solely on scoring *as many points as possible*. Your objective is to keep looking for more chances to score points. When an opportunity arises (defined as your feeling bothered by Anxiety), be glad! It gives you a chance to score again! If an opportunity doesn't arise, create one.

If you plan on facing your threats with great frequency (and I sincerely hope you do), I have an excellent prop for you. Many people I've coached have found it to be quite helpful. It's called a tally counter, and you can pick one up for under five dollars either online or at an office supply store. It's that little, handheld device a bouncer at a nightclub might use to ensure the club doesn't exceed capacity. You can hold it discreetly in the palm of your hand whenever you intend to practice, depressing the little chrome clicker every time you score a point. You can even set a goal to reward yourself after you reach a certain number of points. I encourage you to try it out.

Perhaps you've heard this quote, often attributed to Ben Franklin: "Watch the pennies, and the dollars will take care of themselves." The same is true with facing your difficulties. Keep your focus on scoring points, and soon you will discover that you are moving forward, toward the life you've been wanting for a long time.

BAD DAYS ARE EXCELLENT DAYS

Your challenger is a sly one. Anxiety will start slipping in some new manipulations. One of them is the "take it easy" approach. Essentially,

Anxiety will set aside special times when it's okay not to step into the action. You may have had a long day, or you're not in a very good mood, or maybe it feels like "a little too much right now." So take notice if you find yourself "taking it easy" a bit too often. This could very well be your need for certainty, begging you to play hooky today and put the work off until tomorrow ("and tomorrow, and tomorrow," as Macbeth would say).

Ask Michael Phelps, the most decorated Olympic champion ever— or, rather, ask his longtime coach Bob Bowman—if he would "take it easy" when he was feeling less than stellar on any given training day. At the height of his twenty-year career (since he began competitive swimming at the age of seven), Phelps was in the pool 365 days of the year (yes, even on Christmas), partly because he and Bowman knew that other athletes were taking the day off.

One day while training a teenage Michael Phelps, Bowman put his star pupil through a rather rigorous training session. "I said, 'You should be very tired, that's the hardest practice you've ever done,'" the coach recalled. "I'll never forget. He looked me straight in the eye and said 'I don't get tired.' So I made that my life goal, to see if I could accomplish that."

Bowman's job was not to make Phelps comfortable. "I've had the driver pick us up late so that he missed dinner one time," Bowman revealed in an interview during the 2012 London Olympics. "[Before] one meet, he forgot to take his goggles out, and instead of bringing them to him, I just hid them in my pocket." And as it turns out, despite the sting of the chlorine, Phelps won the race without his goggles.

It's no surprise, really, that Bowman has a degree in developmental psychology. Some might think it cruel that he once stepped on Phelps's goggles before a practice, knowing that they would fill with water once he got into the pool; however, cruel as it might be, this practice became preparation for the now world-famous 200-meter butterfly race in the

2008 Beijing Olympics, when Phelps's goggles filled with water. Phelps took the gold medal in that race and set a new world record.

You are going to face bad days, days when you don't want to practice, when you don't think you have time to practice, when you don't feel like practicing. You need to know that the only way to get stronger is to repeatedly face all your adversities with strength, courage, and commitment. *Bad days are excellent days to practice.*

It's the equivalent of Phelps practicing on Christmas morning. While their friends and relatives sipped cocoa, sat around the tree, and opened presents, Phelps and Bowman were at the pool, committing to the repetition, committing to their 359th practice of the year.

Bowman's coaching model isn't an advocacy for cruelty. It's a model for the expectation of uncertainty and discomfort. If he could catch Phelps off guard, disrupt his routine, or make him uncomfortable, then he could prepare him for the rigors of Olympic competition. If Phelps could win a race under the most stressful conditions and in the most threatening of situations, then nothing could stop him. Eighteen gold medals later, it's hard to argue with this philosophy.

Bad days expose your vulnerabilities and make you more susceptible to your symptoms. So rather than "taking it easy," GO TOWARD THEM! After all, your challenger isn't taking a day off.

If you look back to Figure 1 on page 25, you'll see the pendulum that depicts this hurtful pattern you've been participating in, whether you knew it or not. Anxiety taught you to push away the threat, which causes it to return to you with greater force. Now turn to Figure 2 on page 107. This drawing shows how it looks to take a detached, mindful position by simply stepping back, noticing your thoughts and feelings, and yet not engaging in the urge to push them away. That picture also represents how it will look when you are done with this work, when you are strong and independent again. But you can't get there magically. You get there through work.

Way back in Chapter 8, Sir Isaac Newton showed us that the mass of a body, how substantial it is, makes it more capable of resisting. If it has big mass, it is simply more difficult to move. Anxiety has been manipulating you by increasing the mass of your fear, by getting you to believe that the threat is big, looming, and will hurt you or others, and that you don't have what it takes to handle it, so you had better keep it away.

Figure 15. The provocative stance—"I want exactly this."

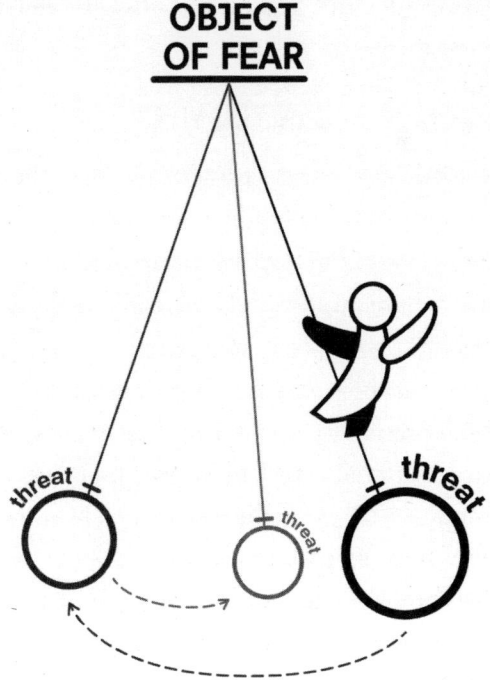

Now we are using that exact same concept of mass to completely turn the tables on Anxiety and stop this hurtful pattern. Check out Figure 15. Instead of pushing that threat away, and instead of stepping back and simply noticing it, your job is to jump onto the bob (that's what they call that swinging ball in physics). Welcome the worried thoughts. Invite Anxiety to send more confusion your way. Remember, big mass = big resistance. So don't shrink away from the threat. Get on and get big. The larger you become while swinging on that bob, the more air resistance you create. Do you know what that does to Anxiety's pattern? You create more air resistance and put a drag on the pendulum's swing. That pendulum will slow down *much more quickly* than if you just step back and mindfully wait. So why wait? Get courageously and aggressively big.

Then you will learn the benefits of your efforts.

And *then* you will learn that you don't have to push away threats.

And *then* you will carry a newfound strength and resilience into your future.

CAN YOU WIN?

Here's the good news. For the past twenty years, clinical innovators and researchers have been challenging our preconceived notions about how quickly someone can start recovering from severe worries and anxiety. Our patients have surprised us! If we can give them the right tools offered through the right delivery system, they exceed our expectations. Our newest findings show that shorter treatments can be just as effective as longer interventions, and brief group treatments can produce comparable results to individual treatment. Even structured self-help materials show potential, such as Internet-based instructions with only e-mail contact with a therapist.

All of this is definitely good news for our task. Whatever your difficulties are with anxiety and worry, we now know that you can change. You may even be able to change sooner than you imagined. And if you will lock in a new belief system about how to face difficulties, your changes can remain stable over time.

Here is another intriguing finding. Researchers are now learning that some people with anxiety make sudden and spontaneous gains during treatment. Although it's not yet proven, it appears that the rapid improvement in symptoms may come immediately after they alter their beliefs. In other words, they start thinking differently about their relationship to anxiety. And this is just what you and I have been focusing on: how to shift your beliefs before you start to change your behavior.

Over my entire career as a psychologist, I have been developing the model laid out in this book, and for the past ten years, I've been teaching all of these newest tactics to clients who face the difficult symptoms of worry, panic disorder, social anxiety, phobias, and OCD. So I believe I have worked out most of the kinks.

It's true that I don't know you. I have no idea what you've been through, and I don't know your current struggles. Can you win back your life by reading a book and applying its strategy to your specific problems? That remains to be seen, doesn't it? However, I want you to know that I have been testing out this idea of knowing very little about someone and still being able to offer them helpful tools. Since 2007, I've been teaching these moves within intensive two-day treatment groups (see Appendix B). Working with eight people at once for such a brief period means that we can't spend much time talking about individual problems and symptoms. We all work together on figuring out this challenger called Anxiety and how to beat it. (And we always use tally counters to help us, by the way.) We have now completed a study on that treatment, and our results have been published in the *Journal of Obsessive-Compulsive Disorder and Related Disorders*.* We chose to study OCD patients specifically because

---

*R. Wilson, F. Neziroglu, B. Feinstein, and R. Ginsberg, "A new model for the initiation of treatment for obsessive-compulsive disorder: An exploratory study," *Journal of Obsessive-Compulsive and Related Disorders*, 3 (2014), 332–337.

they appear to be pretty darn stuck in their beliefs, so they would be a good test of the model. We can't make broad assumptions based on the results, since this was an exploratory study with a number of expected limitations. We didn't compare this treatment with a waitlist or a different treatment model, such as individual therapy. We didn't control for such variables as age, symptom severity, or level of depression.

And yet . . .

Something noteworthy and valuable seems to have happened. The participants showed significant changes in their beliefs and attitudes immediately after the two-day treatment. That's rapid change! And those changes, measured by sixteen reliable scales, held up or improved over the next thirty days without any other treatment intervention using this protocol.

At the end of each two-day group, I ask the participants if they are willing to write a note, which I will hand to the person who literally sits down in their seat at the start of the next group I run. They can say anything they want that might serve as encouragement for someone who is feeling as nervous and apprehensive as they were when they walked in the previous day.

As I read through hundreds of handwritten notes, three primary themes recur in their messages:

- ✧ You need to trust that this process will help you.
- ✧ Keep an open mind, even if you don't get it at first.
- ✧ Do the work; be aggressive with the tactics you learn.

I think it's most appropriate to end this final chapter by sharing a few of those notes with you. Yes, they are talking to someone who's about to engage in treatment. But what you have just learned in this book is identical to the protocol I used in those groups. Those folks have already tested out what you are about to do. So, in a sense, they can speak to you as well.

Hello seat #3 and welcome! As crazy as this process seems, you should know that it works. Follow what Dr. Wilson says, even though it might seem odd or strange. I wish you the best of luck because, if you want it, you CAN change!

Dear seatmate: I want to encourage you to give it all you've got. You have incredible opportunities for growth here. Guess what I did while I was here? I locked myself in the trunk of a car!!!!! Two other ladies did that before me. They were so inspirational. I told them how brave they were. Then I mustered up the courage and strength to do the same. I had to draw deep from the recesses of my innermost being, but I did it. You can too, if you want it. All the best!!! Tears are okay. :)

Dear participant—
Love the fear. Love the anxiety. They hate that. They'll run from it. The more you court them, the more they'll leave you. You can do it. Tell yourself you can, and tell your anxiety you can handle it.
Good luck.

I used to feel like anxiety just happened to me over and over and that my job was to avoid it until I found a way to get rid of it. The thing is, I can't get rid of it. But I can control it and live my life now, because anxiety doesn't chase me anymore. You can't chase somebody who doesn't run. Sorry if that sounds cryptic. He'll explain it better. Good luck!

Hey you!
I came here because I wanted my life back. I came tired and hopeless. It took me a little while to get it, but when that happened, I felt so empowered. It's such a great feeling. I'm leaving today hopeful that this will help me change my life for the good and help me for the long run. So keep your mind open, even if you don't get it at first. Just keep

listening and believe that there is hope, and we will beat this OCD bully. Have fun. Good luck, and God bless you.

Hey!

Congratulations on having the courage to come here. That was a big step for me, and I'm sure for you as well. You made a great decision. I want to let you know two major elements from my session that are helping me through my panic disorder:

1) *Why are you here? What is it that you want or want to improve? Family? Friends? Freedom? Picture it. Whenever you find yourself losing your nerve, then visualize the outcome that you want. Never take your eyes off your prize. The mental image is power-ful, even in the toughest of times. The more you want it, the more empowering it is.*

2) *You must also want the anxiety. The uncertainty. The fear. As ridiculous as it sounds, you must reach the mind-set that you want to put yourself in uncomfortable situations. Seek them out. The cure is in accepting the disorder, provoking the symptoms, and knowing that you are able to not just handle them but control them.*

Good Luck!

To the person who is sitting here. . . .

I was sitting in your chair last weekend and was thinking, "How is this workshop going to help me with my anxiety and panic disorder?" But it did help, and here's what I learned and am trying to change:

✧ Let the anxiety happen. It will be *very* uncomfortable, but it will pass.

✧ Ask for more anxiety and less will happen. (You truly have to want it.)

✧ All the worry thoughts are noise, and if you don't react to the noise, the anxiety gets better.

✧ The noise is stopping you from living your life.

✧ Make sure to do your practices even when you get home.
    It works!

Wishing you the best,
Your Chair Friend
P.S. Reid is nuts, but he is a great coach!

To the person who has taken over my chair,

If you can open your eyes to the possibilities and can welcome the fear of the unknown, there is no doubt you will leave here with the skills and tools you have been searching for. I have felt a shift in my attitude, and I faced some of my greatest fears. I rode an elevator for the first time in as long as I can remember!!! There is no miracle fix to our disorders, and I know that the anxiety/panic will rear its ugly head again. BUT the difference is I now have the tools to handle it! You will leave with some new life mantras, and you'll create some of your own. In the past I tried to use "Let go and let God," but I was struggling with the letting go part. Now I am just going to say, "Do it afraid!" I don't want to miss out on any more of life, so I have to choose to do it afraid and to say to myself, "This may be uncomfortable, this may cause some fear, but I CAN HANDLE IT!" I am confident your time will be as insightful as mine was. Be very excited for the possibilities of living life with FREEDOM from anxiety!

APPENDIX A
Need Coaching? Get Treatment

Stopping the Noise in Your Head is a Step-One intervention in what we call Stepped Care: a system to help those with health problems receive the best, most cost-effective help for their specific problem. Here, of course, we are addressing the mental health problems of anxiety, worries, panic, phobias, and OCD. Stepped Care is designed to use only the minimal resources necessary to get the job done. This book is within Step-One not because it's so simple (although it is) or because it provides only the basic information. It belongs in this category because it is inexpensive, it's readily accessible, and it's one of the least intrusive interventions you can find.

In the self-help field, our questions will always be: How many people can be lifted up, and to what degree, by following the instructions within a Step-One resource like a book? Who can finish their work with this guidance? Who will be more prepared for professional treatment if they begin their work within the Step-One level? I believe lots of people who struggle with anxiety, noisy worries, and fearful avoidance can get stronger by applying the principles of this book. If you're one of those people, then I think you can, too. What we don't know is how strong you can get. Why don't you find out? If this approach makes sense to you, continue studying these principles and tactics and then give it your all as you go into action. Even if you think it won't help you, the only way you can know for sure is to put 100 percent of your effort toward engaging in our strategy. If you get lost, struggle to apply the principles without getting better, or simply don't finish your work, then you can get further help.

If you don't like the approach I've presented here, or it doesn't help you get strong enough, then you still have options within this inexpensive Step-One level. At least a dozen high-quality self-help books and workbooks have been published in this field of anxiety by some of the top experts in the world, and more will be released each year. Pick another one and study it. Keep looking until you find a program you resonate with. Or check out the Internet for free (yet trustworthy) self-help guides. Look for software programs and apps that support your efforts. Then, whatever you pick, work that program. Because getting stronger isn't about reading, listening, or watching, it's about taking actions out into the world that move you toward your important goals.

STEPPING UP TO PROFESSIONAL HELP

If you get stuck or if you haven't gotten as far as you want to, then you can "step up" to a higher level intervention. In case you haven't already done so, start by making an appointment with your primary care physician to check out whether any physical problem or side effect of medication is contributing to your symptoms, because they certainly can.

Warning: In an effort to provide you with the relief you want, your physician may prescribe a medication. While medications can certainly be part of a treatment regimen, they are not the only treatment available, and sometimes they are not even the best intervention. They are *easy*. You just take a pill each day. And we all like easy. But if you've read this book, then you know that "easy" isn't always the best plan. In the territory of anxiety, you gotta be willing to do "hard." Medications, though, can serve as a crutch to help some people do the hard stuff. There's nothing wrong with using a crutch, as long as it is contributing to you taking a bigger step toward what threatens you. But if you only rely on a crutch and otherwise become passive when you really need to be active, then you are not moving in the right direction. So if you decide to take medication, make sure it is part of your action plan to get stronger, but not the only part.

If you do the best you can to work our strategy yet still don't get as strong as you'd like, then an *excellent* next step is to work with a mental health professional who can help you finish what you've started. The good news is that absorbing the principles within this book will prepare you for treatment. If you are able to grasp these concepts, you will be a giant step ahead. Any mental health professional who specializes in anxiety treatment will be pleased to know that you have a basic sense about how to get stronger and have now come to request their help. It means that their time with you will be more efficient, even if you feel stuck. Being stuck is a solvable problem. The more you can enter that treatment session with a sense of how you are stuck, the more you will be ready to collaborate with your therapist in the task of getting unstuck. If you are clear about the task before you, your therapist can serve more of a coaching role, providing firm, dynamic support for your action and offering her expertise when you need it.

If you feel totally confused about what's going on with you, that's fine, too. You don't have to have any understanding about how to get better. You can just say, "I have this problem, I've tried to work on it on my own, I'm stuck, and I need your help." Then you follow that by saying, "This is what I want in my life: [fill in the blank]. And this problem is in my way." It's the therapist's job to guide the conversation at that point, to ask you questions that further his understanding, and then to give you feedback about his perceptions regarding the ways you might be stuck and what you might need to do next.

If at all possible, I recommend that you work with a therapist who is a specialist in anxiety treatment. Specialists can be much more efficient in their work with you because they are more experienced with targeting anxiety disorders. This ought to mean that you will spend less time in treatment than you might when working with someone who works with lots of different problems. Specialists may describe their treatment approach using several different labels. Those who will be more closely aligned with the principles of this book will use terms like cognitive-behavioral therapy (or CBT), exposure treatment, exposure and response prevention, cognitive therapy, or acceptance and commitment therapy.

Even if no anxiety specialist works close enough to where you live, you may still find someone who can help. In your first treatment session, listen for a few qualities.

- ✧ After listening to you for fifteen to twenty minutes, can she offer her perception of your problem in such a way that you think she understands you so far?
- ✧ As you continue to share with him, can he tell you specifically how he might help you if you decide to work with him, and does that sound like a fit for what you are seeking?
- ✧ Does she mention the importance of homework assignments between sessions?
- ✧ Can he help you outline the steps you need to take to get to where you want to go?

Ideally, her end of the conversation will sound along the lines of "I know what you mean. And this is how I think you can get stronger." Just make this request of her at the beginning of the first session (so she saves enough time for it): "Before we're done today, can you tell me your opinion about what I've said, and can you tell me how you might help me?" She should be able to give you that feedback in the initial session. But sometimes, especially if you have a complex story, it can take her longer. One response to be listening for is that every helpful therapist should know that you're going to solve anxiety problems only by your actions. So if she doesn't talk about how she will help you take action, I'm not sure she is the right fit for you.

Another quality that is just as important as all the others is that you need to feel a connection with this therapist. Do you sense that he can be your ally, and that your goals for treatment match? You need to have a good feeling about your relationship with him, his ability to establish rapport with you, his understanding of the problem and its potential solutions, and his ability to collaborate with you. If you don't have that feeling of alliance, or if his goals seem to diverge from yours, then thank him and move on. Yes, it cost you the price of a first session. But step away if he doesn't feel like a good fit. It's similar to what any of us would do in a social gathering. We chat with people for a little bit, and if we don't hit it off, we thank them, move on over to get some chips and salsa, and then look for someone else interesting.

By the way, you can't expect that the therapist will know anything about this book or my strategy. Or if she does, she may not agree with everything I have said here. Some of my ideas might sound pretty crazy to her. "*Talk* to Anxiety? Be *cunning*? Oh, my heavens. I suggest you throw that book into the shower." She still may be a great fit for you.

WHAT WILL YOU TAKE INTO TREATMENT?

You have a responsibility to take an attitude of determination into your sessions. I recommend an "I want this" attitude. Only go into treatment if you *want* to do the work of treatment. You don't have to want to do it with all your heart, mind, and soul. A part of you, like a part of all of us, isn't interested in doing the work, and that's fine. Just don't put that part of you in charge of your decisions. Treatment might be difficult, scary, take time, and cost you money. You have to decide it's worth the investment and worth the risk. And then choose "I want this." Want to be in treatment, either because you're stuck, or you want to get stronger and need some coaching, or Anxiety is kicking your buttocks and you want to take back your life. Your therapist can't give you attitude. You have to bring attitude. And I think it will make all the difference in the world.

SOURCES FOR LOCATING A THERAPIST

Five national and international organizations can help you find a therapist near you who specializes in anxiety treatment. I've provided the hyperlink to their home pages. Once you get there, click on any link that resembles the phrase *Find a Therapist*. Please note that professionals who appear on these lists are not certified in any specialty by these organizations (unless specifically indicated within their individual description). Joining these organizations does not reflect that the professional has any competence in treatment, much less treatment of anxiety. It only indicates their interest in that specialty. Nonetheless, these organizations are *great* places to start your search for a competent therapist who will help you get stronger.

- ✧ Anxiety and Depression Association of America, *adaa.org*
- ✧ International OCD Foundation, *iocdf.org*
- ✧ Association for Behavioral and Cognitive Therapies, *abct.org*
- ✧ Academy of Cognitive Therapy, *academyofct.org*
- ✧ Association for Contextual Behavioral Science, *contextualscience.org* (This group represents acceptance and commitment therapy.)

APPENDIX B
Resources

TREATMENT SESSIONS WITH MARY AND BOB— VIDEOS FOR PROFESSIONALS

All dialogue with Mary and Bob is courtesy of *psychotherapy.net* and is part of the Strategic Treatment of Anxiety Disorders series (Six-Videos) found at *psychotherapy.net/video/Strategic-Treatment-Anxiety-Disorders*. All videos are available as streaming or as DVD.

✧ Mary's two sessions are presented in the video *Exposure Therapy for Phobias*.

✧ Bob's two sessions are presented in the video *Treating the Severe OCD Client*.

SUPPLEMENTAL MATERIALS FOR THIS BOOK

You can download copies of all the major charts and graphics from this book here: *www.anxieties.com/noise*

THE 2-DAY INTENSIVE TREATMENT GROUPS

You can find information on these treatment groups here: *www.anxieties.com/weekend*

Or e-mail *info@anxieties.com*

TO LEARN MORE FROM DR. WILSON

Free self-help: *www.anxieties.com/free*

For e-newsletter: *www.anxieties.com/subscribe*

Twitter: *@DrReidWilson*

Facebook: *www.facebook.com/anxietiesdotcom*

YouTube: *www.youtube.com/user/ReidWilsonPhD*

ABOUT THE AUTHOR

Reid Wilson, PhD, is Director of the Anxiety Disorders Treatment Center in Chapel Hill and Durham, NC, and is Adjunct Associate Professor of Psychiatry at the University of North Carolina School of Medicine. He is author of the bestselling classic *Don't Panic*, and the co-author of *Anxious Kids, Anxious Parents*, as well as *Stop Obsessing*! and *Playing with Anxiety*. He is a Founding Clinical Fellow of the Anxiety and Depression Association of America and a Fellow of the Association for Behavioral and Cognitive Therapies. For recreational competition, he is a charter member of CHAOS Rowing.

INDEX

An f indicates a figure; a t indicates a table.

A

Acceptance. *See also* Paradoxical acceptance
  choose to stop fighting, 140
  of present moment, 138
  vs. resistance, 139t
"Acting as though"
  allows action, 243–244
  anxious worry is irrelevant noise, 288
  content is irrelevant, 244
  and trust, 251
  and skill sufficiency, 244–245
Action. *See also* Stepping forward
  and anxiety resistance, 92–93
  backing away from, 18
  paradoxical, 162–164
  response to signal, 55
  self-talk to, 203–205
  taking before having confidence, 249–251
  taking those you want to take, 162, 163
  taking when uncomfortable, 63
  timing of, 63
  triggers worry, 60

Amygdala
  anatomy and physiology of, 33–34
  catastrophizing and, 40
  fight, flight, or freeze, 118
  and sense of danger, 36, 37–38
  slow track arousal, 38–40
  teaching, 156, 297
Anger, using to transform response, 327–329
Anxiety. *See also* Anxious worrying; Challenger; Threat; Worry
  "act as though" strategy, 242–245, 303–304
  acting opposite to expectations, 89–90
  areas of life suffering, questions revealing, 281–282
  attitude change to combat, 9, 194–195, 312–313
  attributes of, 12
  catching off guard, 260
  competing with broad strategies, 8
  delegating responsibility to, 257
  drag on pendulum's swing, 349, 350f
  experiencing to combat, 126–129
  goals of, 32, 70–71
  interrupting pattern of, 265
  irrational fears, 56
  making stronger, 28

making the protocol your own, 275
"messing with" the pattern, 336–337
moves of, 20, 288
offensive strategy against, 236–239,
    272, 290–291
outcome pictures, 283–286
as person, 259
playing game against, 300–305
points of view of, 289
preoccupation with concern, 28–29
replacing with excitement, 333–335
response to noisy worry, 53–54
response to sensations, 124–125
self-deception and, 19
social, 23–24, 160, 172–173
staying distracted by content, 64
strategies of, 8, 77
talking to, 317–320, 320f
as thriving on worry, 24–26
timing of action and, 73
two choices in, 29
wants resistance, 165
when in the way, 280–281
as worry about legitimate concern, 55
Anxious worrying. See also Anxiety;
    Worry
fight as though in competition, 195
firefighter example, 195–196
illustrations of, 26
Avoidance, and worry, 24

B

Barlow, Dr. David, 335–336
Belief system. See also Thoughts
anxiety and, 69
challenging how much is tolerable,
    226–230
strong beliefs and inertia, 85–86, 91
Blushing bride example, 247–249
Bob, overcoming OCD, 263–265, 266–268
treatment sessions videos, 365
Brer Rabbit offense, 236–239

C

Challenger, know your, 287–289
Challenges, facing challenges, 183.

See also Tough moments
Claustrophobia example (Mary), 66–69
changing beliefs, 120–122
changing interpretation of events,
    129–132
experience to combat anxiety, 126–129
pillowcase exercise, 223–225
practicing new skills, 217–218
self-talk, 221–222
simple cue for complex process, 215–
    216
suffocation experiment, 122–126
treatment sessions videos, 365

Cobblestone streets example, 169
Comfort
challenging commitment to feeling, 31
and self-deception, 19
Competition
as battle inside the mind, 199–203
changing emotions with competing
    point of view, 332
as telling threat, "I want this," 270
Confidence and certainty
challenging commitment to feel, 31
paradoxical best perspective, 133
questions when lack of, 17–18
seeking, 16–17
taking action before, 249–251
Content, 62–70
definition, 75–76
detaching from, 77–82
focusing on wrong topic, 76
irrelevant in OCD, 81
making it not about, 220
pushing away noisy, 70
replacing, 62
shifting from signal to noise, 71t
Craske, Dr. Michelle, 336–337

D

Deep water soloing example, 177–180
Desire, using to transform response, 327–
    329. See also "I want this" strategy
Detachment
three-step process, 294, 295f
trapeze school example, 292–293

Disruptive change
    cobblestones, 169
    mental comfort zone, 169
    weight training, 169
Distressing event, generating distress,
        choice of, 155–156. *See also* Tough
        moments

Doubt, embracing feeling of, 81–82
Dudley-Do-Right, amygdala as, 41

E

Emotions. *See also* Feelings
    competing point of view activates
        competing, 331–332
    replacing anxiety with excitement,
        333–334
    responses to stimuli, 327–331
Excitement, replacing anxiety with,
        333–335

F

Failure
    permitting, 181, 182, 183
    recovery after, 185–186
    trying to fail examples, 188–190
Fear
    activating neurocircuitry of, 154–155
    confronting, 145
    cultivating interest, curiosity, and
        desire in face of, 328
    history of confronting, 325–326
    irrational, avoidance of, 56
    mental rehearsal, 31
    pendulum to push, 25, 25f,
    shifting topic of, to noise, 70
    using to transform response, 327–329
Feelings. *See also* Emotions
    confronting, 220–222
    doubt, allowing in, 80
Fight, flight, or freeze, 99–100
    and point of view, 118
Firefighter example, 195–196
First Responder, voice in self-talk, 214
Focus

detachment and absorption, 208–209
    noise is mistaken as signal, 288
    of OCD, 266
    putting on goal, 209–211
    three components of, 209–210
    UMBC example, 207–208
Frequency, intensity, and duration of
        habituation, 159

G

Game strategy, 301–305, 340–346
    acting aggressive when stuck, 322–323
    how to score points, 325, 344
    pressing through bad days, 346–348
    rules, 324
    winning with altered beliefs, 351
Generating distress, choice of, 155–156
Gulag Archipelago, The, example,
        145–146

H

Habituation
    definition, 159
    frequency, intensity, and duration of,
        159
    need shift in attitude toward threat,
        161
    paradoxical twist to, 164–165
    science of, 158–162
Hrabowski, Freeman, 207–208
Hurricane preparedness example, 59–60

I

Inertia
    explaining unchanging beliefs, 84–85
    moving to position of uncertainty to
        break, 86–87
Interpretation of events, 122–126
    changing, 129–132
    false, 246
"I want this" strategy, 302–303

L

Love the mat, 152–154

M

Mary's claustrophobia example, 66–69
    changing beliefs, 120–122
    changing interpretation of events,
        129–132
    experience to combat anxiety, 126–129
    pillowcase exercise, 223–225
    practicing new skills, 217–218
    self-talk, 221–222
    simple cue for complex process, 215–
        216
    suffocation experiment, 122–126
    treatment sessions videos, 365
Michael Phelps example, 347–348
Muhammed Ali, 233–235

N

Newton's First Law of Motion. *See also*
        Inertia
    acting in ways opposite of what
        Anxiety expects, 289
    how you can change according to,
        87–88
    inertia in unchanging beliefs, 84–85
Noise
    action and, 53
    actions vs. feelings, 65–66
    danger in New York example, 50–51
    shifting topic of fear from signal to, 70
    vs. signal, 49–50, 50–51, 52–53, 61–62
    transferring concern from signal to, 60

O

Obrestad, Annette, 10–12
Observer, 99
    accessing, 108
Obsessive-compulsive disorder (OCD).
        See also Challenger; Threat
    and anxiety pendulum, 26
    Bob's example, 263–265
    content irrelevant in, 81
    discerning issue from topic, 54–55
    illustrations of, 27
    making the protocol your own, 275
    as person, 266–275

principles for overcoming, 298
    and thoughts, 72–73
OCD. See Obsessive-compulsive disorder
        (OCD)
OCD treatment groups, 351–352
    client testimonials, 353–355
    information on, 366
    two-day intensive, 366
Offensive strategy, 236–239, 272, 290–291
    Brer Rabbit, 236–239
Outcome
    Bob's principles for, 298–299
    Mary's principles for, 297
    picture of, 283–286

P

Panic and phobias, illustrations of, 27
Panic attacks, 24
Paradoxical acceptance, 255
    accept the present before changing,
        149
    driving example, 147
    focus on ways to influence the next
        moment, 149
    new attitude in difficult situation, 148
    responding with absurd point of view,
        141
    of situation that already exists, 148
Paradoxical action
    catch Anxiety off guard, 260
    do only what you want to, 162–163
    find ways to want to do hard stuff,
        163–164
    to new point of view, 291, 321f
    want whatever is happening right now,
        301
Personal high standards, lowering,
        191–192
Personify, externalize, and simplify, 255
    anxiety as person, 259
    OCD as person, 266–275
Perspective, new, 79f
Plan
    creating, 59
    instituting master, 207–208
    for anxiety, 273
    worry triggers, 60

Point of view, 113
    adopting new, 307
    in anxiety, 289
    changing, 88, 91, 300, 332
    choosing how to perceive event, 115
    competition between two, 132–133
    directing our next moves, 115
    focus attention for new, 92
    judging current experience and, 118–119
    paradox, 116–117
    placeholder for new, 138
    root of, 117
    synonyms for, 114t
    translate into self-talk, 207
    winning, 190–191
Poker example of studying opponent, 10–12
Practice, helpful but not easy, 222
Prefrontal cortex
    gives danger messages to amygdala, 154
    refocusing, 157
    use to focus on paradoxical statements, 154
Principles
    for overcoming OCD, 298–299
    for overcoming claustrophobia, 297
    self-talk showing, 314–315
Problem identification phase, 58
Problem solving, 3, 58–59
    take action signal versus noise, 48–56
    worry as Step One in, 4
    worry not placed in
Professional help, 358–359. See also Therapist
    "I want this" attitude in sessions, 362
    when stuck, 359–360
Psychological goals, 15
    confidence and certainty, 16–17
    and expected standards, 15–16

Q

Quiet moment, 104–106
    calming down and relaxing, 108–109

R

Reality, and point of view, 115
Resistance. See also Toilet overflow example
    vs. acceptance, 135–136, 137–139, 139t
    Anxiety wants, 165
    to change, 92–94
    doing the exact opposite, 257
    fight, flight or freeze, 99–100
    signs of, 101
    strategy requirement, 330
    strong negative beliefs and, 91
Roller coaster example, 255–256
Rope-a-Dope example, 233–235
Rowing example, 199–203

S

Safety
    and amygdala, 34–36
    crutches, 29–31
    and worry, 21
Self-deception, 19
Self-talk, 39–41, 203–205, 308–312, 315
    and "acting as though," 246–249
    to Anxiety, 317–320
    blushing bride example, 247–249
    examples of, 49, 51, 201–203, 315–316
    First Responder voice, 214
    illustrating principles, 314–315
    motivating messages, 316–317
    positive meaning for why one allows feelings of threat, 330–331
    reassuring, 226
Sharma, Chris, 177–181
Signal
    action and, 53
    negative, 159–161
    vs. noise, 49–50, 50–51, 52–53, 61–62
    as obsession, 54–55
    problem solving and, 48
    simple cue for more complex process, 212–214
    take action, 48
    transferring concern to noise, 60
Stability, and control, 171–172

Stepped Care, 357–358
Stepping back, 96
    awareness of resistance to, 99–101
    biofeedback and relaxation training,
        96–97
    with detachment, 107f, 104–109
    process, 102, 103–104
    to insert pause from worry
    intentional, 106
    from messages of worries and
        obsessions, 269
    practicing, 168, 223
    quiet moment in, 104–106
    reappraise the situation, 129
    wanting it, steps of, 167–168
Stepping forward
    focus on big picture, 193
    hold fast to strategy, 304–305
    practicing skills of, 197–198
    principles, 313–315
    toward problem, 310
    size of step, 302
    steps in, 182–183
    winning the moment, 197
    winning vs. losing, 194
    worst soccer player example, 189–190
    worst therapist example, 188–189
Strategy. See also Game strategy
    "act as though," 242–245, 303–304
    "I want this" strategy, 302–303
    offensive against anxiety, 236–239,
        272, 290–291
    requires resistance, 330
    turning four big tasks into attitude of
        commitment, 328

T

Tabatabai, John, 10
Tae Kwon Do example, 151–152
Take action signal, 48
Therapist
    locating a therapist, 362–363
    qualities of therapist, 360–361
Thoughts
    act as if are noise, 72
    defeating obsessive, 253–254

discerning, 308–309
    separating from anxious, 143
Threat
    asking challenger to increase, 260–262
    paradoxical response to, 268–269, 321f
    seeking out, 220
Toilet overflow example, 135–136
Topic. See Content
Tough moment. See also Challenges
    changing response to, 142
    conquering vs. getting through, 187–
        188
    pressing through, 346–348
    responses to, 139
    purposely choose to step into, 157
    willingness to experience, 150
Track example, 205–207
Trust, "acting as though" and, 251
2-Day Intensive Treatment Groups, 366

V

Viewpoint. See Point of view

W

"Want it" mind-set, 295
Willingness
    to improve, 97
    to lose something of value, 192–196,
        197
Working memory, 139
    accepting rather than resisting and,
        141
    active resistance and resources for, 140
    asking for acceptance, 143
    and long-term memory, 144
Worry. See also Anxiety
    actions and, 53
    Anxiety's four ways to take advantage
        of, 76–77
    automatic responses to, 166
    common stances generating, 22
    competes with broad strategies, 8
    examining, 51–52
    fretting, 2–3
    generates problems as job of, 5

inhibiting our performance, 5
legitimate, 47
as potential to trigger planning,
    preparation, and action, 60
safety and, 21
three moves to manage, 255
signal, as, 47
step back process to insert pause in, 98
use as signal to move to action, 3